Jacques Lacan's Return to Freud

PSYCHOANALYTIC CROSSCURRENTS
General Editor: Leo Goldberger

THE DEATH OF DESIRE: A STUDY IN PSYCHOPATHOLOGY
by M. Guy Thompson

THE TALKING CURE: LITERARY REPRESENTATIONS OF PSYCHOANALYSIS
by Jeffrey Berman

NARCISSISM AND THE TEXT: STUDIES IN LITERATURE AND THE PSYCHOLOGY OF THE SELF
Edited by Lynne Layton and Barbara Ann Schapiro

THE LANGUAGE OF PSYCHOSIS
by Bent Rosenbaum and Harly Sonne

SEXUALITY AND MIND: THE ROLE OF THE FATHER AND THE MOTHER IN THE PSYCHE
by Janine Chasseguet-Smirgel

ART AND LIFE: ASPECTS OF MICHELANGELO
by Nathan Leites

PATHOLOGIES OF THE MODERN SELF: POSTMODERN STUDIES ON NARCISSISM, SCHIZOPHRENIA, AND DEPRESSION
Edited by David Michael Levin

FREUD'S THEORY OF PSYCHOANALYSIS
by Ole Andkjaer Olsen and Simo Køppe

THE UNCONSCIOUS AND THE THEORY OF PSYCHONEUROSES
by Zvi Giora

CHANGING MIND-SETS: THE POTENTIAL UNCONSCIOUS
by Maria Carmen Gear, Ernesto Cesar Liendo, and Lila Lee Scott

LANGUAGE AND THE DISTORTION OF MEANING
by Patrick de Gramont

THE NEUROTIC FOUNDATIONS OF SOCIAL ORDER: PSYCHOANALYTIC ROOTS OF PATRIARCHY
by J. C. Smith

SELF AND OTHER: OBJECT RELATIONS IN PSYCHOANALYSIS
AND LITERATURE
by Robert Rogers

THE IDEA OF THE PAST: HISTORY, SCIENCE, AND PRACTICE
IN AMERICAN PSYCHOANALYSIS
by Leonard Jonathan Lamm

SUBJECT AND AGENCY IN PSYCHOANALYSIS: WHICH IS
TO BE MASTER?
by Frances M. Moran

JACQUES LACAN'S RETURN TO FREUD: THE REAL,
THE SYMBOLIC, AND THE IMAGINARY
by Philippe Julien

JACQUES LACAN'S RETURN TO FREUD

The real, the symbolic, and the imaginary

Philippe Julien

Translated by Devra Beck Simiu

NEW YORK UNIVERSITY PRESS
New York and London

New York University Press
New York and London

Copyright © 1994 by New York University
All rights reserved

Translation of this book from the original French was supported
by the French Ministry of Culture.

Library of Congress Cataloging-in-Publication Data
Julien, Philippe.
[Retour à Freud de Jacques Lacan. English]
Jacques Lacan's return to Freud : the real, the symbolic, and the
imaginary / Philippe Julien ; translated by Devra Beck Simiu.
p.   cm. — (Psychoanalytic crosscurrents)
Includes bibliographical references and index.
ISBN 0-8147-4198-3 (alk. paper)
1. Lacan, Jacques, 1901–   . 2. Psychoanalysis—France—History.
3. Freud, Sigmund, 1856–1939. I. Title. II. Series.
BF109.L28J85   1994
150.19′5′092—dc20   93-40773
                             CIP

New York University Press books are printed on acid-free paper,
and their binding materials are chosen for strength and durability.

Manufactured in the United States of America

10   9   8   7   6   5   4   3   2   1

To those whose passion burned them with the truth and made them prey to the beasts of their thoughts.

Contents

Foreword by Leo Goldberger   xi

Preface by William J. Richardson   xv

Introduction   1

I. The Shadow of Freud

1. The Pain of Being Two   15
2. My Dearest Counterpart, My Mirror   28
3. Paranoic Knowledge   36

II. A Return to Freud

4. The Lacanian Thing   45
5. Exhaustion in the Symbolic   55
6. The Making of a Case of Acting-Out   65

III. The Transference

7. A Change of Place   77
8. An Ethical Question   83
9. A Metaphor of Love   92

IV. Toward the Real

10. A Cartesian Approach	105
11. A Literal Operation	118
12. The Drive at Stake	140

V. Another Imaginary

13. A Hole in the Imaginary	153
14. Imagination of a Triple Hole	165
15. An Imaginary with Consistency	172
Conclusion: The Psychoanalyst Applied to the Mirror	185
Notes	195
Index	215

Foreword

The *Psychoanalytic Crosscurrents* series presents selected books and monographs that reveal the growing intellectual ferment within and across the boundaries of psychoanalysis.

Freud's theories and grand-scale speculative leaps have been found wanting, if not disturbing, from the very beginning and have led to a succession of derisive attacks, shifts in emphasis, revisions, modifications, and extensions. Despite the chronic and, at times, fierce debate that has characterized psychoanalysis, not only as a movement but also as a science, Freud's genius and transformational impact on the twentieth century have never been seriously questioned. Recent psychoanalytic thought has been subjected to dramatic reassessments under the sway of contemporary currents in the history of ideas, philosophy of science, epistemology, structuralism, critical theory, semantics, and semiology as well as in sociobiology, theology, and neurocognitive science. Not only is Freud's place in intellectual history being meticulously scrutinized; his texts, too, are being carefully read, explicated, and debated within a variety of conceptual frameworks and sociopolitical contexts.

The legacy of Freud is perhaps most notably evident within the narrow confines of psychoanalysis itself, the "impossible profession" that has served as the central platform for the promulgation of official orthodoxy. But Freud's contributions—his original radical thrust—reach far beyond the parochial concerns of the clinician psychoanalyst as clinician. His writings touch on a wealth of issues, crossing traditional boundaries—be they situated in the biological, social, or humanistic spheres—that have profoundly altered our conception of the individual and society.

A rich and flowering literature, falling under the rubric of "applied psychoanalysis," came into being, reached its zenith many decades ago, and then almost vanished. Early contributors to this literature, in addition to Freud himself, came from a wide range of backgrounds both within and outside the medical/psychiatric field, many later becoming psychoanalysts themselves. These early efforts were characteristically reductionistic in their attempt to extrapolate from psychoanalytic theory (often the purely clinical theory) to explanations of phenomena lying at some distance from the clinical. Over the years, academic psychologists, educators, anthropologists, sociologists, political scientists, philosophers, jurists, literary critics, art historians, artists, and writers, among others (with or without formal psychoanalytic training), have joined in the proliferation of this literature.

The intent of the *Psychoanalytic Crosscurrents* series is to apply psychoanalytic ideas to topics that may lie beyond the narrowly clinical, but its essential conception and scope are quite different. The present series eschews the reductionistic tendency to be found in much traditional "applied psychoanalysis." It acknowledges not only the complexity of psychological phenomena but also the way in which they are embedded in social and scientific contexts that are constantly changing. It calls for a dialectical relationship to earlier theoretical views and conceptions rather than a mechanical repetition of Freud's dated thoughts. The series affirms the fact that contributions to and about psychoanalysis have come from many directions. It is designed as a forum for the multidisciplinary studies that intersect with psychoanalytic thought but without the requirement that psychoanalysis necessarily be the starting point or, indeed, the center focus. The criteria for inclusion in the series are that the work be significantly informed by psychoanalytic thought or that it be aimed at furthering our understanding of psychoanalysis in its broadest meaning as theory, practice, and sociocultural phenomenon; that it be of current topical interest and that it provide the critical reader with contemporary insights; and, above all, that it be high-quality scholarship, free of absolute dogma, banalization, and empty jargon. The author's professional identity and particular theoretical orientation matters only to the extent that such facts may serve to frame the work for the reader, alerting him or her to inevitable biases of the author.

The *Psychoanalytic Crosscurrents* series presents an array of works from the multidisciplinary domain in an attempt to capture the ferment of scholarly activities at the core as well as at the boundaries of psychoanalysis. The books and monographs are from a variety of sources: authors will be psychoanalysts—traditional, neo- and post-Freudian, existential, object relational, Kohutian, Lacanian, etc.—social scientists with quantitative or qualitative orientations to psychoanalytic data, and scholars from the vast diversity of approaches and interests that make up the humanities. The series entertains works on critical comparisons of psychoanalytic theories and concepts as well as philosophical examinations of fundamental assumptions and epistemic claims that furnish the base for psychoanalytic hypotheses. It includes studies of psychoanalysis as literature (discourse and narrative theory) as well as the application of psychoanalytic studies of creativity and the arts. Works in the cognitive and neurosciences will be included to the extent that they address some fundamental psychoanalytic tenet, such as the role of dreaming and other forms of unconscious mental processes.

It should be obvious that an exhaustive enumeration of the types of works that might fit into the *Psychoanalytic Crosscurrents* series is pointless. The studies comprise a lively and growing literature as a unique domain; books of this sort are frequently difficult to classify or catalog. Suffice it to say that the overriding aim of the editor of this series is to serve as a conduit for the identification of the outstanding yield of that emergent literature and to foster its further unhampered growth.

LEO GOLDBERGER
New York University

Preface

Jacques Lacan's initial attempt to return to Freud seemed in his own eyes to have failed. At least this appeared to be the case when, ten years after he had announced a "new covenant" with the meaning of the Freudian discovery (in the famous "Discourse at Rome" of 1953), he declared the need for its renewal. In this provocative book Philippe Julien reassesses that apparent "failure" and reflects upon its significance for those who come after Lacan.

For in a certain sense the enterprise was bound to "fail," inasmuch as the unconscious, discovered by Freud, is a field that by its very nature disappears in the very moment of its discovery. Hence, there is an inevitable discordance between an experience of the unconscious and any attempt to give an account of it—even that of a Freud. It was precisely this discordance that fascinated Lacan, and the goal of his entire effort was to tease out the import of this discordance, first manifest in the lacunae within Freud's thought itself. It is in this sense that Lacan's effort was and remains a very Freudian exercise.

But if Lacan would begin by filling in the lacunae of Freud's unsaid, this had to be accomplished by following the antecedent logic of the said. Over the long years, Lacan's commitment to this endeavor, wide-reaching though it was, never faltered. As long as his teaching continued, his followers could claim to make this return "with" him. But now that his voice is silenced, how are psychoanalysts to assume in their own name Lacan's profoundly Freudian return to Freud?

Julien considers several options that he dismisses as unsatisfactory. One may declare Lacan's return to Freud a success, for example, and simply repeat his interpretations and interpolations as a closed system that revolves about its own axis in a purely circular fashion. The task, then, would be simply to repeat over and over the words of the master. Or, alternatively, one may conceive the effort as an open-ended spiral meant to continue indefinitely with no possibility of closure. But this would be an exercise in futility, with the constant slippage leaving no means of determining real progress. Julien suggests instead a third model, that of a closed spiral—the image is a kind of three-dimensional figure in the form of the number 8—in terms of which those who come "after" Lacan may accept Lacan's gains but continue to extend and expand them in an enduring effort to carry out the ultimately impossible task of giving an account of . . . dis-cord.

Julien proposes to retrieve Lacan's return to Freud with precisely this model in mind, insisting on the importance of following Lacan's journey in its *entirety*, tracing the twisting and turning according to the historical context in which each shift along the way took place. The journey began in 1932 with the publication of Lacan's doctoral dissertation, *Paranoid Psychosis and Its Relation to Personality*, and would not end until the annual series of weekly (toward the end, bimonthly) seminars, begun in 1953, came to a close in 1980. It was not until 1953 that he introduced the categories that would most distinguish his thought—"symbolic," "imaginary," and "real"—but in retrospect it is clear that from 1932 until 1953, the focus of his attention was on what would subsequently be called the "imaginary."

This focus began with Lacan's attempt to understand the paranoia of his premier patient, Aimée, with the help of certain of Freud's texts on narcissism, carefully chosen to suit his purposes. This was a purely utilitarian reading of Freud (in that respect like many an other), not yet truly a Freudian one. Soon (1936), after further reflection on narcissism, he proposed to conceive of the ego as constituted by the reflected image of the infant's own body as if in a mirror, and, eventually (by 1946), to consider the ego thus understood as itself paranoid in structure. Accordingly, Lacan's conception of the imaginary, based on the specular image, became more and more refined, but its correlation with a primordial narcissism was irreducible.

By 1953, Lacan had discovered Lévi-Strauss. From then on, the structures (and the structuring) of language in the psychoanalytic process became paramount. Accordingly, the focus of his attention soon shifted to the effect of the symbolic on the imaginary. The result was to relativize the imaginary, and, indeed, the subject itself as well through its subordination to the symbolic. This emphasis lasted until the early sixties, when Lacan's interest turned to topology as a way to formalize his thinking. Soon, it focused on the role of the real in this topology.

Julien follows this itinerary, thematizing major aspects of Lacan's thought as they appear. Following the evolution of Lacan's seminars in the fifties, he reviews the highlights, first tracing the relation between symbolic and imaginary in terms of the interplay between ego-ideal and ideal ego in the process of identification. Other issues (e.g., speech versus language, full versus empty speech, symbolic versus imaginary transference, the ethics of psychoanalysis, desire of the analyst) all receive their share of attention. It is with the seminar on *The Four Fundamental Concepts of Psychoanalysis* (1964) that Lacan begins to focus on the role of the real, whose relation to the symbolic functions through the materiality of the "letter," which Julien explains as the localized structure of the signifier.

Once the real has become the focus of attention, Lacan begins to reflect on its relationship not only to the symbolic but to the imaginary as well. Roughly speaking, one may say that this becomes the major interest of the seventies. He conceives all these three modalities as equivalent and takes as his paradigm for this conception the so-called Borromean knot, a triplex unity of spheres ("holes") in which each component functions in complete complementarity with the others—destroy one and the whole knot disintegrates. Julien acknowledges the theological avatar of this trinitarian conception of three-in-one. With it, the imaginary assumes a new importance for Lacan, even a peculiar priority. For, although all three modalities are equivalent, still the consistency of the knot (the oneness that keeps it together) derives neither from the symbolic nor the real but rather from the sheer interrelatedness of the three spheres, that is, from 3 taken simply as a number—hence, as a function of the imaginary. Thus, Lacan: "The Borromean knot, insofar as it is supported by the number 3, belongs to the register of the *imaginary*."

In any case, once the imaginary has been stripped of its narcissistic overtones, it has now a topological function that is absolutely essential. Henceforth, "the *real* effect of the *symbolic* is *imagined*." An analysis may be said to reach its end when the analysand learns how to "deal with" her symptom, and that means, at the very least, to live with and deal with her specular image, that is, to "imaginarize" with it in a mobile, supple, non-narcissistic fashion. "In this way a reversal of the image in the field of the

Other is effected, in the locus of that symbolic pact which is the analytic relation." All this is a far cry from "filling in the lacunae" of Freud, but a Freudian enterprise it still remains.

This penetrating work goes far beyond a mere "introduction" to Lacan and constantly challenges the reader to submit to the rigor of Lacan's sinuous thinking. The rewards for doing so, however, are rich indeed. Though the book's trenchant style is not meant for beginners, Devra Simiu has translated it with meticulous care into an English whose fluidity does justice to the French original. With this study, Lacanian scholarship among anglophone readers reaches a new level of sophistication.

WILLIAM J. RICHARDSON
Boston College

Introduction

Summing up his teaching career about a year before his death, Lacan one day confessed: "I have been traumatized by misunderstanding. I can't abide it, so I wear myself out clearing it up. And what happens—I just nourish it" (June 10, 1980).

In a number of ways, Lacan actually fostered misunderstanding. As a clinician, he was passionately interested in paranoia—at the risk of letting us believe that a touch of madness is preferable to a dreary neurosis. In his rereading of the Freudian texts, he deciphered the enigmas—at the risk of letting us believe that everything is in Freud, if only we read him right. A man of letters, he worked magic with words—at the risk of letting us believe that analysis is but a series of punch lines. A rigorous and precise researcher, he submitted himself to the constraints of science—at the risk of letting us believe that psychoanalysis is either a science or nothing at all. An educator enamored of the young, he encouraged the newcomers to prove themselves—at the risk of letting us believe that proving oneself entailed expelling those who had come before.

But to denounce misunderstanding is not to dissolve it. On April 19, 1970, seeking to dot some *i*'s and cross some *t*'s, Lacan declared: "I must emphasize that, in offering itself to teaching, psychoanalytical discourse brings the analyst to the position of the analysand. This means that, in spite of appearances, nothing masterable is produced, only something like a symptom."[1]

However, simply saying this accomplished little. His listeners understood his words differently. And this was exactly what Lacan would later cite as the "reason for failure": the failure of his teaching and, as a result, the failure of the school he had founded upon it.

We should not be surprised. For it is through misunderstanding that the unconscious lets us glimpse a little of the real. And therein lies the purpose of analysis, which is to replace the misunderstanding inherited from our ancestors with another, the one created by the gap between true-speaking and the real. There is, however, one condition to be met: we must separate out that portion of speech that has been affected by writing, inasmuch as writing prepares a path for itself from speech.

Transition to the After-Lacan

This condition affects us, who are today situated in the after-Lacan. It is not simply that there was Freud, then Lacan, then the after-Lacan. A chronological ordering of this kind is not appropriate. We are not in the after-Lacan period simply because Lacan is now silent, his teaching interrupted. The sequence is neither linear nor ineluctable. The after-Lacan must be established by a subjective position; it is not something that happens by itself, say, in 1985, whether we want it to or not.

The condition for its occurrence is our recognition that, from the time of Lacan's death onward, we are in a *time of forgetting*. It is not that we have lost the memory. Rather it is this: Lacan wished to accomplish a return to Freud. This was his "watchword," as he called it. But the return to Freud necessitated Lacan's constant presence through his teaching, first weekly, then bimonthly, from 1951 to 1980. The necessity comes from the relationship of saying to what is said, a necessity that even today remains intrinsic to psychoanalysis and its transmission. For just as there can be no psychoanalysis without the psychoanalyst, so there can be no return to Freud *through* Lacan without the maintenance of his word. His word is necessary to support, recapture, rectify, confirm, and develop the meaning of the return to Freud, which is embedded in his teaching and in his last, brief communications. These final communications, from 1980, on such topics as how psychoanalysis differs from religion or what it says about the nature of feminine *jouissance,* are reminders of what psychoanalysis is and was for him.

Given the necessity of his presence, Lacan's death stamps his return to Freud as "forgotten." Here we might be tempted to make the following denial: "Not at all! You and I are here to continue and to extend his teaching." To continue and to extend: two admirable verbs, certainly. But

Introduction 3

they only testify to the fact that we strongly resist the transition to the after-Lacan and refuse to recognize the forgetting that results from the absence of Lacan's word as operative in the return to Freud.

Returning to Freud

But this forgetting, is it not constitutive, rather than accidental? Does it not in fact permit the engendering of a transition to the after-Lacan? Such are the questions we must ask ourselves. But to ask them is already to begin responding to them with our work and our presence. Lacan's return to Freud will thus be articulated in the future perfect: it will have been this or that. Today, we are in a period of engendering the "will have been."

To speak of a constitutive forgetting is to designate something other than than a pure, barren loss. It is, rather, a condition that engenders. One day Lacan was recounting the story of a man who had retired to a desert island in order to forget. "To forget what?" he was asked. "Well, I've forgotten!"[2] He had forgotten what it was he had to forget! An amusing story, indeed. Here we have a man who doesn't know why he is there on his island, the image of a man dazed, stunned, stupid in the face of a question that takes him by surprise, as if it were put to him when he was only half-awake: "So, what are you doing on this earth, with this profession, this spouse, these children, these neighbors?" He knows nothing about it. But, on the other hand, what he forgot has not forgotten him. This is the hypothesis of the unconscious: the soil whence he emigrated clings to the soles of his feet forever.

It was precisely on the basis of a story of emigration to another continent that Lacan conceived his return to Freud. He hoped the return would become, in his words, "a flag"[3] and a "watchword" for the "reversal"[4] of Freudianism, in the name of renewing the bond with Freud. Lacan announced this program when he was more than fifty years old, at a lecture he gave in Freud's city of Vienna on November 7, 1955. The lecture bore a double title: "The Freudian thing, or the meaning of the return to Freud in psychoanalysis."

In the "eternal city of Freud's discovery," Lacan called it a symbolic scandal that the commemorative plaque marking Freud's home had been placed there, not by the International Psychoanalytic Association (IPA), to whom he had entrusted guardianship of his work, but by the request of his fellow citizens. This forgetfulness on the part of the analytic establishment was but a sign of another forgetting, one that could be traced to those who, beginning in 1936, fled Nazism and Europe via London or Paris and finally settled in the United States.

In the following statement, Lacan evokes his own past as a young Parisian psychiatrist in the thirties: "It was on the waves set up by the tocsin of hate, the tumult of discord, the panic-stricken breath of war, that Freud's voice reached us, as we witnessed the diaspora of those who were its bearers and a persecution that did not strike blindly."[5]

The emigrants, wishing to assimilate to American culture at any price, forgot both the Freudian message and their own cultural and political past as Europeans, a past that had served as a vehicle for this message. In effect, the price of their forgetting was abandonment of the function of psychoanalysis, founded as it is on remembering and restoring to humanity its past, the source of its twentieth-century modernity. But if the analyst has not submitted to his or her own individual and collective history, if the analyst has not been duped by his or her own unconscious (but properly, not as a function of love or hate), there will be no birth of the desire-of-the-analyst.

Because of their break with the past, these "migrant birds" felt the need to distinguish themselves from their European colleagues. Hence, when the war ended and they were invited to takes their places again at the IPA, they reciprocated by offering Europe the gift of "ego psychology." It was a beautiful example of a return ticket: without their knowing it, their response to persecution had consisted in the promotion of a strong ego and a strategy of breaking down the analysand's defenses. Indeed, the unconscious does not forget. Nor can there be a psychic interior without relation to a cultural and political exterior.

What did Lacan say about this in 1955, when he lectured in the city where Freud had considered himself to be a full-fledged citizen? Of the effacement of Freud and of Europe—corresponding to a repression of unpleasant memories—he said, "We have only ourselves to thank."[6] He meant no reproach, particularly with respect to his own analyst, Rudolph Loewenstein, who left Paris in 1942 for the United States, where he, Kris, and Hartmann formed a troika responsible for new perspectives in psychoanalysis. No, it was not a reproach. Rather, it was an attempt to come to terms with this forgetting, through the *effects* it engendered, in

Introduction 5

order to return to the meaning of Freud's discovery. And how was this to be accomplished? By making explicit the effects of this forgetting.

Put somewhat differently, the previous generation's forgetting could not take place without a return of the repressed. By considering this very return to be the antithesis of Freud's discovery, we can now clarify the latter, now that Freud is no longer here to preserve it "by his unique presence." Lacan's project for a return to Freud thus took the form of an *Auf-hebung,* in the sense of an un-doing—an un-doing both of the statue and statute of the ego, as conceived by the post-Freudian analyst.

Reading Freud

How is Lacan's project to be defined and what are the requirements for its execution?

1. The Freudian text as a whole is to be taken as Freud's *speaking,* as an address, beyond death, both to analysts and to those nonanalysts within the culture who are concerned with the exigencies of scientific communicability.

2. The Freudian text is to be taken as true-speaking. This means accepting it as speech that interrogates us and requires a response. How does it interrogate us? By means of what is missing or absent from the text itself, the lacunae. Because the meaning of Freud's discovery is the meaning of the unconscious, it is not exhausted by the clinical or metapsychological account that he gave of it. "The field which Freud investigated extended beyond the avenues he left in our care, and . . . his observations, which sometimes give the impression of being exhaustive, were little attuned to what he had to demonstrate."[7] It is this gap in Freud that summons us to a "return." In brief, the text does not say everything; therefore, it questions us much more than we question it.

3. To take the text in this fashion is to compel it *itself* to answer the questions it poses, through ex-egesis, the act of "making one text come out of another."[8] The text is considered to be transference, in Freud's first sense of the term; it is as if the place of inscription had been changed, as in a transfer of funds. In other words, the Freudian text is to be read not solely as an analytical text, but analytically, in accordance with the procedures and rules of the unconscious.

This is how Lacan described a "literal" commentary: "One allows oneself to be guided by the letter of the text up to the point of achieving the necessary flash of insight. But one does not make an advance appointment with it, nor retreat before the residue of the enigmatic beginning, rediscovered at the conclusion. And even at the end of the road, there is no release from the sense of wonder with which one started."[9] The reason for this is structural: the truth that speaks through what Freud called a formation of the unconscious is strictly dependent upon the letter of language.

4. To read the Freudian text in this way, by subjecting it to a series of transformations, is to establish a *distance* between Freud's act of transmitting his message and the field that Lacan at once opened up and limited by means of a new writing. The return itself produces distance and heterogeneity, as indicated in the separation of the two proper names: the return to *Freud* by *Lacan*. Two proper names. The truth is that this new writing was elaborated and maintained by the physical presence of just one analyst, speaking and writing under the name Lacan.

These four points define a procedure. But what is important is what each of them *implies,* namely that Lacan's return to Freud be *itself* Freudian. Is the return itself Freudian? This is the decisive question for us today.

A Freudian Return

In January 1964, Lacan resumed teaching, having been forced to interrupt his seminar at Sainte-Anne toward the end of November 1963, for institutional reasons. On the day he canceled his seminar (entitled "The Names-of-the-Father"), he referred to these reasons as "ecclesiastical." At that point, he was alone, without connection to an institution, "excommunicated," as he would later describe it.

When he again took up teaching, in January 1964, Lacan held the post of lecturer at the Ecole Pratique des Hautes Etudes. His new seminar was entitled "The Four Fundamental Concepts of Psycho-Analysis." Later, his remarks of April 15 would be transcribed as a chapter on the "presence of the analyst." What did Lacan say on that day?

"Ten years ago, in my Rome report, I sought to achieve a *new covenant* with the meaning of the Freudian discovery."[10] This was no trifling statement. He was describing his return to Freud as a new covenant,

Introduction

something that, in ecclesiastical parlance, would be termed a New Testament, following upon an Old Testament. The Rome Report ("Function and field of speech and language") therefore established a new covenant. Now, more than ten years later, he was proposing a renewal of the covenant with Freud's discovery, a renewal because the previous encounter had *failed*, the appointment had been *missed*. In brief, the original covenant had not forged a link, in Latin, a *re-ligio;* it had not produced a religion.

The covenant had failed, not by reason of accident, which could always be overcome; nor on account of the analyst's personal weakness, judged in relation to a potential capability. It failed because the field opened up by Freud is that of the unconscious, in other words, a field that by nature disappears, that closes itself up as soon as it is opened. Indeed, it is precisely because of the unconscious that there arises an irreducible discordance between the report of analytic experience and the experience itself.

This is why Lacan's new covenant with Freud was really a noncovenant and why, for us today, Lacan's return to Freud will have been *Freudian*, totally Freudian, to be described by this term and none other, certainly not by the term "Lacanian."

It will have been Freudian for us—future perfect—in the sense that this failure was not just any failure, but a specific sort of failure, *supported* and *identified* as such. How was it supported and identified? By Lacan's presence, bearing witness to the failure through his word, making manifest the loss and its articulation.

It was in this sense, then, that Lacan said on April 15, "the presence of the psychoanalyst, appearing in the same perspective as the vanity of his discourse, must be *included* in the concept of the unconscious."[11] "Included": with this word, Lacan identified himself with the social symptom that the psychoanalyst is today. Isn't this the goal of didactic analysis? One rids oneself of one's own symptom by turning it into a metaphor for the symptom that is the psychoanalyst!

Lacan identified himself with the symptom that is the Freudian analyst in two ways: he intervened publicly in the conflict through his teaching; and he assumed responsibility for the disparity between any account of analytic experience and the analytic experience per se. Thus he demonstrated that the cause of the unconscious is fundamentally a lost cause—and afforded it, thereby, its sole chance to prevail.

Introduction

...y to reopen the unconscious is by specifying the manner ...es itself up. Lacan's return to Freud will itself have been ...... is what it accomplished. Keeping this point in mind, it is up to us—now that Lacan is silent—to show by our presence whether this return has been Freudian or not.

In effect, as long as Lacan was alive, this return was taking place. Note that we have used the *imperfect* here. Lacan insisted on this strange imperfect: one moment later, the bomb was exploding. We can understand it both as a temporal and as an objective description. First this, then an instant later, the explosion of the bomb. Or, on the contrary, as an imminent possibility: if I had not released the detonator, then . . . a little while later . . . the bomb hasn't exploded! In the second case, one situates oneself subjectively inside a lived temporality.

The return to Freud was taking place: what sort of imperfect is involved here? Only today has it become possible to remove the indetermination by transforming it into a future perfect through *discourse,* discourse about what it will have been for us.

It is no longer a question of accomplishing the return day by day, little by little, *with* Lacan. There is no more "with" Lacan. From now on, it is a matter of defining for ourselves a return to Freud, not with Lacan, but *of* Lacan. This return depends on our discourse. It therefore follows that it itself must be Freudian, that is to say, a failed covenant, failed because the cause of the Freudian unconscious "is a function of the impossible upon which a certainty is founded."[12]

In clearing a path, we will begin by uttering the impossible and by upholding the interdiction against constituting Lacan's return to Freud as a certainty. Indeed, if this interdiction is not articulated, there will ensue an actual forgetting of Lacan's failed covenant with Freud, together with the subjective uncertainty that flows from this forgetting.

A Double Turn

For the publication of his *Ecrits* in 1966, Lacan wrote five forewords that were really afterwords. In one of them, entitled "D'un dessein," he defined the meaning of his return to Freud "as belonging to the topology of the subject, which is elucidated only by a second turn upon itself. Everything must be said again on another face so that what it embraces is enclosed. This is certainly not an absolute knowledge *(savoir)* [13] but that position from which knowledge *(savoir)* can overturn the effects of truth. Without a doubt, it has to do with a moment in which there is a suture in a finished joint, so that whatever science we have achieved absolutely is assured."[14]

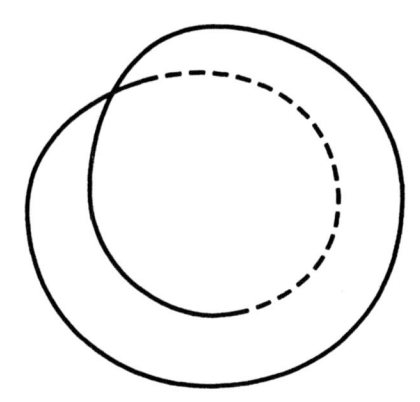

The re-turn is a double turn. Thus it excludes, first, the sphere that turns only once; and, second, the spiral that does not close, that is without suture. A double negation.

1. A Progression

In its first form, the forgetting reduces Lacan's return to Freud to a simple turn, a successful covenant. Freud left us certain aporias, for example, on the termination of analysis, on the ego and the subject of knowledge, on the relationship between moral conscience and the superego as heir to the Oedipus complex, on feminine sexuality, etc. In answering these unresolved questions, Lacan continued what Freud merely began, brought it to completion and went beyond it. In brief, Lacan is seen as the return *of* Freud; he rendered useless the Freudian text, with its lacunae, and *replaced* it with a lacunae-free text. This is the position of those for whom psychoanalysis today is either Lacan or nothing. They hold that with Lacan, psychoanalysis for the first time became theory in the ancient sense of the term, that is to say, a sphere, a sphere that illuminates practice by enclosing it within itself. Therefore, it remains for us to read only the Lacanian text and to put aside the Freudian text, given that the latter has been integrated into the former.

2. A Regression

Opposed to the first (progressive) form of forgetting is a second (regressive) form, which turns Lacan's return into a second turn, the path of which remains suspended, without possibility of suture.

According to this second view, the Freudian text constitutes a closed circle within Freudianism, a fully realized body of knowledge *(savoir)*. Lacan opened it up with his questions and left it gaping on purpose. His was a seductive return, which delighted in prolonging the research indefinitely, lending an aura of mystery. Therefore all dogmatism is to be countered by returning to Freud after Lacan, by putting *everything* on the table again.

In religion, this is called a return to the sources: *"fons et origo."* At the foundation of psychoanalysis is the original experience of one Sigmund Freud: *everything* is contained therein. But in translating his experience into a written text, Freud thereby betrayed it. This is why he was compelled to continue writing until the very end. Lacan in turn took up the game, turning round and round this first experience without ever attaining it, *a spiral without end*. Hence, if Lacan's return to Freud is a failed covenant, it is not because of the object Freud discovered, namely the unconscious, but because Freud's find remains hidden in his thoughts—more precisely, in that part of Freud's thoughts that belong to the past. If Lacan failed in his return, it is because he said: I do not seek, I find—and because he wished to suture the double loop. If we are to reinvigorate psychoanalysis after Lacan, we must do so by reopening research into its origin: Freud's love for Fliess. This love wrought either a miracle, by engendering the *thoughts* of the founder of psychoanalysis, or, inversely, a serious handicap, since it arose in one who never addressed himself to an analyst and therefore was never able to analyze his own transference. In this latter case, psychoanalysis would have been born from an *acting-out*.

In either case, it would be our destiny today, in the after-Lacan, to go back to the source of the Freudian text—Freud's experience—in the hope of being able to assess at last the extent to which Lacan failed in his covenant and reached an impasse.

This second (regressive) view of the return rests on the following presupposition: already existing out there in the past is knowledge *(savoir)* discovered by Freud. Its loss condemns us to renew its meaning endlessly through open-ended research, that is to say, through hermeneutics.

Today, then, Lacan's return to Freud presents itself either as a sphere or as a spiral, and it does so to the extent that Lacan is seen as not truly Freudian. But if we, in opposition to this, bring it about that Lacan's return *will have been* Freudian, then by our speaking, a closed double turn will be engendered, the interior of a figure eight that, when interpreted three dimensionally, establishes an empty space, a specific gap between the first and second turns. The desire-of-the-analyst—if there is an analyst—at once establishes this specific gap and inscribes itself in it, a manifestation that Lacan's return is itself Freudian.

This is our task now, in a situation where passage to the after-Lacan needs to be effected in such a way that the impossible—that is, the double exclusion of the sphere and the spiral—determines a certitude for us.

The Complete Writings

Today we face our task at a moment that is altogether new with respect to Lacan's teaching. So long as it was sustained by his *voice,* Lacan's teaching affected his listeners at *different* times during the extensive period it took to prepare the way. This was how several generations of students were created, each generation different, each fixated on what appeared to be the true Lacan. Now, for the first time, with the silence of this voice, it has become possible to read and to decipher Lacan's teaching in context and to approach it in its entirety, from 1932 (the date of the doctoral thesis) to 1980.

The listener turned reader is now able to realize that each transcribed word, each published writing must necessarily be dated if it is to be read. Lacan's teaching is, in fact, divided into diverse periods that need to be clearly distinguished. To refuse this historization is to sentence ourselves either to denouncing contradictions where there are none or to attempting to justify them as fruitful antinomies.

For us, it is especially critical to be able to approach Lacan's teaching in its entirety and from an historical point of view, for this will finally permit us to show just *where* Lacan met with obstacles on his path back to Freud. This occurred not on his way up, as has often been claimed, but on his way down. In dealing with Lacan's return to Freud, our aim in this book will be to reveal one of the stumbling blocks that Lacan never ceased running up against.

We begin with Lacan's first encounter with the Freudian text in 1932, with what he will later call the *imaginary*. From this original imprint was later generated—by means of an application to the mirror—an elaboration that repeats it in different forms, the last of which, because of its topological nature, both reveals and characterizes the consistency of the Freudian text.

Our purpose here is not to draw up a balance sheet but to reveal the scope of *another imaginary*, different from the one described in Freud's second topography. For through this new imaginary is established the specific gap between the first and second turns of the return's loop. More importantly, we shall see how this other imaginary in the analysand will, at the end of the journey, determine in him a birth of the desire-of-the-analyst.

I

THE SHADOW OF FREUD

1

The Pain of Being Two

What was the nature of Lacan's first encounter with the Freudian text? It began in 1932, with his doctoral thesis in medicine, *Paranoid Psychosis and Its Relation to Personality*.[1] The thesis inaugurated a period that was to end on July 8, 1953, with Lacan's invention of three terms: the symbolic, the imaginary, and the real. On that day, Lacan finally used the term "imaginary" to designate what he had been reading in Freud for twenty years.

In this first encounter with Freud (1932–1953), Lacan was not yet a Freudian but a Lacanian. Like his contemporaries who sought to introduce Freud, he made choices among the Freudian texts. He did not draw on a *whole* text in order to interpret each element by means of the others. Rather, he selected from Freud whatever he found useful, to wit: the second topography (id, ego, superego), but nothing from the first topography or from the first fundamental works on unconscious formations (dreams, symptoms, parapraxes, jokes).

The twenty-year period may be divided into three stages:

1. In his 1932 thesis, and in the very dense pages written in 1933 on what motivated the Papin sisters' crime,[2] Lacan studied paranoia in the psychiatric sense, with the purpose of demonstrating that it was a form of narcissism and one of its avatars. His most important step was to *link the ego in the Freudian text to narcissism*. This he did by interpreting the Freudian ego as the foundation of narcissism, *not* as a principle of objective knowledge, nor as "the system perception-consciousness," that is, "the apparatus by which the organism is adapted to the reality principle."[3]

2. In 1936, Lacan invented the mirror stage. In this theory, presented on August 3 at the Marienbad Congress, he *tied the ego to the imago*. For

every human being, the temporal origin of the ego is in the mirror stage, as a constitution of the image of his or her own body.

3. In 1946, after many years of silence, Lacan embarked upon a rereading of his thesis on madness. He arrived at a generalization that linked the first two stages through the following decisive advance: *the ego* (taken in the Freudian sense) *is paranoid in structure*.[4] Thus, disengaging paranoia from psychosis, he linked the ego to paranoic knowledge, going so far as to define psychoanalysis as "an induction in the subject of a controlled paranoia."[5]

Correlatively, the years 1932–1953 belonged to a period of political torment, which Lacan did not exclude from his analysis. Quite the contrary. Ever since the time of his famous 1938 text on "The Family,"[6] Lacan had found—in Freud's second topography—an adequate means of approach to the crisis of identification precipitated in the twentieth century by the disintegration of Western societies and the ever-increasing impact of science and technology.

The Case of Aimée

Nineteen thirty-two: Lacan was thirty-one. A young psychiatrist, he began his analysis with Rudolph Loewenstein and completed the preparation of his doctoral thesis. His encounter with psychoanalysis came about through his interest in psychosis. In contrast to Freud, who had discovered the unconscious via neurosis, Lacan was gradually compelled to come to terms with Freudian psychoanalysis by way of psychosis, more precisely, by way of paranoia. How did he do this?

Let us look at his thesis. What does psychosis reveal? Lacan was struck by the following: whether or not there is an intellectual deficit is of little importance. Psychosis reveals itself essentially as a mental problem of psychic synthesis. Lacan called this synthesis "personality." Whence the title of his thesis: paranoid psychosis is a crisis *of* personality, defined as the effect and manifestation of a process of synthesis and unification. Paranoid psychosis introduces the reverse: *discordance*.

A second point: Lacan was not satisfied with definitions of the phenomenon of personality. Concerned with clinical facts, he selected one case for the purpose of exploring it exhaustively, so as to extract from it a clinical type heretofore poorly recognized. And because solid synthesis is impossible without rigorous, in-depth observation—observation limited to a few concrete cases—from among forty cases, twenty of whom were psychotics, he focused on a single one. He called her Aimée, after the heroine of one of the novels she herself had written.

By giving the case a name of his own invention, "self-punishment paranoia," Lacan raised it to the level of a *prototype*. The "Aimée case," far from adding a new clinical entity, instead made a case for a *method* of research aimed at personalized intervention. It was a method that, by its refusal of generalities and its respect for the specific features of the subject's history, would take into account *personality*.

And so we have returned to the point! Lacan was committed to the following premise: personality exists, and it is a principle for comprehending what at first appears to be incomprehensible in paranoid psychosis. Moreover, it is that which brings about *con*-cordance where the psychiatrist sees only *dis*-cordance. But of course, it is a concordance that is different from that of the psychiatrist's. And so another discordance emerges, this time between two personalities, that of the "sick person" and that of his or her psychiatrist.[7] Could this discordance be surmounted? This was precisely what Lacan was wagering in his thesis: that it could be surmounted, and that a new understanding of paranoid psychosis could thus come about.

The wager was an ambitious one. Lacan backed it up by actually using the method embodied in his study, a study he described, the following year, as "the first, at least in France," to have been attempted.[8]

On April 10, 1930, at the very moment when Madame Z, one of the best-loved actresses in Paris, arrived at the theater to perform, a 38-year-old woman inflicted a knife wound to her hand. Interned at St. Anne, the woman was "observed" for a year and a half by Lacan. He called her Aimée and made note of two delusions: one of *persecution*, the other of *grandeur*.

The first had to do with her child. Sometime after her marriage, Aimée separated from her husband. It was to him that the child, a boy, was entrusted. According to Aimée, someone wanted to kill him! She said her persecutors had inquired into her past "as if" searching for some indiscretion: She claimed that they suspected her, but wrongly! Was she not describing herself when she wrote in her novel: "Truly evil is around her but not in her"?[9]

Thus, from the beginning, Aimée posed the problem in ethical terms.

There is disorder in the world (Schreber had spoken of an "assassination of souls"), and her mission was to denounce and remedy it. Therein lay the reason for her persecutors' hostility: they were attempting to prevent her from fulfilling her vocation.

Indeed, it was along these lines that a second delirious theme, that of grandeur, became intertwined with the first. This second theme had to do with the difference between social classes, which Lacan prudently called a difference of "milieu." In effect, the persecution was the work of women who, because of their elevated social role, were in the public eye: actresses, such as Madame Z and Sarah Bernhardt; or writers, such as Madame C. What characterized these women were the ideal traits that Aimée was attempting to appropriate for herself. She wrote two novels, "whose literary value impressed many writers, from Fargue and the dear Crevel, who read them before everyone else, to Joe Bousquet, who immediately made favorable comments upon them, to Eluard, who most recently drew from them involuntary poetry."[10]

Self-educated, Aimée tried three times to obtain the baccalauréat[11] in spite of the burden of her professional work. But while she identified with the women mentioned above, she felt her purpose was *opposed* to theirs. Their influence on society was evil; her mission was to create a better world through ideals of purity and devotion. The circle began to close as the reason for her persecution was found. The signs pointing to it were clear: her editors' refusal to publish her writings; her failure to win the baccalauréat; the abduction of her son in order to kill him.

The Psychiatric Explanations

Observing Aimée, Lacan wondered how to account for this double delusion. Was the "causal topography" inherited from his masters sufficient to explain it? The first interpretation, based on the organic theory, explained the triggering of the delusion by means of an occasional cause. The cause could be *either* organic (a morbid constitution stemming from a congenital defect of character) *or* organo-psychic. According to this interpretation, it is the basic phenomena of psychosis (dream states, perceptual difficulties, illusions of memory) that create a problem, to which the delusion is an attempted response. Whether the cause is organic or organo-psychic, psychosis is seen as a deficit.

Lacan was not convinced by this explanation. In effect, the very content of the delusion—its fixation and organization—remained unaccounted for. Moreover, whatever the delusion produces that is novel and therefore discordant within the personality must exceed the scope of the occasional cause.

The second interpretation explained the content of the delusion by means of unusual, traumatic *events* in the history of the subject. These encounters, being conflictual in nature, are seen as the source of the delusion. Such was Aimée's first, failed love affair with a man, a local poetaster. Such was her encounter with Mademoiselle C, an impoverished aristocrat who was the supervisor in her office. When Lacan interviewed this woman, he found she exerted a strong intellectual and moral influence over Aimée. Informing Aimée of the successes of Sarah Bernhardt and of Madame Z (the future victim), she intimated that she and Aimée were also women of a *different* sort, different from the modest milieu in which they were living. This was exactly what Aimée's family had said about her: she was not like the others! Finally, and most importantly, there was Aimée's relationship to her *older sister*. Lacan's lengthy interview with her was a decisive event, one that would be determinative for the whole of his work. For on that day, he had an intuition that would occur again later as he read of the enigmatic bond uniting Christine and Lea Papin.

Who, then, was Aimée's older sister? The widow of an uncle who had made her his wife, she had never borne children. Eight months after her younger sister's marriage, she came to live with the newlyweds in order to offer them her advice and her devotion. Aimée's first child was born dead. The second was a boy, for whom her sister played the role of mother. In this communal life à trois, Aimée felt she was being excluded by her sister, especially in comparison to her husband. Lacan noted: "The intrusion of Aimée's sister was followed by her seizure of the practical management of the household."[12]

Now, what astonished Lacan was the fact that Aimée had not reacted to this. Even later, when he questioned her about her sister's attitude, she never directly admitted her grievances, which—in Lacan's eyes—were well justified. There was a *discordance* between what he expected and what she said, between what he would have done in her place and what she did. His imaginary identification with her failed, revealing a weak point. And the more he insisted, the more she denied:

> We must recognize here a confession of what is so rigorously denied, namely, in the present case, the grievance with which Aimée reproaches her sister for having stolen away her child, a grievance in which it is striking to recognize the theme that will organize the delusion. Now this is the point we have to make: in the delusion, the grievance has been distanced from her sister with a constancy whose true importance analysis will show us.[13]

Lacan concluded:

> Aimée's personality does not permit her to react with a straightforward, combative attitude, which would be the true paranoid reaction, understood in the sense of this term since its establishment as a description. Indeed, it is not from the praise or authority conferred upon her by her entourage that the sister draws her principal strength against Aimée. It is from Aimée's own consciousness. Aimée recognizes as valuable her sister's qualities, virtues, and efforts. She is dominated by her, who represents for her, from a certain perspective, the *very image of the being* that she is powerless to become.... Her silent battle with the one who humiliates her and takes her place expresses itself only in the peculiar ambivalence of the remarks she makes about her.[14]

Thus Aimée makes her complaint against women other than her sister, substituting other, more distant objects of hatred. "For years, therefore, the delusion appears to be a reaction of flight before the aggressive act."[15] But then the question arises: why this *resistance* to a direct battle against her sister? Why this renunciation before her of any moral claim to her rights? Moreover, why, in the delusion, where she does not hesitate to accuse Mademoiselle C de la N of being her persecutor, does she by contrast stop short of her sister?

This transposition astonished Lacan. But the second explanation for the cause of the delusion, that it came about by means of traumatic events, provided no reason for it. Nor could the second explanation account for the "choice" of paranoid psychosis over neurosis.

Recourse to Freud

It was simply not enough to search out the cause of the delusion. For Lacan, the important thing was to lay bare the very foundation of paranoid psychosis. In order to do this, he put forth the notion of personality, conceived as the *totality* of the specialized, functional relationships that adapt the animal-human to society. These relationships are dynamically constituted from social tensions; and what defines personality is precisely the state, either of equilibrium or of rupture, of these relations. Thus personality is "the *unity* of a regular and comprehensible development,"[16] comprehensible, that is, by the psychiatrist.

Now paranoid psychosis does not escape this unitary law. A mode of reaction to life situations of great significance, "most often of the order of a conflict of moral consciousness,"[17] it is one reactional mode among others *of* personality. Therefore, in spite of its apparent discordance, it *too* depends on "the unity of a regular and comprehensible development," insofar as it is a "phenomenon of personality." But how could Lacan back up this claim?

The prototypical case of Aimée, together with that of the Papin sisters, showed the following: at the foundation of psychosis is the unconscious aggressive instinct, camouflaged in the compromise that is the delusion. However, it is not sufficient to say this; it must be demonstrated. To do so, Lacan began from a final, clinical observation: "The delusion vanished with the realization of the *aims* of the act"[18]—the aims of the act of murder. Does the nature of the cure not reveal the nature of the disease?

Yes, indeed, this is the right track: not the act, but its aims, are to be studied. With Aimée, the aim would be self-punishment, the crime an *appeal* to be punished by the judicial arm of society. Her crime gave her a *right* to sanction, *for the sake of* atonement. It was the same with Christine Papin: on her knees, she received the news that she was to be beheaded. Starting then from this therapeutic presupposition, Lacan devoted his thesis to a study of paranoid psychosis as a response to the following question: what is made *of* the aggressive drive?

It was here that Lacan introduced Freud—the Freud of the second topography—into psychiatry. He borrowed from him two arguments, which he linked together in order to explain why Aimée's case was an instance of self-punishment paranoia.

1. A Right to Punishment

The first argument is set forth in Freud's 1924 article, "The Economic Problem of Masochism."[19] In his discussion of masochism, Freud observed: "It is instructive, too, to find, contrary to all theory and expectation, that a neurosis that has defied even therapeutic effort may vanish if the subject becomes involved in the misery of an unhappy marriage, or loses all his money, or develops a dangerous organic disease."[20] Now the patient feels better!

Is this a matter of unconscious guilt *(unbewusstes Schuldgefühl)*? The patient finds it difficult to admit as much and rightly so, according to Freud, for this is not the correct diagnosis. It is rather a matter of *Strafbedürfnis*, a need for punishment, satisfiable by word of law—in other words, a legal demand for sanction, a right to be punished.

How, then, is masochism to be distinguished from moral consciousness? The latter results from a victory over the Oedipus complex, that is to say, from its desexualization. By means of introjection, the *superego* inherits from the parents certain essential traits. But masochism is something else altogether. It *resexualizes* morality by regression. There is fixation at a point of *jouissance* and an interruption in the evolution of aggressivity.

The sense of guilt that follows from this regression is of a different nature. In effect, what occurs is a translation *(Übersetzen)* into "*Strafbedürfnis*," a right to be punished by a parental authority. Whence this fixation, and why this avatar of the superego?

2. *A Conversion* (Umwandlung)

To answer these questions, Lacan turned to Freud's 1922 article, "Some Neurotic Mechanisms in Jealousy, Paranoia, and Homosexuality." This article, together with the one preceding it on the superego, provided the centerpiece for his argument. In 1932, the same year he completed his thesis, Lacan translated "Some Neurotic Mechanisms" into French and published it in the *Revue Française de Psychanalyse*. An essential source, it determined the nature of Lacan's encounter with Freud: a study of the second topography—more precisely, a study of the relationship between the libido and the ego.

It is striking to find that the relationship *between* the libido and the ego is at the center both of Freud's investigation of dementia praecox and paranoia (with Jung as intermediary) and of Lacan's investigation of paranoid psychosis.

Now the leading thread of the 1922 article is the notion of *"narzisstliche Objektwahl,"* narcissistic object-choice. A relatively old idea, it had been advanced by Freud in his 1914 article "On Narcissism: An Introduction." The libido invests not only the other but also the ego itself, resulting in two types of object-choice: the *other* by way of anaclisis, the *ego* by way of narcissism. It is a relationship of reciprocal exclusion, such that what is given to one is taken away from the other, and vice versa.

In the 1922 article, Freud went farther. He relativized, without destroying, this relationship of exclusion by showing that *in certain cases* the second choice, the narcissistic object-choice, includes the other as an *image of the ego*. The other and the ego are correlatively invested by the libido. To achieve greater clarity, Freud complemented the term "narcissistic object-choice" with the term "homosexual object-choice." Thus three times—with respect to jealousy, paranoia, and homosexuality—he demonstrated a "conversion of feeling" *(Gefühlsumwandlung) from aggressivity into love of a narcissistic type.*

Already in 1915, in his article "A Case of Paranoia Running Counter to the Psycho-Analytic Theory of the Disease," Freud had advanced the following idea: "The persecutor is at bottom someone whom the patient loves or has loved in the past."[21] Lacan adapted Freud's assertion to account for the case of the Papin sisters who, according to the police reports, were convinced they were being persecuted. Lacan explained that a homosexual tendency had been expressed, but only through "a desperate denial of itself, that would found the conviction of being persecuted and would identify the loved one in the persecutor."[22] But why this love and why for the persecutor?

In 1922, Freud answered: in the past, there was *first* aggressivity toward an object of the same sex, *then* a metamorphosis into love and narcissistic object-choice as a reaction against the aggressive drive—that is to say, an avatar of the "fraternal complex." This is what happens later to the jealous husband. Normally, jealousy is directed not toward the one who loves (his wife), but toward the one who is loved (the rival loved by his wife). However, at a certain moment, there is a trans-position *(Versetzung)* by means of projection in the optical sense: in the other as mirror, the jealous husband sees himself as loved by the one who loves (his wife). He then abandons his rivalry. The same thing occurs in paranoia: the subject's original rivalry—a rivalry as yet unsymbolized—appears outside in the real in the person of the persecutor. Finally, in homosexuality, during the course of the subject's development, there is abandonment of fraternal competition and conversion of the rival into a loved object.

Freud tied this transformation to a precocious stage of fixation and inertia. What occurs, he said, is an *Übertreibung des Vorganges*—"an exaggeration of the process which, according to my view, leads to the birth of social instincts in the individual."[23] The preceding year, in *Group Psychology and the Analysis of the Ego,* Freud had, in contrast, described the normal development of social feeling: "Thus social feeling is based upon the reversal of what was first a hostile feeling into a positively-toned tie in the nature of an identification"[24]—in other words, identification with a trait belonging to someone outside the group and formation of the ego-ideal.

But in the 1922 article, the metamorphosis is of a different nature. It originates in exaggeration and constraint, and results in an identification that is unsymbolized and unmediated.[25] Freud writes: "homosexual [understand: narcissistic] object-choice not infrequently proceeds from an *early overcoming (Überwindung frühzeitiger)* of rivalry with men."[26] Thus it is a premature overstepping through exaggeration of the process. In other words, social feeling remains fixated to the original object-choice. Freud thus concludes: "The detachment of social feeling from object-choice has not been fully carried through."[27]

Lacan's Interpretation

Lacan explained Aimée's psychosis and that of the Papin sisters by *linking* together two of Freud's articles, the one from 1922 and the one from 1924. Based on the 1922 article, he noted a fixation at the stage of secondary narcissism. In accordance with the 1924 article, he ascribed the reason for it to masochism.

Let us read what he had to say:

> In an admirable article (the one from 1922), Freud shows us that, when there is a *forced* reduction in the primitive hostility between brothers during the first stage of what is now recognized as infant sexuality, an abnormal *inversion* can turn this hostility into desire.... In fact, this mechanism is constant: an amorous fixation is the primordial condition for the first integration of what we call *social tensions* into the instinctive tendencies....

This integration is *nevertheless* accomplished according to the law of least resistance, by means of an affective *fixation* that, for all that, is very close to the solipsistic ego, a fixation that merits being called narcissistic, in which the chosen object is the one most similar to the subject. This is the reason for its homosexual character.[28]

Thus, Aimée's *delusion* was an attempt to free herself from this fixation to her sister by reviving the original *hostility* and directing it onto others. But here Aimée failed. The others were always images of herself, ideal images she could only love. Contained in the "frenzied denial of herself"[29] was a *loving* hatred.

Why a passage to action via self-punishment? Freud's 1924 article allowed Lacan to make this diagnosis: primordial masochism through fixation to secondary narcissism, with eroticization of fraternal objects—a complex Freud called the "brother complex," preceding the Oedipus.[30]

Starting from Freud

This was how things stood in 1932. Thanks to his first encounter with Freud, Lacan had incorporated him into psychiatry, following in the footsteps of Janet and Kretschmer. It was a question of "borrowing from psychoanalysis,"[31] he wrote, in order to arrive at "a science of personality." He did not manage to invent this, but instead produced a thesis in which he sought "confirmation" in the Freudian doctrine for his study of the clinical facts pertaining to Aimée.

Lacan's willingness to incorporate Freud was based on a *decision:* not only did he choose the Freud of the second topography, while ignoring the first completely; he also committed an act of violence *in forging a rigid connection between narcissism and the ego*. This act of violence consisted in reducing the ego to narcissism and rejecting it as a "subject of knowledge" or as the center of the system "perception-consciousness." Lacan compelled Freud to choose: the ego is one or the other but not both. For the principle of objective knowledge cannot emerge *from* narcissism unless it is *already there* from the start, as the rabbit is in the hat, or a little man within a man. If the ego is essentially narcissistic, there is no immanent genesis.[32] Lacan settled the matter by selecting some of Freud and rejecting some. Because "our research on the psychoses takes up the problem where psychoanalysis leaves off,"[33] he set himself a program. The goal was to go beyond Freud by clarifying the notion of *narcissism*, which "remains mythical and unknown"[34] in the doctrine. It was a fine program, exemplifying Lacan's first encounter with Freud from 1932 to 1953 (a date that marks a change in his position).

In effect, to approach Freud by way of narcissism and to make the destiny of the aggressive drive the "basis of psychosis"[35] is, as we have seen, to accept this *Freudian presupposition:* first there is hostility, then narcissistic love when hostility is abandoned. But what becomes of the aggressive drive? Repressed, it would return in the passage to the murderous act. But Lacan found it difficult to accept this thesis with respect to psychosis. For, isn't transition to the act, far from being a reversal of narcissistic love, rather its realization? If the purpose of the act of murder is self-punishment, is this not the supreme confession of a frenzied love of the persecutor's image in the negation of oneself? The act of murder—is it really an aggression against the other, or is it a defensive reaction against invasion by the image of the adored object?

In other words, shouldn't the aggressive drive and the narcissism of the ego be linked *in a manner different from Freud's?* Is their temporal succession not a matter for dispute? These were the questions—left hanging in his thesis—to which Lacan responded four years later with his invention of the mirror stage.

Lacan's Orientation

Lacan's original encounter with Freud and psychoanalysis left him with a double preoccupation.

1. Anxious to understand psychosis, Lacan was intent upon reducing disharmony to harmony comprehensible by the psychiatrist. He therefore focused on what produces accord, unity, and synthesis, namely the ego *insofar as* it is narcissistic. His goal, in other words, was mutual comprehension between patient and psychiatrist. In terms of therapy—since paranoia is a narcissistic illness—he considered "a *psychoanalysis of the ego* more necessary than a psychoanalysis of the unconscious,"[36] with careful attention to knowing the techniques for handling the *ego's resistances.* It was a directive that fit well with the nature of his encounter with Freud: the second topography was severed from the first for the sake of studying the ego as the key phenomenon of personality.

2. In the cases of paranoid psychosis he studied—especially that of Aimée—Lacan was struck by the content of the delusions. Couched in ethical terms from the beginning, the delusions were concerned with *political* and *religious* society, rather than with the family. Like Jean-Jacques Rousseau, Aimée saw writing as a means of socially effective expression, an appeal to a large collectivity for moral reform of the whole of public life. Both were "personalities." Psychosis, therefore, is not a deficit. Lacan described these personalities as

> zealous servants of the State, teachers or nurses convinced of their role, employees, excellent artisans, enthusiastic workers, all with "gifts of self" useful to various religious enterprises and in general to all communities— whether of a moral, social, or political nature—that are founded on a supra-individual bond.[37]

Rather than allow paranoia to "cure" itself through passage to an act of murder, why not treat it by making use of its social efficacy? This was the treatment Lacan favored, but only on condition that the subjects not be left in "the cruel, moral isolation"[38] of modern societies based on a formalized democracy. He therefore advocated "integration" into communities that were religious in nature, with strict rules and an elevated ideal of devotion to a cause: "the army, political and socially militant communities, charitable societies, societies based on moral emulation or on shared beliefs."[39]

Later, in a similar vein, Lacan would define the "madman" as outside discourse, "discourse" understood in the precise sense of that which creates the *social bond*. Thus the following law can be deduced: wherever there is discourse, one prescribes a mild institution; wherever it is lacking, one prescribes a strict institution. Moreover, Lacan was steadfast in his wish that analytic discourse found the analytical institution and not the reverse. As we learn from Antigone, respect for unwritten laws relativizes the laws of the city.

2

My Dearest Counterpart, My Mirror

On August 3, 1936, Jacques Lacan, a young psychoanalyst, was attending the Fourteenth Congress of the International Psychoanalytical Association in Marienbad. On that day, he delivered an oral presentation titled "The Looking-Glass Phase."

He then left the Congress before it concluded in order to take in the games of the Eleventh Olympiad, held in Berlin from the first to the sixteenth of August. He visited the Nazi fair, that typically Nazi ceremonial that, for the first time in history, turned the games into an immense publicity stunt. With his invention of the mirror stage, Lacan had exposed the very source of racism; now, in Berlin, he saw its glaring manifestation. Indeed, the power of racism is rooted in the primordial fascination of each of us with his or her counterpart, in the captivating vision of the *Gestalt* of the other's body as mirror. A specific sort of beauty, silhouette, and muscle tone; the power of the body moving or at rest; the color of the skin, eyes, and hair—all this defines a phenotypic physiognomy productive of kinship along genotypic lines.

On the other hand, this vision excludes the stranger, the one with whom I cannot identify lest he break my mirror. The stranger participates in the *heteros* of a woman and therefore must be reduced to the mother's body, inasmuch as she is the single matrix of fraternal bodies.[1]

Historians of the Berlin games were struck by what had occurred. In a well-documented work, Jean-Marie Brohm showed how the Reich had

---

In French, the title of this chapter is *"Mon cher semblable, mon miroir."* It recalls the last line of Baudelaire's poem *"Au lecteur"*: "—Hypocrite lecteur,—mon semblable,—mon frère!" ("Hypocrite reader!—You!—My twin!—My brother!"). See Charles Baudelaire, *The Flowers of Evil: A Selection*, ed. Martheil Mathews and Jackson Mathews (New York: New Directions, 1955), 4–5. —TRANS.

succeeded in polarizing *vision* and stimulating a phenomenon of *narcissistic* identification, which was easily read in the eyes of the elated crowd in the stadium.[2] Face to face with soft, sophisticated democracies at a time when social decline of the paternal *imago* had left the individual crippled before the collective effects of technological progress, German youth found in the liturgy of the body both temerity and intoxication. Was this a purely Hitlerian phenomenon?[3] Hadn't Freud termed it "narcissistic object-choice"?

Evident here is one of Lacan's constant preoccupations: the questions Freud set out to resolve in his second topography. Indeed, what was at stake in the second topography was the account of the identification process. By what means is transmission effected? Freud answers: by means of a passage *from an outside to an inside*. Lacan took up this question—and in a very fundamental way—by going all the way back to the very birth of the ego.

The Origin of the Ego

We have seen how Lacan read Freud in 1932. He made a choice: the ego is not the subject of objective knowledge, but rather a libidinal object of narcissism. This reading permitted him to "confirm" theoretically his observations in the Aimée case. In 1936, Lacan advanced a step further, beyond paranoid psychosis to the universal. In the mirror phase, he brought to light the very *birth* of the ego, what Freud had called "primary narcissism."

As we shall see, however, by explaining narcissism in this way, Lacan was calling into question its nature *as conceived by* Freud. In Lacan's view, the child is not at all a being originally closed in upon itself, who must little by little open up to the outside world and emerge from narcissism. Primary narcissism defines a being altogether *outside* of itself, given from the start to the other and subjected to events. Is it still narcissistic? Absolutely—this is what the mirror stage demonstrates.

In 1934, Henri Wallon published *Les origines du caractère chez l'enfant*. Among other things, he reviewed existing studies on the child and its specular image:

> Darwin notes that toward the eighth month, he manifests with an "Ah!" his surprise each time his look happens to encounter his image, and Preyer

notes that at the thirty-fifth week, he eagerly extends his hand towards his image.... The reality attributed to the image is in fact so complete that, between the forty-first and the forty-fourth week, not only does Preyer's child laugh and extend his arms toward it every time he sees it, but Darwin's child looks at his mirror-image every time he is called by name. When he hears his name, he no longer applies it, albeit in a passing or intermittent fashion, to his proprioceptive self, but rather to the exteroceptive *image* of himself that the mirror offers him.[4]

It is a decisive moment when the child recognizes himself in the mirror, for *then* he has a representation of his body distinct from his internal motor sensations—a representation made possible by the nature of the image as *exterior*. The child's image of himself is similar to the images he has of other bodies outside himself in the world: he is one body among others. But Lacan effects a subversion of the received interpretation. The ego is not formed by means of *its* exteriorization, by a movement from interior to exterior, that is, by projection. Rather, the reverse occurs: the ego is from the start exteroceptive or there is no ego.

To begin with, Lacan borrowed Wallon's example solely in order to illustrate "a particular case of the function of the *imago*."[5] This case is the mirror stage, a universal phenomenon occurring between the sixth and eighteenth months of life, even where there is no such material object as a mirror. In fact, strictly speaking, it is the other who functions as a mirror. For the wolf-child, it is the wolf! Thus the mirror stage is but a paradigm. In the revelation experienced by the child, the observer *identifies* something else that is accomplished: the birth of the ego.

Four Elements

Lacan's invention is a synthesis of four elements, which are constitutive of the birth and nature of the ego.

1. Organic Discord

The human infant is born prematurely. This is in contrast to the majority of baby animals, whose mobility and capacity to feed themselves allow them to survive on their own. Instinct directs them to accomplish many more things and to learn how to do so much more rapidly than the human baby, who has almost everything to learn. In effect, the human infant is delivered over, from the start, to the other's goodwill: it is a question of life and death! The developmental insufficiency of the nervous system renders the human newborn radically dependent on the action of others. Thus, from the start, the baby is condemned to be social or to die. The human child's biological inferiority in comparison with animals opens up a gap that delivers it into the hands of the other.[6] Freud speaks of a *Hilflosigkeit* that stamps the human child forever.

2. Diachrony

By means of vision, the infant anticipates its future mobility: what it cannot accomplish today in its own, anaclitic situation, it sees realized in the other. Thus is born a *temporal* split between vision and the other sensory powers. The primacy of the visual permits the child to see the future of its body: its fascination with the other's image arouses, stirs, and drives it. It is as if its eyes impelled its acts. Soon it will smile at the mother's smile, which it locates and contemplates with its look.

The primacy of the visual induces a rupture with that which is animal; in culture, it determines the anticipatory power of theory over praxis. In effect, when from *speculum speculatio* is born, it engenders and justifies action, not the reverse. Indeed, one observes that the first recognized ethic is that of the master: a man of the *schole* ("leisure" and "school" combined), he dominates his body (and that of the slave). His body is a locus of struggle and work, while the eye is a metaphor for mind: *intuitio mentis!*

3. A Unified Totality

As early as 1934, Wallon had suggested that in the specular image the infant sees itself no longer in parts, but for the first time as a whole.[7] This is a particular case of how a *two-dimensional*, clearly exposed, total image of the *other* functions. The mirror effects a victory over the fragmentation of the disjointed members and assures motor coordination. A sense of unity, mastery, and freedom of stature is achieved.

The other's body—insofar as it is seen as a *Gestalt*—is the *source* of the feeling that one's own body is a unity, a spatio-temporal continuity akin to any other object in the world. Thus it is insufficient to say that the mirror stage may begin within days of the child's first smiling response to its mother's smile. The mirror stage takes place later, between six and eighteen months, depending on the individual case, precisely *because* what is at stake is something different, namely the ego itself (as we shall see) and not some partial image of the body.

4. *The Libido*

What was novel in Lacan's invention was the light it cast on the libidinal investment that characterizes the mirror stage. Wallon had discussed the cognitive aspects of the specular image, the image as representation: the infant recognizes itself; it thus makes progress in coming to know its body as an object in the world. Without denying this fact, Lacan put the accent elsewhere: on the "Ah!" of the infant's *jubilation*. The image of the counterpart delights the child because it loves the image. The child finds in the image what the child lacks: unity, mastery, freedom of motility. For, by means of the look, the child is entirely outside.

Now—and this is what is essential—the image has a *morphogenetic power*. It is not a pure, passive reflection but the engendering of the infant's ego. What we call the feeling of one's own body, or intero-ceptive sensation of the body, comes from this *matrix* that is the image of the other. The child does not exteriorize itself. It does not project itself in an image. Rather, the reverse occurs. The child is constituted in conformity to and by means of the image, in keeping with the process described in Freud's second topography. There is transmission by means of identification, that is to say, by a passage from the outside to the inside. The *imago* is an *Urbild,* a psychic causality with effects that are both informative (identification of . . .) and formative (identification to . . .): "In his feeling of Self, the subject identifies himself with the image of the other, and the image of the other comes to capture in him this feeling,"[8] that is, the feeling he has of his body.

Such is the transitivistic love of one's neighbor: I feel the pain in your chest, in your slapped cheek. It is an homage paid to my counterpart for making me feel my bodily being: "It is the stability of the standing posture, the prestige of stature, the impressiveness of statues, that set the style for the identification in which the ego finds its starting-point and leave their imprint in it for ever."[9]

Thus, by delineating the foundation of the Freudian ego in the mirror stage, Lacan subverted the nature of primary narcissism. It is not an inside closed in upon the self, but an outside constitutive of an inside, an original alienation.

The Term "Imaginary"

Later, much later, Lacan would use the term "imaginary" to describe this identification. What is the imaginary?

1. Is It the Illusory?

"He is imagining things!" Following the philosophical and theological tradition from Plato to Spinoza, the imaginary is what leads us to deception.

2. Is It the Unreal?

In contrast, in the romantic tradition, the imaginary has a *poetic* function, with art as its privileged witness (cf. André Malraux). Bachelard wrote: "Thanks to the imaginary, the imagination is essentially open, evasive. In human personality, it is the very experience of openness, the very experience of novelty."[10]

3. Is It a Pregnant Representation?

According to certain modern historians, the imaginary is neither good nor bad, neither Pascalian nor Jungian. It is what defines the collective representations a society gives itself, with respect to the diverse functions that organize it. Each culture will have its own, social imaginary.

In the mirror stage, Lacan went back to the common source of these three meanings—and thereby ruled them out. The imaginary just is the *corporeal,* taken not as an object of study for the biologist but as an image of the human body. The Latin term *"imago,"* which designated statues of divinities, once more came to the fore. Certainly, *Gestalttheorie* and ethology had restored it to its pedestal, but only with Freud and his concept of libidinal investment was its involvement in narcissism finally demonstrated.[11] "We psycho-analysts," said Lacan, "are reintroducing an idea abandoned by experimental science, i.e. Aristotle's idea of *Morphe*."[12]

In order to make psychoanalysis into a "veritable, scientific" psychology, it was necessary to reintroduce into Galilean science what it had nullified: the Aristotelian "form" as an explanatory cause. What Freud had rediscovered under the name "libido" was the *imago's* formative power in the organism, in accordance with a cause/effect relationship based on *similarity*. The vegetable, animal, and human soul was not a platonic idea, but the peculiar power of a body to engender another body in its image . . . in the mirror![13]

Endless Oscillation

We have seen in the preceding chapter that Freud explained "the narcissistic object-choice" by means of a conversion *(Umwandlung)* of aggressivity into love, a metamorphosis stemming from a repression of the aggressive drive following an "exaggeration" of the socializing process. There is, in other words, a passage—both precocious and unhappy—from one stage to another.

In the mirror stage, Lacan compressed the two phases into one. At the very moment when the ego is formed by the image of the other, narcissism and aggressivity are *correlatives*. Narcissism, in which the image of one's own body is sustained by the image of the other, in fact introduces a *tension:* the other in his image both attracts and rejects me. I am indeed nothing but the other, yet at the same time, he remains *alienus*, a stranger. This other who is myself is other than myself.

From this is born an aggressivity that is inherent to love in any dual relationship. There is mutual *exclusion:* either . . . or . . . , one or the other. The one I love excludes me; I exclude the one I love. *Yet*, every exclusion leads to its opposite by virtue of a pendular motion, in such a way that no resolution, no conclusive negation, is possible. Such is the "fraternal complex": an instability that lacks real process. For example, a woman sees a beautiful blouse in the window; desire is born, and she procures it. But, alas! As she leaves the store, she meets a neighbor who is wearing the same blouse. Once beautiful, it has now become ugly!

Lacan would little by little discover that this erotic-aggressive relationship corresponds to what Melanie Klein had called the *depressive* position.

Either the other kills me or I kill the other. This is a result of the imaginary discord that is intrinsic to the constitution of the ego and is its essential sign. But *before* the formation of the ego, Melanie Klein situated the *paranoid* position, which appears retroactively in a phantasm or hallucination of multiple images of a fragmented, egoless body. The fragmented body, wrote Lacan, "appears in the form of disjointed limbs, or of those organs represented in exoscopy, growing wings and taking up arms for intestinal persecutions—the very same that the visionary Hieronymus Bosch has fixed, for all time, in painting, in their ascent from the fifteenth century to the imaginary zenith of modern man. But this form is even tangibly revealed at the organic level, in the lines of 'fragilization' that define the anatomy of phantasy, as exhibited in the schizoid and spasmodic symptoms of hysteria."[14]

In other words, the enigmatic relationship between these two Kleinian positions is clarified only if the mirror stage intervenes at their juncture, with the paranoid position occurring before, the depressive position after. But what is the destiny of this tension between the ego and the other? That's the question to be resolved!

The only resolution possible would be *real* suppression of the beloved *image* by means of a passage to action. This is what happens in paranoid psychosis, as Lacan had discovered four years earlier. Aimée physically assaulted Madame Z at the entrance to the theater. However, not everyone can go mad!

3

Paranoic Knowledge

In his 1932 thesis on Aimée, Lacan linked the ego to narcissism: the ego is purely narcissistic. In 1936, with the mirror stage, he linked the ego to the image of one's own body: the ego is purely imaginary. Finally, in the postwar period (from 1946 on), he devised the term "paranoic knowledge" to indicate *the paranoic structure of the ego*. Borrowing the term "paranoia" from psychiatry, he turned it into a specific qualifier for the ego and saw there the fundamental structure of madness.

These three stages constitute a single period (1932 to 1953), during the course of which Lacan *made selections* in the Freudian text in order to tip the balance. He was thus an heresiarch in the most original sense of the term, and the period was more Lacanian than Freudian. Typically, in addressing himself to an audience of psychiatrists, he spoke of paranoic knowledge as "*my* conception of the ego."[1] Already—and still—he was far from Freud, somewhere in between!

Paranoic knowledge is the effect of what is illustrated in the mirror stage, namely, imaginary identification. The sign of imaginary identification is the child's transitivism when faced with an other who is slightly older than itself. Here we have an example of the sympathy Max Scheler so aptly described as the basis of moral feeling, in accordance with which I laugh when I see the other laugh and suffer at the sight of the other's suffering.

From this origin flows a process that may be defined by these three characteristics: stasis of being, misrecognition of self, and suicidal action.

1. Stasis of Being

Human knowledge is paranoic in this sense: through vision, I am captured by the other's *space,* fascinated by the other's spatial field, which is outside myself. Indeed, during the temporal unfolding of the intersubjective relationship and of the dialectical production of meaning, the image of the other suddenly fixes my gaze. There is a moment at which visual spatialization brings social temporality to a halt, a critical moment punctuated by a piercing look. Such is the nature of human objectification: I pose in front of . . . through "the objective," understood in the optical sense. Thus the image takes on the qualities of the ob-ject: permanence, identity, substantiality. This is well shown in surrealism, for example, with Dali and his miniature spectacles.

Thus memory is not the power of synthesizing past-present, but an album of souvenir photos, of images that are immobile, scattered, juxtaposed. Lacan called it *kal-eido-scopic:* beautiful-image-examined. Roland Barthes, in *La chambre claire,* admirably described this phenomenon of the photo-image:

> In photography, the immobilization of Time is only given in an excessive, monstrous mode: Time is blocked. . . . That the Photo is "modern," intermingled with most burning aspects of our daily life, does not prevent there being in it, like an enigmatic point of inactuality, a strange stasis, the very essence of a *stoppage* . . . nothing but *the exorbitated thing.* Photography is violent, not because it depicts violence but because, in every instance, *it fills up sight by force,* and nothing in it can withhold itself or transform itself.[2]

The event "takes place," according to the genius of our language: it has taken place, and thus I know it. All knowledge is spatializing, in the other's space, in the other's light. Such is the nature of the *imago,* the third element between the *Innenwelt* and the *Umwelt:* "I have three brothers, Peter, Paul and myself," the child tells itself, for this is how the child sees itself.

This primordial alienation determines a fixation. Captured by the image, I become it, a subject infatuated with *himself* or *herself.* He thinks he is so and so, she takes herself for so and so, because they believe it. One develops a passion for being a man or a woman. "This stasis of being in an ideal identification"[3] is, as we have seen, without mediation and is therefore expressed in terms of *being.* Whence Lacan's famous formula:

"If a man who believes himself to be a king is mad, then a king who believes himself to be a king is no less so."[4] Edifying speech about the dominance of being over having is a kind of madness; in it, fanaticism and bureaucracy find their justification.

2. Misrecognition of Self

Paranoic knowledge is knowledge, a lucidity that is *right on target* with respect to the evil and misfortune diffused in the space of the universe. It knows very well how *to see* what is external, but misrecognizes what I am. It assigns to the other—who remains outside me, *alienus*—all *kakon*, complete responsibility for disorder in the world. Thus I have no role whatsoever in what happens to me. Objectification is objection to my responsibility. By this negation, this paranoic enunciation, I exclude myself: "It is not me . . . but him!" (I do not say: ". . . but you!" For this would be to address myself in you, in a locus where I appeal to your faith, thus to something that is beyond my knowledge.)

What has happened? Has the mirror turned opaque? In the other, I clearly discern the bad object; in the other, I see *myself*. Yet I fail to recognize in the other what is in me. Misrecognition, however, is not ignorance: what is denied is in some way known. But is it possible to know in the other what I know about myself without recognizing myself there?

3. Suicidal Action

It is possible for a third person to know it. Precisely because I do not see myself, I act by attacking the bad object in the image of myself that is the other. Hence Aimée's aggression against Madame Z at the entrance to the theater, Jean-Jacques Rousseau's diatribe against his persecutors, Alceste's anger upon hearing Oronte's sonnet. "The words of the infuriated clearly reveal that he seeks to attack himself."[5] But what is revealed appears not to Alceste but to the audience!

The other is always—and exactly—my own mirror image. But I fail to recognize myself in the other and, *for this reason,* proceed to the act: "In the object he assails, the deranged seeks to attack nothing other than the *kakon* of his own being."[6] Whether as an agitator for justice, a prophet of doom, a critic of moral decline, or a denouncer of deviance, by designating my scapegoat, I *proclaim* my own malice against myself. Thus the erotic-aggressive tension reflected in the mirror, with its incessant oscillation (*either* I exclude the other *or* the other excludes me), finally finds its *resolution* in a blow that brings matters to a halt, a blow by which I exclude myself by excluding the other.

It is no longer a question of sympathetic aggressivity or of competitive complicity, but of *hatred* proper. In destroying the other, I destroy myself. In the process, the *imago* as such is reduced to pieces, and I am returned to a period *preceding* the mirror stage: Freud's primordial masochism, Melanie Klein's paranoid position.[7]

The establishment of narcissism by means of the mirror stage had effected a *rupture* of the subject with himself or herself. The passage to the suicidal act suppresses this rupture. There is a return to the body in pieces, haunted by the *kakon,* a return to what appears retroactively in the symptoms, structured as they are as "excluded islets, inert scotomas, or parasitical compulsions in the functions of the person."[8] Thus hatred of the *imago*—a hatred *enacted* upon it—is a sign that the mirror stage has failed as a necessary, imaginary identification and foundation for narcissism. But then the sign shows us, *a contrario,* another possible path, a path *other* than passage to the suicidal act for resolving the hatred, another way of "dealing with" the *kakon:* that in which the *imago* triumphs.

Indeed, the *imago* as psychic cause of identification "has as its function to realize an identification that *resolves* a psychic phase, in other words, a metamorphosis of the relationship of the individual to his counterpart."[9] This is why problems with space and time (the "elementary phenomena" of paranoid psychosis) are deficiencies *of* the imaginary mode, that mode in accordance with which the subject constitutes his or her world within the confines of social reality.

The Image of the Psychoanalyst

Therefore Lacan defines the analytic experience as a process in which the image is "reconstituted" and "restored to its proper reality" as psychic cause.[10] Whence his famous definition of the analytic process as "inducing in the subject a controlled paranoia."[11] Paranoia is not provoked but rather directed *onto* the image of the psychoanalyst, in such a way that all the *kakon* unknown to the subject is progressively projected onto it. Identifying the *kakon* according to its historical origin, the analyst then returns it to the subject. In the same measure as the image is reattached to the real through being projected onto the image of the psychoanalyst, it is dissociated from the real *through* its identification, which returns it to its proper status as image. In this way the image, "diffuse and broken" as it was, achieves *unity* in the subject's consciousness and brings about the mirror's success: at last, the subject recognizes himself or herself in it.[12]

But one condition must be met, an absolute condition of asceticism: the personality of the analyst must be "the pure mirror of an unruffled surface,"[13] a personage "as devoid as possible of individual characteristics."[14] Then, upon this immaculate, immobile screen, an "imaginary transfer" of the subject's archaic *images* can be effected. In 1936, the same year as the invention of the mirror stage, Lacan described the unfolding of this strange phenomenon in three stunningly graphic pages (part of his article "Au-delà du 'Principe de réalité' "), pages that claimed to convey to the reader the nature of Freudian technique.[15] The silent image of the psychoanalyst is a blank page on which are imprinted traces of the image that *activates* the talking, suffering subject. A family portrait is thus drawn little by little: "image of the father or of the mother, of the omnipotent adult, tender or terrible, benevolent or punishing, image of the brother, rival child, reflection of the self or companion."[16] To the subject who still fails to realize what explains him or her, the analyst—*through* the interpretation—presents a portrait: "You are this."[17] By means of the word issuing from the subject's image, the analyst offers the subject a mirror in which finally the subject can recognize himself or herself in the unity of his or her ego, established at last.

Such is the other path to resolving the hatred. In place of suicidal action through the "crime," there is passage to an act-of-projection: an image is projected onto the virgin screen that is the analyst. A wondrous moment it was, that first encounter, when Lacan discovered in Freud "the brilliant use he knew how to make of the notion of *image*."[18]

Destiny of a Text

At the Marienbad Congress, Lacan read his text on the mirror stage but admitted ten years later: "I did not deliver my paper to the proceedings of the congress."[19] Whatever Lacan's reason for withholding this text, from the ensuing void there emerged a series of presentations on the mirror stage. The series, stretching over many years, was not homogeneous in nature. Nevertheless, the presentations may be grouped into clearly discernable periods:

1. 1938–1952.[20] In each of the articles published during this period, Lacan revealed the specificity of the imaginary mode. It is not something illusory but a "psychic object," with its own causality and in no way reducible to the organic.

2. 1953–1960. Lacan described the effect of the symbolic *on* the imaginary, modifying the presentation of the mirror stage in his articles and seminars in such a way as to relativize it and subject it to the symbolic order. He also formalized it with his introduction of the optical schema.

3. 1961–1980. During this period, Lacan gave the mirror stage a different—topological—treatment, introducing the *gaze* as *objet petit a* in the field of the Other. Far from being relativized, the mirror thus took on its irreducible dimension as imaginary.

Three presentations, three periods, determined by Lacan's reading of the Freudian text. But always this reading was marked by what had been Lacan's first, unforgettable encounter with Freud: with respect to paranoia, the question of narcissism and its relation to the second Freudian topography.

II

A RETURN TO FREUD

Language
Whenever do words
become again Word?
When does the wending wind while with clearer wisdom?

When words, [these] gifts from far away,
come to utterance—
    not [simply] proffer meaning through signs—
when they show forth the wealth they carry
in the place
of age-old appropriation
    —mortals making them their own through use—whither the sound
of stillness summons,
where pristine Thought of [first] At-tunement
echoes clearly to dwellers nearby.

    —Martin Heidegger,
    translated by William J. Richardson

4

The Lacanian Thing

> For my part—I am an epigone—I have tried to make manifest the coherence, the consistency of what Freud thought. This is the work of a commentator.
>
> —Lacan, November 2, 1976

Before 1953, Lacan was not yet a commentator on Freud. Rather, he would pick and choose from within the Freudian text, forging and severing connections. Thus he linked "The Ego and the Id" (1923) to "On Narcissism: An Introduction" (1914) while disengaging the *Ich* (ego) from the function perception-consciousness. He appealed to the need for such selection, explaining that it was a question of "considering as obsolete whatever in fact is, in the work of an unequaled master."[1] In 1946, then, Lacan resembled other analysts. Each wished to contribute his or her stone to the analytical edifice, *choosing* part of the Freudian text for revival (a cherished word in hermeneutics!), extricating that part from the part to be abandoned. He was, in brief, a Lacanian.

In 1953, Lacan moved from heresy, which makes selections in the text, to schism, which effects an institutional rupture. Breaking with the Société psychanalytic de Paris, he adopted the *whole* Freudian text. What pretentiousness—bolstered by an ideology of progress—to believe one can go beyond Freud! One either takes him or leaves him. One either follows him or quits. Voila! Lacan had become both a Freudian . . . and a commentator on Freud!

Inviting Jean Hyppolite to present Freud's "Negation" ("Die Verneinung")[2] at the first seminar at Saint-Anne (1953–54), Lacan stated without reservation: "This paper shows once more the fundamental value of *all* Freud's writings. Each word is worthy of being measured for its precise angle, for its accent, for its particular turn, [each word] is worthy of being subjected to the most rigorous of logical analyses."[3] And in his response to Hyppolite (rewritten in 1956) Lacan explained that it is not a question of interrogating the Freudian text "in its relationship to the one who is the author" (one does not explain the Oedipus complex by means of Sigmund's relationship to his father and mother), but of treating it "as a true word" in accordance with "its value as a transference."[4] In other words, in this text, Freud addresses himself to Lacan (and not the reverse). It is Freud who questions Lacan—through what is missing from these lines. Lacan in turn must *make* the text itself respond to Freud's questions. This is the nature of exegesis: to make one text come out of another. Thus Lacan became Freudian by accepting the text as full speech, in "the terms of vocation and of calling."[5] This put him in the position of one summoned or "convoked," as he would later describe it in February 1969 at a lecture by Michel Foucault at the Collège philosophique.

The method therefore consists in taking the *whole* of the Freudian text as a speech addressed to analysts, a speech that questions them through aporia in the text itself. The text does not say everything about the discovery of the unconscious; it is this "not-everything" that questions us, not we who question the text on the basis of our own problems. Hence Foucault's definition of commentary: "Its only role is finally to say what was therein silently articulated. . . . It permits us to say something other than the text itself, on condition that the text itself be said."[6]

With Freudianism, Freud's saying *(le dire de Freud)* was forgotten, obscured behind what he said. However, it was not lost to understanding, for like anything forgotten, it could be rediscovered. In rediscovering this saying, what did Lacan *read* in what Freud said?

July 8, 1953

An important date. After twenty years of marking time—from his thesis in 1932 to his paper, "Some Reflections on the Ego,"[7] read to the British Psycho-Analytical Society on May 2, 1951—Lacan at last began *a return to Freud* in an exposé inaugurating the Société française de psychanalyse.

What made Lacan's return to Freud a necessity was his revelation, for the first time, of a tripartite terminology: *symbolic, imaginary, real.*[8] Recalling that date on November 16, 1976, Lacan said: "In '53, I enunciated the symbolic, the imaginary, and the real by titling an inaugural lecture with these three nouns, turning them, in short, into what Frege calls proper names."[9] Drawing on Frege's "Sinn und Bedeutung,"[10] Lacan was making the following point: these three terms—"symbolic," "imaginary," and "real"—do not simply evoke a representation in the minds of his audience. Nor do they simply express a sense *(Sinn)*, as does any translation of the Freudian text into French, or any hermeneutical commentary that seeks to reactualize the meaning—always new, never exhausted—of Freud's thought. Rather, these three terms are linked to the act that founds their definition in their reference or denotation *(Bedeutung)*, for they designate the very object of the Freudian discovery and derive their truth-value from it. To say these words is thus to confirm Lacan's statement from "The Freudian Thing" (Vienna, 1955): "If Freud had brought to man's knowledge nothing more than the truth that there is such a thing as the true, there would be no Freudian discovery"[11] but at best a work of art, at worst an imposture. Such, then, is the nature of Lacan's return to Freud: through reference to Freud's speech addressed to him, Lacan "extracts"[12] these three terms. Indeed, if "psychoanalysis takes its consistency from Freud's texts,"[13] under pain of having none at all, this consistency will still have to be demonstrated at the level of terminology. This is why, on November 16, 1976, he immediately added: "It is Lacan's extension to the symbolic, the imaginary, and the real that allows these terms to consist,"[14] by which we understand: to consist *together*, in the same way as Freud's texts give consistency to psychoanalysis.

Thus on July 8, 1953, Lacan "founded" three terms, thereby inaugurating his return to Freud. But how did he pursue it in the ten years that followed? During this phase,

— the *real* is named only, not yet demonstrated;
— the *imaginary*, first revealed in 1932, is taken up and transformed in its relationship to the symbolic;
— the *symbolic* is promoted and brought to the fore, especially in its *primacy* over the imaginary.

In the first decade (1953–63), the novelty of Lacan's return to Freud consisted essentially in his introduction of the *symbolic*. Preparing the ground, he moved from the *imago* to the unconscious *by inserting the latter into the symbolic.* This was the program he announced two months later in his famous first Rome Discourse (which was never actually read, but written, distributed, and discussed at the congress in September). To make plain the necessity for introducing the symbolic, Lacan began with a harsh critique of the relation known as imaginary.

A Restatement of the Mirror Stage

The three orders mentioned above—symbolic, imaginary, real—are there in the Freudian text. Still, this had to be demonstrated, which is what Lacan began to do in 1953 at his seminar at Sainte-Anne, exhibiting the *primacy* of the symbolic in its *relationship* to the imaginary.

Now this position must be read in the Freudian text; otherwise, it lacks consistency. But in which texts? Not in those of the first topography, as one would think, but in those of the second. From his thesis in 1932 until his last lecture in 1980,[15] Lacan's research was centered on the second topography. His public lectures from 1953 on were devoted to a new reading of the second topography and were designed to show that the dominance of the symbolic over the imaginary was equivalent to that of the ego-ideal over the ideal ego.

This new reading was decisive in that it called into question the mirror stage as Lacan had repeatedly presented it since 1936. Lacan's mirror stage, read *in* Freud's second topography, now demanded a Freudian writing—in other words, a radical recasting that would eliminate the simple adding together of an original, imaginary mirroring in the child and a later, secondary founding of the symbolic through the presence of an adult. No, it had to be the case that, from the outset, the symbolic superimposes itself upon the imaginary and determines it.

This version of the mirror stage, begun in 1953, was given its conclusive statement in 1958, in Lacan's "Remarque sur le rapport de Daniel Lagache: Psychanalyse et structure de la personnalité."[16] (A completely fresh examination of the theory would have to wait.) In the course of those five years, Lacan, as he often did, made use of an intermediary (in this case Balint, then Lagache) as a mirroring *alter-ego* to challenge his own first presentation of the theory. Corrections were necessary on two essential points: first, that analysis is a process that "reconstitutes" and "restores" the narcissistic *imago;*[17] and second, that successful restoration of the *imago* is the result of an "imaginary" transference onto the person of the analyst.[18]

It is not possible to comprehend what is at stake in the second topography, in "The Ego and the Id" (1923) and "Group Psychology and the Analysis of the Ego" (1921), without taking into account "On Narcissism: An Introduction" (1914). Indeed, what is worked out between 1914 and 1920 is the problem of identification, that is to say, the problem of the relationship of an outside to an inside.

What Freud introduced in the relationship of the ideal ego *(Idealich)* to the ego *(Ich)* was imaginary identification, revealed in Lacan's mirror stage in all its purity. If the infant is jubilant when it anticipates, in the mirror of its counterpart, the mastery, presence, and stature it itself does not yet possess, this is because the ideal ego—which is what the image is—is the formative matrix of the ego. Through this identification, the infant achieves a representation of itself as a body image. In this way, the ego is constituted. For, according to Freud, "The ego is first and foremost a bodily ego; it is not merely a surface entity, but is itself the projection of a surface."[19] Now, as we have seen, this first alienation is one not only of knowledge but also of love. It precludes mutual coexistence and nourishes an endless oscillation between capture by the other, who mesmerizes my look, and destruction of the other, *precisely insofar as* he supports and sustains the ego. In this state of tension, characterized *either* by euphoric elation *or* by aggressive depression, no attention can be paid to the being of the other. Such is the narcissism of *Verliebtheit* (being in love). Within its framework, there can only be established a dual relationship, with the drive organized in accordance with the following alternatives: to swallow or be swallowed, to expel or be expelled, to see or be seen. In the third stage of the drive, which just is reflected action or *making oneself,* there is no room for a new subject (in Freud's words, "Ein neues Subjekt").

To put it differently, the image is never quite "fixed" in the optical sense, if one remains at the imaginary level of the ideal ego/ego. This impasse is the sign of an abstraction. Its pathology tells us that, retroactively and *a contrario,* another dimension superimposes itself on this relation, regulates it, and brings about its resolution: that of the *symbolic,* the dimension of the *ego-ideal.* For this is how Lacan read the third agency in the Freudian text and used it to modify his writing of the mirror stage.

Even before birth, the child is inscribed in a symbolic universe that determines its place. Indeed, the symbolic order subordinates the imaginary, and the speech that names the subject in the Other (locus of signifiers) eventually coincides with the vision of the other. The imaginary alienation, in which the subject *sees* his or her own desire in the image of the other, is coupled with symbolic alienation, in which the subject's desire is *recognized* as desire of the Other's desire. The subject sees the ego in the ideal ego, but without recognizing it there. However, on the return trip the subject can, by means of the *speech* that answers the subject's demand for love, come to recognize himself or herself in what he or she sees. Thus the third, symbolic element situates the subject at a point where his or her own image is "fixed."

To the symbolic introjection of the ego-ideal into the ego, there comes to correspond an imaginary projection of the ego onto the ideal ego. Such is the incessant movement of *going and coming* that marks the history of the subject.

On July 7, 1954, at the end of his first seminar, Lacan offered the following schema: [20]

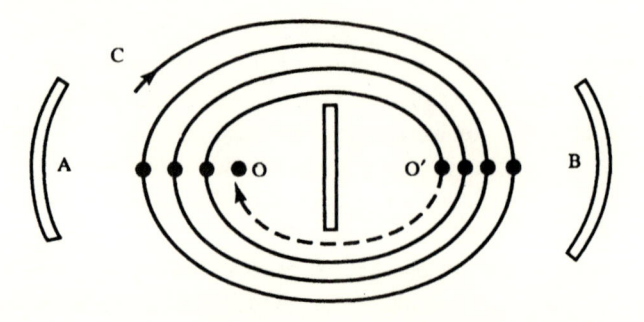

The analytic process is represented by the spiral that goes from C to O. Whatever is said in A, the side of the subject, is understood in B, the side of the analyst. Now this progressive, spoken assumption of the subject's history has the effect of *complementing the imaginary:* whatever is on the side of O' (the ideal ego) passes to the side of O (the ego). In effect, if the analyst truly understands this discourse, *on the return* the subject also understands it. Now, "the echo of his discourse is symmetrical to the specularity of the image."[21] And this is why the subject, *through* the spoken assumption of his or her history, gradually accomplishes the realization of his or her imaginary: from point C to point O.

As a result of this, the imaginary relation of love and war between equals finds its resolution: struggle to the death (one *or* the other) is superseded by coexistence (one *and* the other) in pact and symbol *(symbolon)*.[22] Such is the subversion of the mirror stage by triangulation: the child, seeing itself in its counterpart, turns toward the adult to glean from the adult's word a sign of approval, *on the basis of which* the child can eventually see itself as lovable and acceptable.

Another example of the ideal ego may be found in the son who shows off in a sports car, taking risks in order to demonstrate his strength, shock the onlookers, and dazzle a girl. But if this is how he sees himself in that gorgeous automobile of his, he does so from a *vantage point* located in the symbolic, inasmuch as he is the son *of* his father and nothing else, a daddy's boy. Now here the signifier of the father goes to work, so that, to the extent that he has "introjected" the constellation of insignia that make up the symbolic ego-ideal, the boy will *next be able to see himself* sporting in his car *outside* the social universe of his father.[23]

During the fifties, then, Lacan once more pushed forward in his reading of the second topography, in order to reveal the specificity of the symbolic and of the imaginary. How to arrive at the clearest distinction between them? By reading what Freud had written on identification in chapter 7 of "Group Psychology and the Analysis of the Ego" (1921): "Die Identifizierung eine partielle, höchst beschränkte ist, nur einen einzigen Zug von der Objektperson entlehnt."[24] But how should one translate this without equivocating with respect to the imaginary nature of the relation of ideal ego to ego? ". . . the identification is a partial and extremely limited one and only borrows a single trait *(einen einzigen Zug)* from the person who is its object."[25] Is the *Zug* a trait that belongs to the *Gestalt* and that sends a message? Or is it a signifier in a battery of signifiers? Similarly, is the *einzigen* the one that gives corporeal unity to the image, or is it the one responsible for its outline? Such are the questions posed by this gamble we call conducting an analysis.

The Non-completeness of the Image

At some point in the subject's past, this function of recognition through establishment of the ego-ideal *may* have failed. Anomalies in the subject's history may have caused certain parts of the ego's image to remain forever unseen because they have not been recognized. Lacan remarked: ". . . that is the unconscious!"[26] A surprising statement!

Some psychoanalysts, such as René Spitz, have explained certain of these anomalies by means of early hospitalism, a condition that results when newborns are separated from their mothers after the age of two or three months. These infants, turned over, a dozen to a nurse, do not suffer from any physical lack of food, shelter, cleanliness, or medical care. Nevertheless, when compared to other newborns of the same age who have been tended by their own mothers in a less up-to-date nursery, these infants exhibit a clear retardation in motor development, toilet training, and the acquisition of language. What have they missed?

Is it sufficient to explain this stagnation as an affective deficiency, the result of a nurse caring for ten while the mother cares for only one? Why should it be so disastrous for "brothers" to receive a one-tenth share in the demand for unconditional love? The decisive factor certainly seems to be the formation of the ego-ideal. In what we call the "libidinal object relation" with the privileged adult—either biological mother or nurse!—what is at stake is not the "goodness" of this object. Rather, it is the removal of *anonymity* within this relation, and the possibility this affords of a symbolic identification as determinative for the status of the image.

Along similar lines, when a woman giving birth in a maternity ward cries out in pain and feels ashamed of her *image,* what prevents her from falling prey to the conviction of having been abandoned or even persecuted? Is it the level of medical care and technology? Is it the attentive presence of a team, where everyone is interchangeable? Or is it something altogether different? Is it not the unity of *one* face and *one* proper name, guarantors, beyond the rhythm of presence and absence, of a power of response (responsibility), out of which can be reactualized the symbolic reference of an *"einziger Zug"*?

In the process of analysis, it is precisely unconstituted, regressive images of the subject, linked to various moments and events of the past, that are encountered. How are they encountered? Through free association, through the liberation of speech from its moorings in stable and actual images, the analytic process causes the mirror to oscillate and successive identifications (imaginary and symbolic) from the subject's history to appear. Now in this process of historization holes are revealed, points of fracture, everything nonhistoricized that became a *fixation:* whatever is not-seen in the mirror. All of this because, in the history of the subject, a word was missing, blocked, to be found only in latent form in symptoms, inhibitions, anxieties.

What fresh contribution does analysis make? What is its aim? Must there be completeness of the imaginary, effected through constitution of the ego-ideal? If the analytic process, through liberation of the mooring ropes of speech, truly does permit a maximal, narcissistic projection and a progression into the mirages of *Verliebtheit,* can we say this is its aim? From 1953 on, Lacan's response to this question was no, a correction of his earlier positions. Did Freud have to recognize in Frau K—the woman from Dresden—Dora's *Ichideal* (ego-ideal), the mainstay of her narcissism, the support of her being-loved? Certainly not. If he left Dora's analysis unfinished, it was not because of this failure.

Something else was at stake: not completeness of the narcissistic image, but recognition of desire through naming, inasmuch as the subject's desire is desire of the Other (*de Alio:* in the objective and subjective sense). Now, what would achievement of such recognition suppose, if not integration of the subject into *his or her own* symbolic system, not that of the analyst? This is where we have to choose: the analysand, in search of his or her symbolic realization, will demand it from the side of the analyst. If the analyst, by virtue of an ill-advised desire-to-be-an-analyst, satisfies this demand by personal opinions and the proposal of his or her own system of values, then in effect he or she has made the goal of analysis completion of the narcissistic image through identification with the analyst's ego-ideal. This is a utopian ideal, the very same as that of *Verliebtheit:* indefinite analysis, indefinite because one has resigned oneself, out of sheer fatigue, to the deception induced by dull reality: "Go out there. Now you're a good child."[27]

Two years later (November 16, 1955), in a still stronger statement, Lacan said: "To authenticate all that belongs to the imaginary order in the subject is truly to make analysis the antichamber of madness."[28] Now analysis properly conducted does not lead to this; it is a *reading* of the subject's symbolic universe, *of* his or her singular history with its gashes and holes, its blind imperatives with their obscene and ferocious figures—in brief, of all that has remained unrealized in the symbolic order. The gift of speech effectively brings to birth whatever has not been *in this order* through mutation into a "will have been": elevation of the particular to the universal, in the fall of the accidental.

And so Lacan replied to himself during these years, correcting himself in his answers to his "friend" Balint and his "colleague" Lagache:

1. Far from constituting or from restoring the *imago*, analysis produces a "depersonalization,"[29] a sign, not of running up against some deplorable limit, but of having gone beyond it (with no offense intended to those who defend personalism and respect for the total personality!).

2. Far from being merely imaginary,[30] a projection onto the empty mirror of the analyst's ego, the transference is *symbolic*, an inscription in another locus, the locus of speech. From the moment a subject speaks to another, he causes the Other (with a capital "O") to exist: "Each time a man speaks to another in an authentic and full manner, there is, in the true sense, transference, symbolic transference."[31]

This was a double change of direction for Lacan, one that certainly, in its turn, posed new questions. What, then, is the unconscious? If there is no completeness in the image, is there by contrast any completeness in the symbolic? Is analysis a *totalization* of the subject's history within Heraclitus's *En Panta,* so dear to Heidegger?[32]

5

Exhaustion in the Symbolic

Certainly Freud had good reason for introducing the second topography, which is what drew Lacan to the Freudian text in the first place. But what about the unconscious? How did the introduction of the unconscious determine the practice of analysis? For therein lies a difficulty unique to psychoanalysis, the more so as the unconscious does not plainly reveal itself. Now we will see how Lacan, going back to the *first* topography, linked the unconscious to the symbolic. At first he proceeded pedagogically, with a *formal* distinction of the two sorts of relation present in any human exchange. He did this to locate the point from which analytic practice operates. The first sort of relation belongs to the imaginary order and is between two *egos*. The second sort is symbolic, between two *subjects*. On this basis, the following table of equivalences is founded:

imaginary	*symbolic*
—paranoic knowledge and and spatialization	—recognition in the symbol and historization
—*visualization* of the other as known	—subjectification of the Other in *speech,* which recognizes that which is beyond the known
—the *Gestalt* determines signification	—the *letter* of the signifier determines the subject
—destruction of the other	—coexistence by pact
—love, hate, and ignorance as passions of the ego	—the subject's desire as desire of the Other
—life drives and the pleasure-unpleasure principle	—death drive and what is beyond the pleasure-unpleasure principle

Now these two paths are *mutually exclusive*. "For this desire itself to be satisfied in man requires that it be recognized, through the agreement of speech *or* through the struggle for prestige, in the symbol *or* in the imaginary."[1] Thus, to analyze is to choose the first path. However, in Lacan, this theoretical distinction fades before another: the fundamental distinction between speech and language.

Speech or Language?

Exploring the symbolic itself in his diagnostic of society, Lacan was struck by three paradoxes concerning the relationship of speech and language within the subject:[2]

1. The paradox of madness, in which there is language without speech, especially in those who today have been relegated to "social services involving language."[3]
2. The paradox of neurosis, in which speech exists but is fixed in symptoms and separated from language by repression *(Verdrängung)*.
3. The paradox of modern man, alienated in scientific civilization, his speech objectified in a universal language, his sense of existence lost in a common work. With this point, Lacan launched a thesis that was dear to him: the *wall* of language in its opposition to speech.

Thus three times we note a failure in the requisite identity of universal language and particular speech, of an I that would be an us and an us that would be an I (Hegel). Today, "as language becomes more functional, it becomes improper for speech, and as it becomes too particular to us, it loses its function as language."[4] Meaning: it does nothing but reinforce the ego's narcissism.

In short, speech and language are opposed, and therein lies the real difficulty for psychoanalysis. Indeed, this opposition will come to be *superimposed* on the distinction between imaginary and symbolic. Hence it was an important moment (May 25, 1955) when, during the course of his seminar, Lacan presented—in Schema L—this crucial objection to psychoanalysis:[5]

```
         (Es) S ●--------▶--------● ⓐ' other
                  ╲      ╱
                   ╲ⁱᵐᵃᵍⁱⁿᵃʳʸ ʳᵉˡᵃᵗⁱᵒⁿ
                    ╲  ╱
                    ╱ ╲ᵘⁿᶜᵒⁿˢᶜⁱᵒᵘˢ
                   ╱   ╲
         (ego) ⓐ ○◀─────○ Ⓐ Other
```

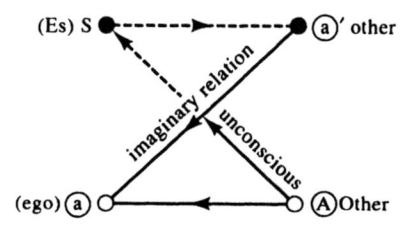

Opposed to the specular plane and the imaginary relation a-a', we find the symbolic relation, which would be the unconscious (S-A). But does the unconscious belong to *the order of speech or of language*? That is the question.

Lacan began his second seminar by describing Newton's achievement: with three little letters, he inscribed the law of gravitation in a field unified by language and rendered the planets silent. Thanks to language, the planets no longer speak. In other words, having lost their value as natural symbols, they no longer have the power to lie to us. This is what language is made for: to create a wall.

What does Schema L show? "So there's the plane of the mirror, the symmetrical world of the *egos* and of the homogeneous others. We'll have to distinguish another level, which we call the wall of language."[6] Lacan continues:

> The imaginary gains its false reality, which nonetheless is a verified reality, starting off from the order defined by the wall of language. The ego such as we understand it, the other, the fellow being, all these imaginary things are objects. To be sure, they aren't homogeneous with moons—and we are liable to forget that all the time. But they are indeed objects, because they are named as such within an organized system, that of the wall of language.[7]

But the subjects are on the other side: "Fundamentally, it is them I am aiming at every time I utter true speech, but I always attain a', a'', through reflection. I always aim at true subjects, and I have to be content with shadows. The subject is separated from the Others, the true ones, by the wall of language."[8] It was to answer this weighty objection that Lacan invented the notion of *full* speech, which at last would break down the wall of language.

The Fiction of Full Speech

Full speech belongs to the psychoanalyst. It is neither powerless nor utopian. In order to grasp this, Lacan identified the psychoanalyst with the figure of the ancient master. Imagine, not a society (the word is too modern), but a city of masters, where the "I" would be an "us" and the "us" an "I"; where the outside (social) would be an inside (psychic) and the inside completely outside; where the good of each would coincide with the good of all. When the master speaks, everything works. Why? Because what sustains the *intersubjective* cohesion of this city—whether it knows peace or war, happiness or unhappiness—is an orthodoxy, that is, what opinion recognizes as right in terms of the ethical conduct to be maintained. (Of course, "opinion" refers to common opinion, without which no city is possible!)

Effortlessly, spontaneously, the master utters the words that move the entire city to action, for they correspond to the *orthos already* there in its *doxa*. The master says the right thing and makes all the right moves because he employs the master-signifiers, the very ones that *organize* the city into a city. He gives no explanations: they are not necessary (not yet!). In one who is simultaneously an orator, a politician, and a lover of language, the art of elocution suffices.

Who does not dream of such a city? For Hegel, for those nostalgic for the *Volksgeist*, for Maurras, wasn't it Athens in the age of Pericles? For an ethnologist, isn't it this or that primitive society? For contemporary man, isn't it that intense moment of unanimity during a soccer championship or a bullfight? For members of a so-called national community, isn't it the tone in which a de Gaulle speaks to France?

In the course of his seminar (October 24, 1954), Lacan chose to speak about Themistocles and Pericles:

> They are at the heart of this historical reality in which a dialogue is taken up, when no truth of any kind can be located in it in the form of a generalizable knowledge that is always true. To give the reply that one has to in response to an event insofar as it is significant, insofar as it is a function of a symbolic exchange between human beings—it could be the order given to the fleet to leave Piraeus—is to give the right interpretation. And to give the right interpretation at the right moment, that's to be a good analyst.[9]

This was still possible because the Sophists had not yet introduced doubt about the primordial signifiers by questioning what they signified. And it was still possible because Plato and Aristotle, educators of future masters, had not yet responded to the divided orthodoxy by introducing a desire for *episteme,* for *knowledge about what is said* and a corresponding need for schooling.

The best demonstration of this is found in Seminar III (June 6, 1956), where Lacan, moving from Athens to Jerusalem, analyzes act 1, scene 2 of Racine's *Athalie.*[10] What does the High Priest Joad (Jehoiada) do when he instills the master signifier—that is, fear of God—in the officer who has lost faith? He transforms him into a firm believer, establishing intersubjectivity, not with new information or new knowledge, but with full speech. Contemporary culture continues this work: a creative subjectivity works subterraneously "to renew the never-exhausted power of symbols in the human exchange that brings them to the light of day."[11] And what example does Lacan give of this? One that Freud did not have the preparation to see: "More than ever, on the other hand, the strength of the churches resides in the language that they have been able to maintain: an authority, it must be said, that Freud left in the dark in the article where he sketches for us what we would call the collective subjectivities of the Church and the Army."[12]

For Lacan of the fifties the paradigm is found in *You are my wife* and *You are my master,* where the creative power of speech and inter-subjectivity are one and the same. And the point of his argument is this: the analyst *is* the modern figure of the masters who, over the ages, have promoted a speech capable of surmounting the wall of language. In a lecture on "the individual myth of the neurotic," given in 1953 at the Collège philosophique, Lacan did not shy away from defining the analyst as one

> who, albeit almost clandestinely, assumes the position, in his symbolic relationship with the subject, of that personage—very much obliterated as a result of our historical decline—who is the *master,* the moral master, the master who raises the ignorant to the level of fundamental human relations and arranges for him what one might call access to consciousness, indeed, even to wisdom, in his grasp of the human condition.[13]

Ten years later, when the Société française de psychanalyse split apart, Lacan reaffirmed his conviction: "If a society of masters is possible, it will come from the analysts."[14]

Isn't it the analyst, with his or her gift of speech at just the right moment (Freud likens him to the lion who springs only once)[15]—isn't it the analyst who today embodies (following Max Weber's distinction) the *charismatic* power necessary to bring about a *Gemeinschaft* (community), above and beyond the *rational* power of a modern, scientific *Gesellschaft* (association), founded on knowledge *(savoir)* and technology?

The analyst's speech is an act that, like poetry, cannot be explained... except by destroying it:

> One tap of *your finger* on the drum releases all sounds and begins the new harmony.
> One step *of yours*, it's the levy of new men and their order to march.
> *Your head* turns aside: the new love! Your head turns back,
> —the new love!
>
> (Arthur Rimbaud, "A une raison")[16]

Truth and Poetry

In a letter dated May 15, 1971, Arthur Rimbaud wrote: "Poetry no longer gives rhythm to action; it *goes ahead of it!*" Psychoanalysis allows anyone at all to liberate the speech frozen in the symptom and to give free rein to the Freudian unconscious, that assiduous worker that *speaks* through its formations. It serves as a new lung, a locus of respiration for the *poetic* speech lost and forgotten in modern man, and it does so in two ways.

If indeed speech is "ahead," this implies a double detachment:

1. Speech is not an organ for communicating knowledge *(savoir)* nor a tool for transmitting information. But it *is* a house of truth, a *dit-mension*.[17] "I, truth, am speaking," said Lacan, allowing it to speak (Vienna, 1955). For truth does not exist except in speaking. Its home is opinion *(doxa)*, that is, everything actually said and recognized in society, by at least some. Its kingdom is the realm of "they say..."—tales and gossip. All of us are housekeepers, with all due respect to learned academicians and militant missionaries.

2. "It no longer gives rhythm to action." Speech is no longer a *theoria* that exceeds and illuminates action, a light to be contemplated, then applied in practice. It is "in advance" because it creates a path for *itself,* without the "I" knowing what it says or who says it. It runs ahead, and

the "I" cannot keep up with it. There is no metalanguage. Only waves of proper names remain to cover up its absence. Anyone can say of himself or herself, "I always speak the truth." This is not a pretentious affirmation by the ego nor, conversely, an attempt to fade into anonymity through denial: "It is not I who speak." It is speech itself, moving through each one of us, not through one more than another: it is "the precedence of poetry," according to Heidegger. And no one is excluded from it by reason of the language he or she inhabits.

Lacan asks:

> Is it not an act of charity on Freud's part to have permitted human beings in their misery to tell themselves there is—since there is the unconscious—something transcendent, truly transcendent, which is nothing other than what this species inhabits, that is, language? Yes, is it not an act of charity to tell them the news that, in their everyday life, language offers them a support that contains more reason than it might seem and already has within itself wisdom, that unattainable object of vain pursuits?[18]

Analysis as Exhaustion in the Symbolic

The fiction of the analyst's gift of full speech could easily lead to tyranny and aggrandizement. Lacan attempted to remedy this by letting go of his historic description of language as nothing other than a wall that reduces the other to an object. He took the first step with his introduction of Schema L at the end of his second seminar (1955). He then posed the question: what is it that makes speech full? Why is speech not reduced to pure "bla-bla-bla?" If the efficacy of the master's speech comes from a supporting *orthodoxa*, what then supports this? Lacan gave the following answer: language is "the radical condition"[19] of speech as full.

This was a veritable reversal that surprised and astonished his listeners! Beginning with his seminar of March 30, 1955, and continuing with his commentary on Poe's story "The Purloined Letter," Lacan introduced the *symbolic* order, strictly speaking: pure language, a combinatorial system for the inscription of places. Among his diverse explanations, two were particularly striking. One made use of cybernetics, in which the minimal binary choice of 0 and 1 inscribes presence against a background of absence, and absence is the condition of symbolic presence. Another consisted in a commentary on the first verse of the Gospel of John, where—in spite of resistance on the part of his listeners—Lacan demonstrated that *in principio erat verbum* (in the beginning was the word) establishes the primacy, not of speech but of language. If speaking is more than simply naming what is, if it can bring into being what is not and generate a 1 from a 0 (ex nihilo), it is by virtue of the structure that is language, as a condition *(principium)* of speech in operation.

From that time on, the *unconscious*—structured like a language—was conceived as belonging to the symbolic order and therefore as determining the structure of analysis. What, then, is the Freudian unconscious? "The unconscious is that part of concrete discourse, in so far as it is transindividual, that is *not* at the disposal of the subject in re-establishing the *continuity* of his conscious discourse."[20] This definition, from the Rome Discourse, meshes with that of the analytic process: "*restoration* of continuity."[21] The analytic process works via full speech, since it is a matter of establishing an "intersubjective continuity of the discourse in which the subject's history is constituted."[22] Whatever has not achieved recognition in the subject by means of the symbol is left hanging. But in the analytic process, inasmuch as it is symbolic, "non-being came to be, because it has spoken."[23] This is possible because the truth of the censored chapter, of the blank page, of the non-recognized and sense-less in the history of the subject can be recovered in his or her symptomatic displacements. Where there was mis-understanding, let understanding arise! Thus, Lacan presents the end of analysis as a work of achievement in the symbolic: "What we teach the subject to recognize as his unconscious is his history—that is to say, we help him *to perfect* the present historization of the facts that have already determined a certain number of the historical 'turning-points' in his existence."[24]

Such a turning point occurred in 1953: the essential incompleteness of the *imago* was met with the *completeness* of meaning. This took place by way of the *symbolic,* wherein are reconciled the universal of language and the particular of speech. Thus the primacy of the symbolic rests on a *triple* supposition: full speech, intersubjectivity, and exhaustion of the subject in the symbolic.

Logically this leads—Lacan admits it, since desire is desire of "nothing"—to an assumption by the subject of the very limit of his or her historicity, that is, of his or her being-for-death, a limit "at every instant *present* in what this history possesses as achieved."[25] How can this come about? Only through voluntary death, which "constitutes in the subject the eternalization of his desire."[26] "Empedocles, by throwing himself into Mount Etna, leaves forever present in the memory of men this symbolic act of his being-for-death."[27] So ended the Rome Discourse in 1953.

The Irreducible Imaginary

From 1964 on, Lacan distanced himself from the period of the fifties. More and more, he came to doubt the creative power of speech, asserting finally in 1980 that it has none. He mocked the title of his Rome discourse, "Fiction and song of speech and language,"[28] adding that the attempt to designate the unconscious resulted in "the fiction of the incomplete text."[29] He said there is no intersubjectivity (only a delirium à deux), that talk of full speech is nothing more than words, "the song of a starling."[30] Full or not, it is not *"You are my wife"* that holds a couple together; on the contrary, if they remain together, it is "in spite of that,"[31] and for reasons having nothing to do with the order of speech.

In applying this light-hearted irony to his own past teachings, Lacan's purpose was to reveal what analytic experience had gradually taught him: that the analyst, by giving *primacy* to the symbolic over the imaginary and the real, makes it impossible for an analysis to end. More specifically: "Stressing the function of knowledge of the one-slip *(l'une-bévue)* — which is how I translate the unconscious — can effectively straighten out a person's life,"[32] but is this the purpose of analysis? No. The "preference given in every matter to the unconscious" will require that the analysis be redone, that the analyst provide the patient with an additional "slice" *(tranche)*, as it is called in popular parlance.[33] The price is therefore a heavy one. But Lacan was not yet at that point. It was the *irreducibility of the imaginary* that he was stumbling up against. Schema L testifies to that. The dotted lines clearly show the lack of direct relation between A and S. A horizontal arrow indicates the only possible path, which leads from the Other (A) to the ego.[34]

There can be no getting around it: only a madman can believe in an I who is on a first-name basis with his or her partner, that is to say, in intersubjectivity. But there is another way, that of Aristotle, who said man thinks *with* his soul. Hence the subject speaks *with* his or her ego to another who is not a thou, but a him or her (with all due respect to Martin Büber and his theses of the I and Thou and the life of dialogue!).

Thus, in the *Traumdeutung*, the beautiful butcher's wife speaks to her gluttonous husband, whose preference is for full-figured women; but she speaks to him *with* the image of her close friend: if there is no caviar for the wife, then the husband will remain desirous, that is to say, unsatisfied!

But if symbolic and imaginary are not concretely opposed to each other, how then is their function to be conceived?

Is the Analyst a Master?

This exaltation of the symbolic during the fifties, its primacy over the imaginary, did not go unquestioned. In particular, there was the question of the irreducibility of the imaginary.

In a similar vein, Lacan would need time—a long time—to free himself of his fascination with the figure of the master. Not until the seminar of 1969–1970 would he show that the social bond—which analysis is—is *the opposite* of the master's discourse: more precisely, its polar opposite. Indeed, the master is supported by these three passions: love, hate, and ignorance.[35]

Was this correction a result of the conclusions he drew from the "events" of May 1968? Speaking to hundreds of students on December 3, 1969, at the Centre Universitaire de Vincennes, Lacan told them: "Revolutionary aspirations have only one possibility: always to end up in the discourse of the master. Experience has proven this. What you aspire to as revolutionaries is a master. You will have one!"[36] And when the master appears, then psychoanalysis disappears: all that remains is strict obedience to orders.

Whatever the value of this hypothesis regarding the importance of May 1968, one thing is certain: Lacan reached this turning point at a time when he was concerned not only with the end of analysis but, even more, with the transition from analysand to analyst. With a master there is no way to know anything; there are only a number of truths.

6

The Making of a Case of Acting-Out

> The imaginary is the place where every truth is enunciated.
> —Lacan, March 18, 1975

This epigraph, from Seminar XXII, condenses a late point of view. Dating from 1975, the final period of Lacan's teaching, it represents his ultimate position on the imaginary: it, not the symbolic, is the place where every truth is enunciated. However, in the fifties, Lacan was far from having arrived at this new topographical perspective. Isn't it the case that this new perspective presupposes another imaginary?

Before measuring the gap between them, we must again emphasize what is presented in Schema L. As we showed in the preceding chapter, the subject speaks from the place of the Other—locus of signifiers—but *with* an ego that is situated in and constituted by its imaginary relation to its counterpart. Thus it is not enough to affirm the primacy of the symbolic; it must be seen *how* the symbolic and the imaginary are conjoined. The subject speaks *with* his or her ego. Thus the symbolic is not on one side or the other of the imaginary. They are not opposed to each other such that a (symbolic) depth is concealed by an (imaginary) surface. Rather, the depth is read right there, *on* the surface itself, "for it is at the surface that it is seen as imperfections on the face of feast days."[1] Hence "another topology is necessary if we are not to be misled as to the place of desire."[2]

Lacan found an occasion to demonstrate this in connection with an article by Ernst Kris, "Ego Psychology and Interpretation in Psychoana-

65

lytic Therapy," published in January 1951 in the *Psychoanalytic Quarterly*.[3] Is it not the timely occasion that makes the case?[4]

No doubt Lacan remembered the sharp reprimand he had received from Kris in August 1936. He had delivered his lecture on the mirror stage and was preparing to leave the Marienbad Congress in advance of its closing (to attend the Olympic Games in Berlin) when Kris issued a call to order: "It's not done!"[5] How could a young psychoanalyst, freshly admitted to the Société psychanalytique de Paris (and not even licensed yet!) permit himself to do such a thing? It may have been that Kris was among the 43 percent of Americans who, in 1935, favored boycotting the Berlin Games because of anti-Jewish discrimination by the Nazis.[6] We don't know. In any event, Lacan did not comply.

But eighteen years later, liberated from his worries associated with the SPP[7] and its affiliation to the IPA, Lacan returned the compliment by responding to Kris on the terrain of psychoanalytic practice. It was a typical example of how a case is made through successive writings and ends up with a label that is the result of interpretation, in this case, the label "acting-out." Below, the five steps:

1. In February 1954, in the course of Seminar I, *Freud's Papers on Technique,* Lacan affirmed: "There's no question about it, the interpretation [by Kris] is valid."[8]

2. In January 1956, in his seminar entitled *Les Psychoses,* Lacan briefly reviewed the case.[9]

3. In 1956, Lacan reworked his position in two articles published in *La Psychanalyse* 1 under the titles "Introduction au commentaire de Jean Hyppolite sur la 'Verneinung' de Freud," and "Réponse au commentaire de Jean Hyppolite sur la 'Verneinung' de Freud."[10] The term "acting-out" appeared.

4. In July 1958 Lacan advanced further with his report to the Colloque de Royaumont: "The Direction of the Treatment and the Principles of Its Power."[11] This time he wrote: "This intervention [by Kris] may be presumed to be erroneous."[12]

5. Finally, on March 8, 1967, in his seminar *La Logique du fantasme,* he concluded more firmly: "I am in disagreement."

Ego Psychology and Interpretation

In his article, Kris revealed changes in technique and theory resulting from new clinical observations. Christening these changes "ego psychology," Kris argued that Freud himself had been moving toward it: to begin with, Freud, stimulated by the Zurich group and, in turn, by his own clinical findings on the psychoses, had introduced the concept of narcissism; next, there had been the introduction of the superego, in order to account for the phenomena of guilt and negative therapeutic reaction; finally, Freud's clinical impressions of resistance and defense (Kris lumps them both together!) facilitated formulation of psychoanalytic theory in terms of ego function. Thus, from 1910 on (according to Kris), Freud had been led to modify his own technique, anticipating both ego psychology and new interpretive techniques in the psychotherapy of adults and children (developed by Anna Freud), as well as interventions with delinquents, borderline cases, and psychotics.

Kris summarized all this in what he called an analysis "near the surface." This concerned typical patterns of behavior in a subject, conceived as defensive operations of the ego. Far from taking the ego as an obstacle, the technique consisted in making it an ally in order to establish with the subject a zone of cooperation between analyst and patient. The analyst, instead of confining himself to interpretation of the unconscious in accordance with the "old procedure," could explore the mechanisms of the ego and, seeing how the analysand reacted, come to an understanding with him or her.

Thus, from the start, a *choice* is made: the ego in Freud is not the foundation of narcissism but the system perception-consciousness and the principle of objective knowledge. From this choice flows Kris's interpretation. To strengthen his demonstration, Kris chose a particularly significant example: the case of a man who had gone through "traditional" analysis with Melitta Schmideberg (Melanie Klein's daughter) and, grateful for the improvement he had experienced, some years later asked Kris to resume the analysis.

The analysand was a man of thirty who worked in scientific research. His symptom was an inhibition to publish his work, which inhibition was jeopardizing his hopes for advancement. His explanation: he was convinced he was a plagiarist and felt himself under constant pressure to borrow ideas from others, for example, from his best friend, a young colleague whose office was next to his own. For these reasons, he felt guilty about publishing anything in his own name.

First Step

During his analysis with Kris, the scientist was finally at the point of publishing an article. Then, one fine morning, he arrived for his session and announced he had unearthed at the library a book he had previously consulted. Lo and behold, the book contained the "basic idea"[13] of his work!

Alerted by his state of "satisfaction and excitement,"[14] Kris lost no time in asking which book it was. He then inquired "in very great detail"[15] about the passages in question and, after a painstaking comparative search, concluded they contained no trace whatsoever of the analysand's essential argument. Kris *assured* him of this: you are making the author of the book say what you yourself wish to say (implying: the author did not say it!). It was an appeal to the healthy part of the ego. With the birth of suspicion in the analysand, everything got reversed. Now he said it must be his office-mate who was stealing his original ideas and repeating them without acknowledgment: the inverse of his original claim. And when the analysand next received his own ideas from his colleague's mouth, he heard them as if for the very first time, without recognizing them as his own. "The whole problem of plagiarism appeared in a new light," wrote Kris.[16]

Second Step

Kris had noted a connection between the patient's intellectual inhibitions and his father. While the grandfather had been a renowned scientist, the subject's father had left no mark in his field of research. Thus the subject's compulsion to find mentors was born of a wish for a "grand" father, an ideal father. On the basis of a dream, Kris uncovered a wish to incorporate the paternal penis: father and son were fighting; the father's weapons were books, which the son managed to seize and *swallow*. Kris offered the analysand the following interpretation: the "tendency to take, to bite, to steal was traced . . . until it could be pointed out one day that the decisive displacement was to *ideas*. Only the ideas of others were truly interesting, only ideas one could take; hence the taking had to be *engineered*."[17]

Kris waited for his words to take effect. After a long silence, the analysand, associating to the last phrase, responded with this story: "Every noon, when I leave here, before luncheon and before returning to my office, I walk through X street (a street well known for its small but attractive restaurants) and I look at the menus in the windows. In one of these restaurants I generally find my preferred dish—*fresh brains*."[18] Kris was satisfied with the patient's reaction. In it he saw an indication that his technique had been effective in helping the patient overcome the feeling that he was "in danger of plagiarizing."[19] The patient now *knew* how "to take" good things and good ideas from the right place.

Text on Text

Taking up the case five times between 1954 and 1967, Lacan evolved a different reading.

1. The subject speaks *with* his ego (cf. Schema L). In the other who is my companion and my ideal ego, I see my own ego in reverse: the other *has* original ideas (hence taking them from the other would be plagiarism). Moreover, I do not recognize myself in him.

But to this imaginary relationship, the symbolic order is *conjoined*; the subject speaks *with* this perspective: he speaks of himself under the *symbol* of negation, he speaks of his being under the form of nonbeing. Freud, in his article "Die Verneinung," wrote: "Recognition of the unconscious on the part of the ego is expressed in a negative formula."[20] In fact, "performance of the function of judgement is not made possible until the creation of the symbol of negation."[21] Thus, by employing the *Verneinung* in discourse, the subject accomplishes the integration of his ego—under the form of inversion. But while he admits to his being, he does not, for all that, recognize himself: for this, he will need the Other's speech.

But what speech? Doubting the subject's words, Kris answered with an appeal to "reality," which he had carefully examined in order to offer the patient "objective" assurance that nothing had been taken from the other's book. The subject replied by again putting into play the subjectivity of his imaginary relationship in its conjunction with the symbolic. That is, he replied by *turning around* the intention: if I cannot plagiarize anymore, then it must be the other who is plagiarizing me. Once again, the other has ideas without my being able to recognize them as my own.

2. What, then, did ego psychology achieve? Kris gave no credence to the subject's speech: after all, had he told the truth when he claimed to have plagiarized the book? Hence it was necessary to seek verification in "reality," by finding a criterion for truth, conceived as *adequatio rei et intellectus,* adequation of thing and idea. But there is no brute reality, only judgments about reality. The criterion will therefore be the analyst's ego, presupposed to be the system perception-consciousness and principle of metalanguage, an ego stronger and more objective than that of the patient. This is once again to stumble over the famous "reality testing," that positivistic red herring that is dragged out whenever a powerful but imperiled position needs shoring up.

But, one will retort, why should Kris have believed what the analysand was saying? Even the analysand was not demanding it; indeed, at the beginning of analysis, he had failed to recount an important event for fear the analyst would rush into believing him and end up mistaken. The Freudian discovery introduced something different, namely a distinction between "I believe *you*" (as speaking subject) and "I believe *it*" (the content of your speech). This approach is Cartesian in that it marks the birth of the subject and the revival of the *cogito* through the Freudian *Wo es war* (there where it was, there must I as subject come into being).

"I believe you," because the imaginary is not the illusory. When Kris's analysand declared, through the *Verneinung,* that he perceived no original ideas except outside himself in the mirror, he was not under any illusion. He was misrecognizing himself. That is, he was sticking to the *only* possible path for eventual self-recognition. In short, his subjectivity was operating as the effect of an "I believe *you*" spoken from the field of the Other.

3. Kris, on the other hand, firmly believed in his analysand's "defenses." By spotting them, he could learn *what it was* the patient was defending himself against, and this would be the *truth* of his desire. On every street corner, a "psychotherapeutic" voice is advertising: "Feeling inhibited? Just say by *what,* and you will learn what you desire. The quick way is the best way!"

For Kris, then, defense and drive are two faces of the *self-same* mold: if you refrain from plagiarizing, this is because you really wish to plagiarize. If you have a compulsion to plagiarize, this is because you have not satisfied the drive. The analytic move is to seek *adaptation* to the object, in this case, the taking of ideas from others. Two presuppositions underpin this goal:

1. The patient believes he is a plagiarist *because* he wishes to be one.
2. The patient is not really a plagiarist (I ascertained this myself!) *because* he defends himself against this wish.

The trick works; the circle is closed. Double causality is the explanation. All that remains is to draw the practical conclusion: it is well to act in accordance with "reality"—that is, in accordance with the ethics of the analyst's ego.

4. Before injecting this into the patient, Kris drew his attention to his wish for a great and successful father. Playing on the equivalence between fish (in the father/son rivalry on fishing trips), books (in the dream), and, finally, original ideas, Kris confirmed what was at stake in the analysand's wish: "incorporation of the father's penis."

What conclusions did Kris draw from this? "Only the ideas of others were truly interesting, only ideas one could take."[22] Go ahead, then, take ideas where they are found! The important thing is to know how to do this! The ideal father was thereby preserved—and in better condition than before. There *is* something in him. All that is needed is to begin participating in the mechanism of "give and take."

Now, this interpretation by Kris preserves the patient's foreclosure (*Verworfen*) of the oral drive, in effect fostering misrecognition of the place of "nothingness" in the Other. In the symbolic order, there is no ownership, nothing of a proprietary or privative nature. Hence the subject—with his oral drive to absorb—could have been recognized as he inserted, in this empty place, the screen of his fantasy, fantasy to be strictly distinguished here from "reality." At that point, the subject could have been recognized as able *to have* ideas and risk publishing them, without worrying about effecting a split—now acknowledged and mastered—between what is yours and what is mine.

However, in the absence of the above interpretation, the subject, after a period of silence, responded by verbalizing the acting-out he had begun some time ago, namely, fulfillment of his compulsion to absorb fresh brains wherever they could be found. Thus he had responded in the same register . . . much to Kris's satisfaction!

Two times, at two different stages, Kris had clearly indicated this register to him: first, by telling him he had, in reality, examined his mentor's book; and second, by urging him to learn how to cope with this reality, as defined by ego psychology. The patient's wish to incorporate the paternal penis was thus fulfilled through introjection of the analyst's ego-ideal.

The Acting-Out

The acting-out may be characterized as follows:

1. It is an acting that has remained opaque, uncomprehended by the subject. The compulsion to eat brains persists as something foreign, something he has stumbled into from his "successful" plagiarism.

In effect, the acting-out is a *response* that conforms to a certain type of interpretation: a response situated in the same order as the interpretation. The analyst takes his ego for the system perception-consciousness; the analysand provides him with a correlative response: "a zone of cooperation between two strong egos," according to Kris.

2. Unlike a purely silent passage to the act, the acting-out includes a deferred verbalization. A report is made and addressed to the analyst. It is both a reconstruction and a *manifestation:* see where I am . . . without my understanding what it means! Thus it is a *demand,* ignorant of its own meaning, addressed to the analyst. To one who knows how to listen, it will be perceived as an appeal that raises the analytic stake, an appeal that aims to put the analyst in position for another intervention. The appeal must be understood this way: I demand that you refuse what I offer you, because this is *not it*.[23] Why? So that the brains in your head be even fresher! In other words, the acting-out is a demand that the object of the drive as cause of desire be placed within the analytic relation in the locus of the Other, not that it be made present in the guise of brains served up on a platter by a restaurateur. Hence:

3. Finally—and fundamentally—the acting-out is a substitute in acted form for a lack of *Bejahung,* a lack of symbolic recognition through the word. Thus, in the final version of this case, Lacan availed himself of English to gain precision: "to act out" appeared where "to read" had failed.[24] When a reading goes badly, then one acts out the role for the audience; through mime, one makes the spectators see what has not been read. The acting-out becomes a substitute for a failure of *reading*. We say

of someone: "He's making a scene!" because *previously* there had been a failure to read the event, to integrate it into the symbolic.

Now, in the transference during treatment, the return of the repressed is inscribed in the field of the Other while awaiting the right interpretation, that is, decoding, which is what the reading is. If the analyst does not allow the analysand to do this, then there is an acting-out: a scene played *outside* the locus of recognition, yet *for* the analyst. Indeed, the acting-out not only substitutes for the reading, but at the same time serves as an appeal for the necessity of taking it up again.

Is Everything Readable?

Whatever has not been decoded by reading appears in the "performance." In the early years of Lacan's return to Freud, this definition of the acting-out process was encompassed in the more general formula, "Whatever does not come to light in the symbolic appears in the real"[25]: a real that is suffered through hallucination, a real enacted through an *acting-out*.[26] In every case, something *from* the symbolic, something foreign to and unrecognized by the subject, appears ... *in* the real. This crucial assertion—in addition to the question it posed about the primacy of the symbolic over the imaginary—now generated two new sorts of questions, which Lacan left pending:

1. If there is some signifier in the real, then what is the real itself? If it has been correctly identified as such, what is its *relation* to the symbolic?

2. Does the analytic process aim for complete *Bejahung*, total exhaustion in the symbolic, *such that* nothing appears in the real? Is it even possible, given that Freud recognized an *urverdrängt*, an irreducible repressed, that precludes the saying of *everything*?

Starting in 1964, Lacan began to confront these new questions. It was a ground-breaking step—one that would, at that point, affect the meaning of the epigraph to this chapter. Here then is the epigraph in context: "Negation is also a way to affirm—Freud insisted on it from the beginning—a way of affirming *there where* alone affirmation is possible, because the imaginary is the *place* where every truth is enunciated, and a truth denied has as much imaginary weight as a truth affirmed, *Verneinung, Bejahung*."[27]

III

THE TRANSFERENCE

7

A Change of Place

In each period of Lacan's teaching he took a different approach to the transference, each approach displaying some of its constitutive elements. The different approaches were not actually opposed to each other; rather, they comprised separate elements of the reply to a new question addressed to Freud. Their only point in common was purely negative: a refusal to be satisfied with a crude, overly simplistic definition of the transference as the sum of positive and negative feelings experienced by the analysand for the analyst. Certainly these feelings are not to be denied, but they are effects of the transference, not the transference itself.

What is most important lies elsewhere, in a point Lacan kept stumbling up against, indeed kept turning around, in his successive advances on the transference. It was a question that constantly preoccupied him: is the position occupied by the analyst a place of support for the *objet petit a*, cause of desire, or not? We will see how his research (from *circare*, "to turn around") permitted Lacan to happen upon some essential discoveries with respect to the transference—without, for all that, exhausting the investigation.

The Transference Belongs to the Imaginary Order

During the fifteen years from 1936 to 1952, Lacan made it clear that the transference was a phenomenon of the *imago*. As a matter of fact, what had seduced him in Freud's second topography was "the ingenious use he knew how to make of the notion of the *image*."[1]

The transference is the presence of the past in the present. But this succinct definition demands questioning with respect to the nature of this presence. Is it *erinnern,* a remembering? If to analyze is to recollect, then analysis will be an art of interpretation. This is what Freud believed for a long time. But in 1920, in chapter 3 of *Beyond the Pleasure Principle,* he wrote, in the imperfect: "Psycho-analysis was then first and foremost an art of interpreting *(Deutungskunst)*."[2] Here was his recognition that psychoanalysis was an art of interpreting, but is no longer, because the presence of the past in the present does not belong to the order of memory. This is *why* there is transference. Doubtless Freud found this regrettable, but he would have to live with it. For transference is something the analyst can neither prevent nor spare the analysand from. In effect, it is *another* mode of the presence of the past: a repetition *(Wiederholung)* that is a reliving *(wiedererleben)*. The analyst must get the analysand "to reexperience some portion *(ein Stück)* of his forgotten life."[3]

Forgotten, but not lost: a portion returns. In what manner? In "*die anscheinende Realität,*" wrote Freud. In reality, but not in apparent reality (as it is usually translated)—rather, in a reality that appears here and now, in a phenomenal given that is there to see. Freud makes it more precise—"*als Spiegelung,*" as a mirror reflection of the forgotten past—and Lacan even more so: this optic reflection occurs in the mirror that is the *image* of the analyst. What he discovered in 1936 in the mirror stage, Lacan now read in Freud's 1920 text. Thus the transference is another mode of recalling and recollecting, not intra- but extra-psychically, via the detour of a third, namely, the presence of the image of the analyst.

In "Au-delà du principe de réalité" (1936), in three pages that are a tiny literary jewel,[4] Lacan described the analytic process in terms of the *imago* and the transference as a change of place *(Übertragung)* for the image, which passes from an original person to the person of the analyst. The analysand gives material form to and actualizes what he or she is: an image by which he or she is activated. He stamps its characteristics onto the image of the analyst, then misrecognizes it in the sense that he or she is unaware either of its nature or of its importance. But the psychoanalyst returns the image, to which—by means of his or her word—he or she has restored the unity, lost over time, in its dimension as imaginary and not real.

Thus, in 1948, Lacan could describe the transference as the projection of an image:

This phenomenon represents in the patient the imaginary transference on to our person of one of the more or less archaic *imagos,* which by an effect of symbolic subduction, degrades, diverts, or inhibits the cycle of such behavior, which, by an accident of repression, has excluded from the control of the ego this or that function or corporeal segment, and which, by an action of identification, has given its form to this or that agency of the personality.[5]

Finally, in "Intervention on the Transference,"[6] his 1951 study of the Dora case, Lacan showed that analytic experience belongs essentially to the order of speech as locus of truth. It is therefore a dialectical experience, where strides toward subjectivation of the analysand depend on the analyst's response. The transference, defined as a dual relationship of image to image, interrupts this process, creating an "obstacle" (Freud called it *das Hindernis*) to intersubjective truth. The transference is thus a *stagnation* of the dialectic, due to the influence of the imaginary in the intersubjective relation. For the analyst to be an accomplice in this is enough to short-circuit the analysis, as happened in Dora's case. If, in 1905, Freud wrote that Dora was transferring onto himself the image of Herr K, this was because he believed Dora loved Herr K (as he would state in 1923). Dora, however, did not love Herr K. He was for her only an identificatory support (not an object), enabling her to question Frau K . . . in her feminine mystery.

Thus, for Lacan at this period, the transference, because merely imaginary, was resistance to truth, a mere trans-port of images. It is important to emphasize this, because Lacan's later approaches to the transference would not succeed in erasing his first encounter with Freud, which was bound up with his discovery of the *imago*. Indeed, far from obliterating his first love of Freud, these approaches are suffused with the following question: is the imaginary mere resistance and stagnation, or is it something else? Is it an obstacle to be avoided or a necessary support?

Because Symbolic, the Transference Is Not an Obstacle

Beginning in 1953, Lacan changed his position and identified the transference with the act of speaking: "Each time a man speaks to another in an authentic and full manner, there is, in the true sense, transference, *symbolic* transference."[7]

Why this new locution? Returning at last to the Freud of the first topography, Lacan reinstated the original, Freudian meaning of the word *Übertragung*, taken in the plural. This sense of the word did not pertain to the analysand's relationship to the analyst but to something that precedes analysis, namely, the work of the unconscious, in accordance with which an unconscious representation is represented by a preconscious one. The transferences are transpositions *(Übersetzungen)* resulting from a change in the place of *inscription*. Freud always retained this fundamental meaning, from his letter to Fliess (May 30, 1896) to his final work, *Moses and Monotheism*.[8]

Now this process does not belong to the order of the image, but is eminently symbolic: its material consists in nothing but discrete, literal elements, in accord with "the essentially *localized* structure of the signifier."[9] Thus the transference is not just any repetition, but repetition of a *demand* addressed to the field of the Other, the return of a past demand. Because the demand was not previously recognized, it returns in unconscious formations (symptoms, dreams, parapraxes, jokes). Thus, as soon as one subject addresses another subject in full, authentic speech, there is transference, such that recognition occurs at the very point where before there had been none: a blank page, a censored chapter, a rejected *(verworfen)* fragment from his history.

Symbolic, then, this repetition is an appeal for nomination. Like Hegel's "concept," the *nomen* is the duration of the thing. Such is the creative power of speech, which makes the thing exist in time, generates identity within difference. The motivation for these "transferences" is not so much the feelings that are experienced as faith that the Other will *be able* to respond to them.

This is why when, eventually, the analyst comes to occupy the place of the Other, he has only to insert himself in an already existing process, a habitual, general process of messages that call for responses in inverted form. This new definition of the transference, originated by Lacan in 1953, is of major significance. It implies that transference *is not an obstacle* to analysis, but the road that leads to it.

This definition is truly Freudian, provided one doesn't forget that Freud's first sense of *Übertragung* also founds the second, which concerns the analytic relationship. Let us take the following example: On March 15, 1923, Lou Andreas-Salomé wrote Freud to let him know the results of an analysis. The patient's symptoms had disappeared, with the exception of some stomach pain. "It appeared," she said, *"just where* the unfolding of the memories stopped at this nodal point."[10] On March 23, Freud responded: "This residual symptom relates to you, the transference mother, and will be waiting for you in Königsberg. Old rule of grammar: whatever does not lend itself to declension, attribute to—transference."[11]

According to this rule of grammar—Freud used it to appeal to the symbolic order—nouns that cannot be declined (gender, number, or case) do not belong to the mother tongue but have a foreign origin ... via transference from one language to another, through a change in their place of inscription. Similarly, this residue of the symptom (stomach pain) cannot be "declined," that is, cannot enter into the subject's psychic elaboration of himself with his material signifier. Unintegrated into the subject's native language, coming from elsewhere by way of the transference, the residue remains suspended. It therefore *summons* speech from elsewhere, from the Other, the very place from which it was transferred: It "relates to you, the transference mother, and will be waiting for you in Königsberg"! Because Lou occupied the place of the addressee (the transference mother) she *alone* could, she *alone* had to—through her speech—restore to the subject his own message, embed it in his own language and "declensions," and thereby make it arrive at its proper destination.

Thus the transference, because symbolic, is not an obstacle to analysis to the extent that it is, as Freud said, a "way of remembering."[12] On this key point, Freud's 1914 article "Remembering, Repeating and Working-Through" is of utmost importance. The purpose of analysis is "a tracing ... back to the past" via an "ideal remembering"[13] by means of a working-through, which allows for situated, dated historization. Now this work encounters a limit, the very limit of remembering: an empty place remains. The function of the transferences is to occupy this place *(an Stelle treten)*. They appear in the *place* of the missing remembrance.

But are they, for all that, a remembering? Remembering is the actual presence of the past, located in the past as distinct from the present. The transferences, on the contrary, are the presence of the past in repetition *(Wiederholung)* and acting-out *(agieren),* in other words, without "an escorting back into the past." Whence the Freudian law of disjunction: either remembering or the transference. The transferred is the *not yet* remembered; the remembered is the *never again* transferred.

For Freud in 1914, the goal of analysis was victory of *das erinnern* over the transference. But by 1920, he had ascertained the impossibility of reducing the one to the other and would eventually affirm the irreducibility of the two paths, remembering and acting-out. The analyst would simply have to make do with it.

Such was the state of affairs when Lacan took up the question. Is the aim of analysis complete satisfaction of the demand to recognize the past, through total exhaustion of this past in the symbolic? We have seen how Lacan twice answered in the affirmative: the transference is a repetition in the *imaginary (imago* to *imago)* or in the *symbolic* (an appeal to the Other, locus of speech). Repetition is a demand for recognition, to which the analyst must respond, not from the field of the other, but from the field of the Other (cf. Schema L).

Eventually, Lacan would answer "no" to the question in the previous paragraph. Analysis is neither the unveiling nor the acceptance of the laws of one's destiny: "This is what you are!" The transference is not only a demand for recognition of an unrecognized past. Within the analytic experience, it is not solely a question of transference in the general sense, the sort that takes place each time a subject speaks authentically to the Other. Within analysis, the transference is characterized by specificity, by reason of the presence of the analyst. In other words, the two paths— that of *erinnern* and that of *Übertragung*—have two different functions. This is what Lacan showed, beginning in 1960, in his seminar on the transference.[14] There he distinguished between *Widerholung* (repetition), which arises from the symbolic (unconscious) and *agieren* (acting-out), which arises from the instinctual, from the ensuing *Trieb* (drive). The *agieren* emerges there where, because of the irreducible repressed *(urverdrängt)*, the symbolic is lacking. Not an identical repetition but a new production, the *agieren* is original in nature, a result of the analysis itself.

8

An Ethical Question

> Beauty also has its arguments.
> —Baltasar Gracián

Lacan's 1960–1961 seminar on the transference[1] marked a turning point. In it, he broke with his two preceding approaches in saying that the transference comes not from the analysand but from the analyst—more precisely, from the desire-of-the-analyst, of which it is the effect. But before he could say this, he needed to establish the meaning of desire; hence the preceding year (1959–1960), he presented a seminar on the ethics of psychoanalysis.[2] Only ethics can clarify the nature of the transference; it serves as its *introduction,* insofar as the Freudian enterprise is, properly speaking, neither religious nor philosophical, but ethical. It comes after religious or philosophical ethics, pointing toward another ethics.

But which ethics? Before drawing the consequences for the transference, Lacan took a year to extract what lies at the heart of the ethics of psychoanalysis: *pure desire*. This is not pure desire in the sense of pure versus impure desires. What is at stake is the birth of desire as such: either it is there or it is not. From this point on, "pure" designates independence with respect to a content such as *this* desired object, or *that* fortunate or unfortunate consequence for the subject. The absolute nature of the god Eros is captured in Lacan's formula at the end of the seminar: "The only thing one can be guilty of is giving ground relative to one's desire."[3]

The ethics of pure desire is born from aporias encountered by the analysand in his or her traditional ethics. In the West, these aporias are precisely three in number.

1. The Ethics of the Sovereign Good

This is the ethics of the common man, of common sense, of civic and medical sense—from the Greeks to our time. Lacan quotes Kant: "Man fühlt sich wohl im Guten,"[4] one feels good in the Good. It is a eudaemonic morality, in which accomplishing good implies more or less long-term happiness, in which well-being is ultimately an index of good, like fruit appended to a flower, beauty to youth, beautiful legs . . . to a virtuous woman. Such harmony rests on the *supposition* of a finality inscribed in the nature of the living being's every *intentio*. Aristotle said: "Every art and every inquiry, and similarly every action and pursuit, is thought to aim at some good; and for this reason the good has rightly been declared to be that at which all things aim."[5] Now this "natural" inclination is identical to a wish for happiness, in accordance with the classical maxim: everyone, without exception, wants to be happy (Plato, Aristotle, Cicero, St. Augustine).

Indeed, the supreme Good attracts everything to itself by giving finality to our actions; through it, they are said to be good. It is the great beloved, the ultimate desirable, the universal attraction, cause of all true desire. Hence education is nothing other than an education of *judgment* to discern between true and false goods, since only the latter participate in the Sovereign Good, in the Good that is their final cause. True goods may be discerned by the durability of the pleasure they produce. In our sublunar world, there is only change and instability: nothing is sure, nothing guaranteed. But the Good is that immobile sphere that moves the finest part of our soul, that is, the mind; this in turn moves the other parts by subordinating them to itself. Such is the future master's task: to educate himself and others for life in the polis.

The result of this view is a sense of measure and of prudence; a temperament opposed to excess, expenditure, and the violence of passion; nothing taken to the extreme. It is precisely what Freud would call the principle of constancy and of least possible tension, the very principle of pleasure-displeasure. It is the ancient wisdom transmitted to the child in the judgment of implication: if . . . then. "Darling, if you eat too much chocolate, you will end up with a stomachache!" Mismeasure brings misfortune.[6]

The radical limitation of this ethics is revealed in those who exceed it, that is, the tragic hero or heroine: Antigone chose misfortune; she went beyond serving the goods to which Creon, guardian of the city, had dedicated himself. There is excess in human beings; it is, according to Freud, a formation of the unconscious in the passage *beyond* the pleasure-displeasure principle. The tragic hero is not a mistake, though he is diagnosed as such by the psychoanalyst established in truth. Rather, he is a social symptom, a sign that, within society, there is a limit to the ethics of the good.

Now this stumbling block that is the tragic hero is not confined to the Greeks. It has multiplied. There is a growing sense of alarm in the West, corresponding to the extent that a eudaemonic morality has become generalized. Among the ancients, it had been the preserve of the *aristoi*, of the masters who, because they had leisure (work was for slaves) could accede to knowledge *(savoir)* of their own good. Now a passage to the universal has occurred: there can be no satisfaction for the individual without satisfaction for all. Thus the ethics we call utilitarian has succeeded the ethics of the Sovereign Good by universalizing it. Our modern, industrial societies are governed by the principle of utility, in accordance with Bentham's formula: "the greatest happiness of the greatest number." What is morally good is not what is expedient for me personally but what is useful to the most people. The principle is therefore to seek the greatest happiness for the greatest number by identifying the individual's interest with the universal interest.

Egoism and altruism are thus correlative *on the level of the useful*. For man, there are no natural needs. Using as a yardstick the mirror of the other, everyone imagines what is useful to himself or herself. Goods are produced in accordance with their value for exchange and distribution among one's fellows. It is this value that determines their value for the individual. The function of goods is defined by cultural artifice and opinion, what Bentham calls *fiction*. It is neither illusion nor deceit but the symbolic order that language is, insofar as it says what *must* be and not what is. Because today's societies are saturated by the media, they function more than ever according to the *law of the counterpart:* the good is the maximum utility for the greatest number. The good is what everyone wants to make everyone share.

Nevertheless there is a malaise in our civilization. This universal eudaimonism based on the law of the counterpart encounters its own limit. We can easily grasp this by describing where in fact this ethic leads, this ethic of love one's neighbor, of the neighbor *as being oneself.*

2. The Ethics of "Love Thy Neighbor"

Here the concern is not only my good but also the good of the other. To do good is to love the other, in this precise sense: to want the good of the other, *velle bonum alicui.* Thus, the good "therapist" wants the good of his or her patient.

Bonum: what good? Whatever I wish for myself I wish for the other. I see myself, I feel myself in the other. As Madame de Sévigné wrote to her daughter, who was suffering from angina: "I have a pain in your chest." Here distributive justice finds a foundation for the sharing of goods—and even more so, in the expansive generosity of the Good. St. Martin gave half his cloak to a beggar. Each half was identical to the other: your good is made in the image of mine.

All this is of little value. The other doesn't even want this good. Freud discreetly termed this phenomenon "negative therapeutic reaction." It is enough for me to want the good of the other for the other to turn and run in the opposite direction. What then is this wanting?

Velle. Velle implies this: I want it to be *me* and no one else who accomplishes your good. Bumping up against the other's refusal, I must choose. *Either* I decide to love with a reasonable love, with a measured altruism: if you do not want bread though I am hungry, so much the worse for you . . . and for me! I regret that you demand caviar from me, which I don't like, but I resign myself to drawing back: go ask next door! *Or,* I move one step beyond, beyond "wisdom," and hold firm to my *velle:* you will achieve happiness through me. I impose myself on you, I am eager for your enjoyment: you will enjoy thanks to me!

At this point the mirror shatters: beyond the other who is my counterpart, I encounter the *ill will* of the Other. The Other does not enjoy. I then accentuate my *velle:* you will have to yield for the sake of your salvation and your happiness. Surprise! I reveal myself as wicked, too. This is a perversion of the love-passion, or, to define it precisely: a pretense to *knowledge (savoir)* about the Other's *jouissance,* which serves to support my devotion to it. A new stumbling block appears: it is no longer the tragic hero advancing into misfortune, but the Other's wickedness, the encounter with which reveals my own wickedness. Each encounter exposes an excess, a beyond-good, which the mirror relation of friendship (recall Aristotle's dictum: the friend is a "second self") fails to explain. To seek refuge there is to perpetuate the politics of *autruiche,* to use Lacan's term.[7]

3. One's Fellow-Creature Is Not One's Counterpart

To account for this penetration beyond the pleasure-displeasure principle, a different step forward was required, one that would take into consideration human-inhuman desire. In his 1895 *Project for a Scientific Psychology,* Freud provided a striking description of it, as embodied in the child's first encounter with his fellow-creature or *Nebenmensch,* for example, the mother. My fellow-creature brings about a *Spaltung,* a split between the thing *(das Ding)* and what appears to me as my counterpart, a split in the self-image (but not in the subject). In paragraph 17, part 1 of the *Project,* Freud writes about the *Nebenmensch,* whom the child perceives and who arouses the child's interest:

> The theoretical interest taken in it is then further explained by the fact that an object *of a similar kind* was the subject's first satisfying object (and also his first hostile object) as well as his sole assisting force. For this reason it is on his fellow-creature that a human being first learns to cognize. The perceptual complexes arising from this fellow-creature will in part be new and noncomparable—for instance, its features (in the visual sphere)—but other visual perceptions (for instance, the movements of its hands) will coincide in the subject with his own memory of quite similar visual impressions of his own body—a memory with which will be associated memories of movements experienced by himself. The same will be the case with other perceptions of the object; thus, for instance, if the object screams, a memory of the subject's own screaming will be aroused and will consequently revive his own experiences of pain.[8]

Freud then concludes about this differentiation between counterpart and noncounterpart,

> Thus the complex of a fellow-creature falls into two portions. One of these gives the impression of being a constant structure and remains as a coherent

"*thing*" *(als Ding)*; while the other can be *understood* by the activity of memory—that is, can be traced back to information about the subject's own body.[9]

Beyond what is understood in my image, there is *das Ding:* empty and impenetrable, a vacuole that resists being shaped. There is division in my fellow creature, and it founds my own division. This primordial, unforgettable thing is a stranger, at once external and internal. The child is subjected to it as to a capricious law, good or ill will, a good or bad object. What is involved here is making the "thing" into pure *nihil,* subjugated, stripped bare, cleansed of all good as well as of all evil. There will be *desire,* a desire for nothing that belongs to the order of the Good or of goods. This nothingness of the thing in the Other, the locus of desire, *founds* the subject's desire: the subject's desire is the desire of the Other. Lacan illustrates this with a bit of humor: the emptiness of the mustard pot is the same as that of any other pot. Heidegger wrote of *das Ding:*

> The potter . . . shapes the void. For it, in it, and out of it, he forms the clay into the form. . . . The jug's void determines all the handling in the process of making the vessel. The vessel's thingness does not lie at all in the material of which it consists, but in the void that holds.[10]

This is why the *nothing* is not pure negation. It produces an effect: ex nihilo, the signifier arises, that is to say, the *Vorstellungen* that revolve around *das Ding.* These *Vorstellungen* are subject to the regulatory principle of reduction of tension (pleasure-unpleasure), but they refer to a beyond, what Freud will later name the "death drive." Indeed, the relation of desire to death is foundational, beyond anything belonging to the order of the Good or of goods and their service: such was Oedipus at Colonus, alone and betrayed by his people; such was Antigone before Creon and before the chorus that feels *fear* and *pity.* As a work of art, Sophocles' *Antigone* purifies the spectator of these two emotions.[11] Antigone herself leads the spectator beyond, to *pure desire,* in the assumption of her being-for-death.

This results in relativizing and relegating to second rank all ideals of goodness and happiness, ideals that foster both hatred toward the one who deprives me of my good and guilt for having given up my desire in order to serve the good. Herein we encounter the imperative of a debt to be paid in order that one may assent to desire. The imperative may be stated as follows: desire must maintain its relationship to death, because it is based in such a relationship. The "must" comes from a law that founds desire: the law *of* desire. It is on this point that we come face to face with another ethical tradition, Kant's, the closest to the Freudian approach. But is there a link between them?

4. Kant . . . with Sade

It is not the Kant of the first *Critique (Pure Reason)* who concerns us here, but the Kant of the second *(Practical Reason)*. That is to say, we are concerned with pure will. Its purity consists in the exclusion of everything "pathological," of everything belonging to the order of "suffering" (passion or compassion) or of the drive. Pure will flows from what may be expressed in two principles: the *categorical,* that is, action carried out for the *sole reason* that the imperative demands it and not because it conforms to what the imperative states; and the *universal,* that is, action required, not just of everyone, but in all cases and at all times.

Now there can be no imperative without enunciation. Whence the question: *where* does the enunciation come from? *Who* enunciates it? Is the imperative's law derived from itself? Kant answers: its origin is the *inner* voice of conscience. Now psychoanalysis shows that there is no inner without an outer and, in addition, that the inner derives from the outer. This is why it is necessary to link Kant with Sade: the moral law comes from the *voice* of the Other, a voice I send back to the sender, to the Other. Indeed, I complement the Other by filling in what the Other lacks, in accordance with Sadian (not sadistic) staging: the voice of a tormentor enjoying his victim. Thus is Kant reinforced by Sade, reinforced by Sade's rejection, destruction, and sacrifice of every object of human tenderness, through the endless repetition of bodily pain (the only *pathos* accepted by Kant).

Such is the function of the Sadian narrative where, in imagination, Sade calls forth what he desires: a state of eternal torment for his victim, who doesn't manage to die in the continually aborted attempt to achieve . . . what? The *nihil* of pure desire. The usual path is not suited for what is at stake here. Strictly speaking, this position defines masochism: one secures *jouissance* for the Other (locus of the voice) so as not to open oneself to the question of the Other's desire.

If Sade brings to light the Kantian fantasy, this is because the voice of the imperative does not falter. The Freudian approach succeeds here by setting a *limit* to the masochistic position of Kantian ethics so that, from this limit, may be born a question concerning the Other's desire. How is it that love allows *jouissance* to condescend to desire?

5. *An Ethics Linked to an Aesthetics*

A constant theme runs throughout Lacan's 1959–1960 seminar on the ethics of psychoanalysis: the path that brings us to pure desire is a language, a language that knows how to *really-tell* (*bien-dire*) the lover's desire as it appears *in* the lover's image. Only the beautiful can establish a *limit* to wanton *jouissance*. In Lacan's words, it establishes "an extreme barrier that prohibits access to a fundamental horror,"[12] that is, to wickedness. Beauty—because it does not experience outrage—prohibits obscenity and shamelessness.

The figure of Antigone serves as the paradigm. Having trespassed the limits of good, Antigone has moved beyond life to that zone where death encroaches. She is resplendent in the eyes of the choir, which knows how to *really-tell* the "visible desire" (ἵμερος ἐναργής) *in* her face. Purged at last of all fear and pity, the choir "reads" the lover's beauty, as it speaks of Eros's triumph (verses 781 ff.):

> Eros, ever the victor
> Eros, swooping down upon the flocks,
> Keeping vigil through the night
> *in* the delicate bloom of a young girl's cheeks
> Over the seas you wander, dwelling in faraway places
> ....
>
> And so desire *(himeros)* triumphs,
> Visible *(enarges)* desire *in* the eyes of a bride
> Awaiting her nuptial bed.
> You are present in primordial law,
> For Aphrodite, invincible, divine,
> Enjoys us all.

At this very moment, language demands that we recognize Antigone as not of this world. She has escaped it in the pain of existing (Oedipus experiences the same pain: "Better never to have been born!" *Oedipus at*

Colonus, verse 1224). *Now* language can celebrate the *libido* that appears in Antigone's face. For, in exchange for pure desire, which is the death drive, there is a *visibility* of desire, revealed in the *Gestalt* of the human form, sung by the tragic poet.

The real barrier to evil is not discourse about good but discourse about the effect of beauty (not the beloved) upon the lover. Lacan provides many examples in his seminar: courtly love of the Lady; Kant's *Critique of Judgment;* baroque art of the Counter-Reformation. This is by no means a matter of desexualized idealization.[13] Rather, it is a question of that speaking which goes in circles around the impenetrable emptiness of the unforgettable "thing," and which, moreover, is born from the *nihil* that life need not resist, since this is what supports life.

Thus pure desire, in its fundamental relationship to death, is not without libidinal effect, for it returns in visible form on the lover's *imago.*

But, if this is so—the ultimate question of this journey—can one still speak of pure desire in the ethics of psychoanalysis? Certainly not, to the extent that psychoanalysis parts company with Kant and Sade with regard to the *way* the law of desire is established. Kantian law, according to Lacan, "is simply desire in its pure state, that very desire that culminates in the sacrifice, strictly speaking, of everything that is the object of love in one's human tenderness—I would say, not only in the rejection of the pathological object, but also in its sacrifice and murder."[14] And indeed, it is true that access to desire presupposes giving up love of the object, of that sovereign good that is the mother. On this point, analysis and Kant intersect.

The Freudian approach, however, is not content with this and goes further. Desire is not pure; it has libidinal consequences. If love does not lead to desire or to its law, then it will make its *return* in accordance with the law of desire "where alone it may live."[15] Far from excluding love, desire permits it, but strictly in accordance with the luck of fortunate encounter *(entuchia).*

This is why the desire-of-the-analyst is not pure desire. To demonstrate this, a detour through ethics was necessary. Only then could the transference be approached *insofar as it* derives from the desire-of-the-analyst. In his seminar of 1960–1961, Lacan indicated all this through a change of tone, moving from the tragic figure of Antigone to the comic god Eros in Plato's *Banquet.* In a discussion of the transference, the elevated tone, the *Schwärmerei* of the tragic hero, simply would not do.

9

A Metaphor of Love

As we have seen, the ethics of psychoanalysis is the ethics of desire. It is exemplified in the figure of Antigone: the glow of visible desire *(himeros enarges)* on the human *Gestalt,* a dazzling radiance that is the effect of beauty. Linked to this ethics is an aesthetics of *bien-dire,* of really-telling this visibility.

For the chorus that sees and hears Antigone, this is not without consequence. By really-telling what they receive from her, they produce an effect *on* the audience. There is, in other words, a transmission, and this was the starting point for Lacan's discussion of the transference the following year (1960–1961).[1] When Freud spoke of the transference in 1914, he distinguished between remembering and what may occur in its place, namely, a simultaneous acting and repeating. But is every acting only a repeating? If the transference is a transmission through production of something new, is there not—in acting—innovation within analysis itself?

A Reading of the Banquet

Drawing on the forgotten heritage of Plato's *Banquet*[2] Lacan would respond to these questions with a new definition of the transference. Indeed, this new definition involved jettisoning several centuries of academic censorship that, following neoplatonic lines of thought, had put Diotoma's speech at the high point of the *Banquet*. The scandalous nature of the final pages, where the relationship between Alcibiades and Socrates is described, effectively topples this reading of the *Banquet*. Lacan breaks with the tradition that interprets Greek *paiderastia*, love of children, as *paideia*, education of the young by the old for the sake of initiating them into civic life (Pausanias's speech) or into the knowledge of Being that is philosophy (Diotima's speech).

According to Lacan, Socrates is the "precursor of psychoanalysis"[3] when he says he "knows nothing, unless it concerns desire" (*Banquet*, 177d). It is a question of *episteme*, of knowledge *(savoir)*, not only about the discourse of those who discourse *on* love but also about him who declares *his* love publicly, namely, Alcibiades. *Paiderastia* is a privileged place, for only from there can knowledge *(savoir)* of love be *elaborated* (in the Freudian sense) through speech. This knowledge *(savoir)* is indispensable, inasmuch as eros is a per-version with respect to a *physis,* a deviation from a teleological, universal, internally consistent norm. At stake here is mastery of knowledge *(savoir)*, knowledge of eros—that per-version that sexuality quite "naturally" is: how to live with eros, other than by way of neurosis, which is the result of societal rules. Aside from sublimation (which is not desexualization), purely active, silent eros—heterosexual or homosexual—teaches us nothing new. As for *paideia*, it is only the application of an already existing knowledge *(savoir)*.

This comes out quite clearly in the first five eulogies spoken by the guests at the banquet: Phaidros, the theologian; Pausanias, the teacher of politics; Eryximachos, the physician; Aristophanes, the comic poet; and Agathon, the tragic poet. Their speeches have two features in common:

1. Love is presented under the figure of a "full cup" (175d). Love lacks nothing; rather, it contains every virtue and every quality (Agathon). Love is a "sphere," a perfect whole, an image of completeness, in which two separate halves are reduced to one (Aristophanes). Love has no father, no genealogy; he is uncreated. The most ancient of the gods, he is the cause of our greatest good (Phaidros).

2. This exaltation of love rests on the presupposition of an *already existing* knowledge *(savoir)* of eros, which therefore needs only to be retrieved, not produced. Love conforms to a knowledge *(savoir)* that is already inscribed somewhere: either in eulogies to the gods (Phaidros); or in the myth of the original unity of our *archaia physis* (Aristophanes); or in Athenian law (Pausanias), which requires the beloved to grant favors to his lover in accordance with established rules, in accordance with a knowledge *(savoir)* of civic ethics wherein love is viewed as education. If the beloved accepts to be loved, he does so to acquire honor, courage,

and virtue from his lover. Prudence, moderation, modesty, and testing permit discrimination between what is beneficial and what is useless.[4]

But we simply cannot believe that eros is exalted and conforms to an already existing knowledge. The tone of the five eulogies is one of irony, parody, even buffoonery. The real key to the *Banquet* are the hiccups that trap Aristophanes amid the howling laughter produced and merited by the eulogy of the "full cup."

When Socrates takes over the floor, a dividing line is introduced. The preceding discourses had described love as plenitude, in other words, as an attribute of the beloved, not of the lover, as if to love were to wish to be loved and to be lovable. Those discourses are beautiful, true, and good; by virtue of this, they belong to the order of opinion, myth, and fiction. But Socrates aims at something else: knowledge *(episteme)*, that is, what turns true, beautiful, well-spoken discourse into *reason*. To possess the eros of knowledge *(savoir)* is not to know. For eros is lack. It is therefore imperfect, an "empty cup," the absence of what one lacks, desire *(epithumia)*. There can be no knowledge *(savoir)* of eros without an eros of knowledge, without nescience. And so Socrates keeps still at the very point where he doesn't know, allowing Diotima to speak through his lips, there where he lacks knowledge *(savoir)* of desire.

Of what does Diotima speak? Of good Platonism. Eros is sublunar, a realm of instability and uncertainty, for his mother was Penia (Poverty). But he may become celestial, a realm of certainty and immortality, for his father was Poros (Plenty). He is something in between, this "daemon" who—by germinating *in* beauty—causes us to pass from one world to another, to ascend from the beauty of bodies to that of the soul *via* beautiful speech.

On this ascending march toward pure, invariant being, a change of direction occurs. Beauty—once the guide—becomes the goal: Beauty itself, the One. At stake here is an identification with *being*, to be accomplished through idealization. This is precisely what Freud called the ego-ideal *(Ichideal)*, foundation of narcissism. From a point in the *Ichideal* (I), I see myself as lovable, beloved. A final transformation from lover into beloved: such is the path indicated by Diotima, in her exortation to being-more. Our tradition has retained this in particular from the *Banquet*.[5]

The Meaning of Love Is Transference

To break with this tradition is to perceive its collapse in the arrival of Alcibiades. For this is the point of the *Banquet,* what it teaches us about the transference. With Alcibiades we no longer hear a eulogy to Eros, but a lover's eulogy to his beloved. *In* Alcibiades, a transference is accomplished in accordance with Lacan's formula: the desire of the subject is the desire of the Other. How?

Transference is not simply the re-inscription that occurs each time a subject addresses himself or herself authentically to the Other. This definition is too general. In analysis, transference is a specific process, one that Plato spells out in the last pages of the *Banquet,* in Alcibiades' speech. The transference comes from the desire-of-the-analyst, from the analyst occupying the empty place of the Other's desire. If somewhere there is desire, then what may come about is a metaphor of love (if one speaks Greek) or a transference of love (if one speaks Latin), in other words, a *substitution* of places: the analysand as beloved becomes in turn the lover, putting the analyst in the position of beloved. There is, however, a double condition. The analysand may become the lover to the extent that *he doesn't know why* he is beloved. Corresponding to this nescience on the part of the analysand is a second, correlative nescience on the part of the analyst, whom the analysand may put in the position of beloved to the extent that the analyst *doesn't know* himself as the object he harbors, namely the object-cause of the analysand's desire. In brief, what happens is not a pure repetition of the past, but production of a new *agieren.*

Analysis is not only the symbolization of a repressed past; it is an innovation: a fire is kindled; out of the flame a hand appears and attempts to join the hand already there for a long time, stretched toward it. To see how the final pages of the *Banquet* enact this process, we need to distinguish three stages:

First Stage

This metaphor of love presupposes a prelude: Socrates' desire. Alcibiades had been Socrates' first beloved. But the anteriority of Socrates' love is veiled, a veiled anteriority of the Other's desire, because Alcibiades doesn't know *why he has been constituted as a beloved*. Whence the question:

che vuoi? What do you want of me? At last let me know this, so that starting from this knowledge *(savoir)*, I may know what I am *for* you!

Lacan illustrates the beloved's nescience regarding the desire of the Other by citing this verse from Victor Hugo's poem, *Booz endormi:*

> Booz ne savait pas qu'une femme était là.
> Ruth ne savait pas ce que Dieu voulait d'elle.[6]

Second Stage: The Birth of the Metaphor

The phenomenon of exchange of places has been perfectly described in the *Phaedrus,* with suitable importance given to the vision of the lover by the beloved. Thus Plato writes: "For as the effluence of beauty enters him through the eyes, he is warmed."[7] This effluence is a stream (*himeros* in Greek, the very word Sophocles used to describe Antigone's desire), and it explains the exchange of places:

> Just as the wind or an echo rebounds from smooth, hard surfaces and returns whence it came, so the *stream* of beauty *passes back* into the beautiful one through the eyes . . . filling the soul of the loved one with love. So he is in love, but he knows not with whom; he does not understand his own condition and cannot explain it; like one who has caught a disease of the eyes from another, he can give no reason for it; he sees himself in his lover as in a mirror, but is not conscious of the fact.[8]

Now this is exactly what will be acted out in the *Banquet,* in Alcibiades' public confession. What, then, does Alcibiades say? That he invited Socrates to dinner and to pass the night with him, so that, having seduced him, he might receive a clear *sign* of love: Socrates before him with an erection (217–19)! To this unconditional demand for a sign, Socrates did not respond. He didn't say he didn't love Alcibiades—he simply didn't say anything. If Socrates had responded to the demand for a sign, the metaphor would have failed. Alcibiades would have remained a beloved, Socrates' beloved. But what Socrates sought in Alcibiades was not so much the desirable as the desiring, that is, the lack in himself.

More specifically, Socrates desired Alcibiades as desiring . . . not as desiring *him.* If it had been otherwise, Alcibiades would have continued to love himself in Socrates, inasmuch as to love is to wish to be loved. So Alcibiades changes places: he becomes the lover. And the moment he does, as written in the *Phaedrus,* "he sees himself in his lover as in a mirror, but is not conscious of the fact." Alcibiades was unaware he had become the lover, but Plato—through the wisdom of Socrates—knew it.

Third Stage: The Realization of the Metaphor

This intimate scene, in which Socrates is a guest in the home of Alcibiades, does not remain intimate. Alcibiades inserts it into a second scene, Agathon's banquet. He turns the first scene into a public confession, made *in front of* a chosen public, a public that will become—through Aristodemos and then through Plato—the anonymous public that we constitute today, as readers. Alcibiades takes the risk, steps forward alone, because he is not a neurotic who persists in demanding signs of love or in keeping silent. He speaks his passion: of how the voice of Socrates possesses him, troubles him, makes him weep; of how he has obeyed Socrates' words, and how ashamed he has been to show his dependence in public. Today, in the absence of a fear of castration, he confesses—without shame—his "feminine" passion.

Through really-telling *(bien-dire)*, he accomplishes the metaphor of love: he *constitutes* Socrates in the place of the beloved, the one who harbors the object of his desire. It is a horrifying confession, in which Alcibiades expresses the rage of a man wounded and insulted, "suffering . . . from a strange wound,"[9] his "masculine" honor breached.

But through his speaking, he brings to presence the object of his fantasy, precisely there where the cause of his desire is found. The eulogy he makes to Socrates *produces* the object Plato calls *agalma*. This is a subversion of the common meaning of the word: *agalma* here is neither a beautiful image nor a figurine of a god. Socrates' *imago*, what appeared on the outside *(exoden)* when he "put on that innocent air,"[10] is nothing but a crude and rustic box. But beyond it, on the inside *(endoten)*, are jewels, *agalmata*. Socrates is put in the position of beloved by Alcibiades, in whom is realized a metaphor of love, that is to say, love's very meaning.

No longer does Alcibiades desire in Socrates the prettified, dressed-up image he (Alcibiades) has clothed him in, so as to identify himself with it and see himself there as lovable. He no longer demands signs of love. Beyond love, which in essence is narcissistic, there is desire, caused by the hidden *agalma*. Beyond the dressed-up image, there is the residue, which Lacan calls the *objet petit a* and which makes the image *hold*.

This illuminates the nature of the transference in psychoanalysis: it is a substitution of places. But this is not the whole story. When Socrates does respond, what does he say? That in truth (as opposed to opinion), there is no *agalma* in him, that everything Alcibiades has said concerns not Socrates but Agathon. He shows Alcibiades his true beloved and, in addition, accompanies and sustains Alcibiades by presenting the eulogy to Agathon. Through this *triangulation,* Socrates satisfies Alcibiades, satisfies him by furnishing him an image of himself (Socrates) as a lover desiring the same beloved: Agathon.

But how does Socrates know there is no *agalma* in himself? How does he know that, for Alcibiades, the *agalma* resides in Agathon? Certainly there is a forced interpretation here that the analyst must guard against. Nevertheless, the direction is right, inasmuch as the analysand *himself* must accomplish the passage to triangulation. Once he has constituted his fundamental fantasy, the analysand must henceforth live out his drive beyond the analyst, in accordance with the contingencies of fortunate encounter *(eutuchia)* with this or that Agathon, this or that Agatha—not in accordance with the idealizing path indicated by Diotima.[11]

But what place should the analyst occupy so that the analysand may accomplish this passage?

The Place of the Analyst

This new definition of the transference as metaphor of love makes it plain that it originates in the desire-of-the-analyst. The analyst occupies a place that he or she leaves vacant for the analysand's desire, such that the analysand may realize himself or herself as the desire of the Other. Why is this necessary?

From the time of birth, the human subject poses—or rather *is,* with all of his or her being—this question: what does the Other want? The question is addressed to a place occupied by a diverse assortment of names, which follow upon the first: most often, in our culture, that of the mother (we are not doing comparative ethnology here!). There is something the speaking being wants to know. Hence he or she questions this place or, more precisely, *from* this place he or she questions: what am I for you? This demand to know is a demand for signs of love and, on this basis, the subject will identify himself or herself with the features of the ego-ideal, the point from which the subject sees himself or herself as loved.

But this narcissistic outcome remains unsatisfying, for nothing can put an end to demand or to the parade of signifiers. What finally halts this dance is the *signifier of the desire of the Other,* insofar as it is missing from the symbolic order: the phallic signifier (which Lacan denotes by Φ, capital phi). The only signifier that signifies itself, it would—if it were not absent—abolish all other signifiers, to which it gives meaning by its very absence. Irreducibly repressed, *urverdrängt,* it leaves the question of the Other's desire with no final response. The Other is barred by the bar of symbolic castration. Incompleteness inheres in the Other.

This is why the subject must complete *himself or herself.* Turning the demand to know "what I am for you" into a demand to know "what you are for me," the subject finally provides an answer when he or she puts the fantasized *objet petit a* into *this* empty place in the field of the *Other:* S($\bar{A}$) (to be read as: signifier of the barred A).

So ends the parade of signifiers. It is brought to a halt through fixation of the fundamental fantasy at the place of the object—cause of desire: barred subject lozenge little *a,* written $ \$ \diamond a $; the bar is same one as the bar in S($\bar{A}$). In the very place where the Other is barred and where anxiety about the desire of the Other can arise, the fantasy serves as bolster and support: at this window, this empty place in the Other, the fantasy-screen is installed. In the otherness of the Other the subject cannot and must not find either his identity or a guarantee of his place. Hence the subject removes himself by identifying with the object of the fantasy. The fantasy is not a stumbling block but rather a stepping stone . . . a footbridge toward encounter with the enigma of the Other.

This is how Alcibiades proceeded, and so must every analysand at the end of analysis. However, there is a condition: the analyst must occupy this vacant place *for* the analysand. On this point, Lacan's return to Freud is crucial. Freudianism was in large measure a reading of the second topography, with analysis viewed as the constitution of an ego-ideal in accordance with the ideals of the individual. On the other hand, Freud had described this identification as an obstacle to be removed during analysis rather than strengthened or established. *Group Psychology* (1921) is completely clear on this. But through their training standards, analytic institutions have turned education into identification with the analyst (perhaps the so-called therapeutic has a somewhat greater chance of avoiding this educational impasse). Lacan, with his return to Freud, put analysis back on track. He contested the official training of analysts, in which—admittedly or not—the analysand makes of his analyst his ego-ideal. The analyst must guard against this by occupying the vacant place of the desire of the Other: S (Ⱥ). Let us now specify in detail what is at stake here.

In the Imaginary Relation

We turn again to Schema L (see chapter 5), not in general, but as applied to the particular relationship between analysand and analyst, what Lacan calls the analytic game of bridge. Analysis is a game for four players, arranged in accordance with Schema L: two follow the imaginary relation (between the other and the ego), while two conform to language and its effect, that is, the unconscious (between the Other as locus of speech and the subject). In this game of bridge, the analysand plays his or her own hand. To do that, it is necessary for the analysand—in accordance with the imaginary relation—to come face to face with a *partner*. The analyst need not refuse or work against this. As the analysand's other, the analyst occupies the place that in bridge is called the dummy (*le mort,* death). In other words, the analyst leaves the cards *for* the analysand's destiny exposed on the table, cards with which the analysand will put into play his or her own existence. However, the analysand will not be able to do this unless the analyst truly does play dead. What does this mean?

It means to act as if one were dead, to turn oneself into a cadaver, to resist the temptations of an imposing or seductive presence, to offer "the subject the pure mirror of an unruffled surface."[12] But is this model of abstinence practicable? Should the analyst try not to have feelings or passions? And if the analyst can't do this, should he or she pretend to?

Or should the analyst, like Melanie Klein, use his or her own feelings and passions in order to better perceive those of the analysand? This "understanding" based on sympathy and care, is it not a refuge for misrecognition?

The answer, which comes from the ethical order, excludes both of these positions. It is the desire-of-the-analyst, a desire *stronger* than any passion, a desire that raises the stakes and is in turn circumscribed by them. The following is at stake.

To Separate the Objet Petit a *from the* i(a) *and Restore It to the Field of the Other*

In his "Remarque sur le rapport de Daniel Lagache: 'Psychanalyse et structure de la personnalité' " (a text from 1960, the same year as his seminar on the transference), Lacan had this to say about the *objet petit a:*

> As partial object, it is not only a part, or detached piece, of the apparatus that here *pictures* the body,[13] but is, *from the beginning,* an element of the structure, one might say, part of the deal in the game being played. Having been selected in the appendices of the body as an index of desire, it is *already* the exponent of a function that sublimates it even before it exercises it, [the function] of an index raised toward an absence about which the *is-it* has nothing to say, except that [the absence] is from there where it *(ça)* speaks.[14]

Thus, detaching itself from the corporal *imaginary* of *i(a),* the object of the drive (breast, feces, gaze, voice) is positioned in the *symbolic* order— where it was from the beginning—in order to become the *cause* of desire.

> This is the real reason why, reflected in the mirror, it doesn't only give back *a'*, the standard exchange, the fee required of the other's desire for entry into the circuit of the Ideal Ego's transitivisms. It is *restored* to the field of the Other with the function of exponent of desire in the Other.
>
> This is what will permit it, at the true termination of analysis, to take on its elective value, to figure in the fantasy where the subject sees himself abolished through *realizing himself* as desire.[15]

For will to condescend to desire in accordance with the fantasy that has been installed—this is the purpose of analysis. To this end, let the subject be sure this is what he or she wants! In effect:

> In order to reach this point beyond reduction of the individual's ideals, it is as *objet a* of desire, as what he has been for the Other in his erection as a living being, as *wanted* or *unwanted* when he came into the world, that the subject is called upon to be reborn in order to *know* if he wants what he desires.... Such is the sort of truth that Freud brought to light with the invention of psychoanalysis.[16]

With these lines, Lacan set forth the process, the wager, and the termination of analysis. *However,* its achievement is conditioned, not only by the primacy of the symbolic over the imaginary, but also by the *incompleteness* of the symbolic, for without $S(\cancel{A})$ there can be no $\$ \diamond a$. Without a lack in the symbolic, there is no fantasy. Now, this lack cannot be established unless the analyst—through his or her position—makes it present, that is to say, unless the analyst occupies the gap that is the desire of the Other, at the place where the signifier of desire is summoned. Occupying this place, the analyst is the real presence of what is silent insofar as it is lacking.

Such was Lacan's teaching on the transference and termination of analysis in 1960–1961. Let us note that everything depends on the precise relationship *between* the symbolic and the imaginary dimensions. But what about the *real*? Lacan had used the term since 1953 but had not yet introduced the *real* as such. He did so beginning in 1964. As we shall see, this would not be without consequences for the definition of the transference.

IV

TOWARD THE REAL

The very idea of real entails the exclusion of any meaning. Only insofar as the real is emptied of all meaning can we apprehend it a little.
—Lacan, Seminar XXIV, March 8, 1977

10

A Cartesian Approach

November 20, 1963

On that day, Lacan presented the first lesson of the seminar he had planned for the academic year 1963–1964. The title of the seminar was "Les Noms-du-Père" ("The Names-of-the-Father"). It would be Lacan's last encounter with his audience at Sainte-Anne. He was interrupting his teaching, certain prominent members of the Société française de psychanalyse (SFP) having just implemented a request by the International Psychoanalytical Association (IPA) to strike his name from the list of training analysts and teachers.

The lesson contained both a response to the IPA and an announcement of the new direction his teaching would take, beginning in 1964: "For a long time now, the name of Freud has not stopped becoming increasingly nonfunctional"[1] as a result of what the analytical establishment—under cover of his name—has made of the Freudian text. Essentially, the matter involved the function of the father, *beginning with* the Oedipus complex and the myth of *Totem and Taboo*. "The entirety of analytic theory and praxis appear to us at present to have come to a halt for not having dared, on the subject of that question, *to go further than* Freud."[2] To go further than Freud with respect to the paternal function means questioning him on this: how, in the Freudian myth, the requisite conjunction of law and desire is generated out of "the *supposition* of the pure erotic bliss *[jouissance]* of the father viewed as primordial."[3] To accomplish a return to Freud is to read in the Freudian text how Freud himself authorizes questioning this presupposition. "He allows us to trace the cleavage of a path going beyond—deeper and more structural than the milestone that

105

he placed there in the form of the myth of the death of the father."[4] To read a text is to generate another text from it.

In psychoanalysis, what is at stake is effecting a split between the Other's desire and his *jouissance*. Establishing this gap permits desire—insofar as it is perverse—to recognize, as its law, the Other's desire and not the Other's *jouissance*. The stake is primordial when it concerns the father, since the father's function is precisely to effect this cleavage. To demonstrate this, Lacan relies on the biblical story of Abraham's sacrifice of Isaac. Breaking with edifying interpretations of Abraham's oblation (the gift of his son to Elohim), he reveals the motive behind this story: "sacrificing one's little boy to the local *Elohim* was quite common at the time."[5] In the regions surrounding Israel, it was customary to offer one's baal what was most precious; in Israel, this was forbidden, but repetition of the interdiction clearly indicates that sacrifice persisted, among kings and people alike.[6]

As Kierkegaard noted so well in *Fear and Trembling*, Abraham is being tested. He is in a state of anxiety on account of the Other's desire—the Other from whom he received a child on the sheer strength of a promise, who made him a father by a barren woman. He defends himself against this anxiety through "sacrifice" of his only child. For three days and three nights, he walks without flinching, like a crusader devoted to the Other's *jouissance* (subjective genitive).[7] Once on the mountain of sacrifice, the hand of God's angel stays his arm. This gesture that bars him is the "no" of the law of desire: there can be no knowledge about the Other's *jouissance* (as in perversion); nor can there be satisfaction of the Other's demand as something identical to his desire (as in neurosis). Thus the "no" opens a gap between desire and *jouissance*.

In this gap, something appears to Abraham that he knew nothing about: the ancestor, that is to say, our "biological origin." It is the primal father who is figured in the ram that hurls itself onto the sacrificial stone, the primal father whose pure *jouissance* Freud supposed at the origin. Thus, according to Lacan, what Elohim indicates to Abraham as the sacrifice in place of Isaac is "his eponymous ancestor, the God of his race."[8] And Abraham, by killing him, extinguishes his voice. In causing his downfall, he turns his voice into the cause of his desire. Such was the revelation contained in his fantasy.

Lacan's allusion to his present situation is clear. It is up to his listeners to choose: *either* maintain the voice of the establishment (the IPA), "sacrificing" Lacan in the name of Freud, the ancestor; *or* take the Freudian text beyond Freud. He ended by saying: "I have never, at any moment, given any pretext for believing that there was not, for me, any difference between yes and no."[9]

Proscribed by the IPA, Lacan found himself alone with his students and outside the establishment. Ten years after its foundation, the Société française de psychanalyse could no longer serve as locus of realization for the Rome Report (1953) or the Vienna conference (1955).

This institutional void marked a turning point in Lacan's teaching. For ten years, he had attempted a return to Freud, reading in the Freudian text a relationship of the primacy of the symbolic *over* the imaginary. But continuing to define this relationship with increasing precision would still leave hanging the question of its meaning for the end of analysis. Is the hysterization provoked by the law of free association terminable? Does it or does it not generate *knowledge (savoir)*?

In brief, the interruption of his seminar on November 20, 1963, left two problems untouched: the end of analysis and the analytic institution. As a result, it became imperative to open up the question of the extraterritoriality of psychoanalysis: can it be practiced and taught publicly without the analyst's having to reckon with the *internal limits* of the discipline, with consideration only for *external* limits, that is, the scientific and juridical exigencies imposed by society in the face of imposture? An inevitable question, but constantly avoided.

Lacan set out to answer it by resuming his seminar in January 1964, founding the Ecole freudienne de Paris (EFP) in June, and introducing the *real* in its *relation to the symbolic:* "No praxis is more orientated towards that which, at the heart of experience, is the kernel of the real than psycho-analysis."[10]

The orientation is to be understood on the basis of the following definition: the Freudian approach is *Cartesian,* and in that respect, ethical. Upon this preparatory basis, *two texts* of fundamental importance would be engendered: "La science et la vérité" (read December 1, 1965, as the opening lecture of the 1965–1966 seminar, now the closing essay of *Ecrits,* published the following year); and the "Proposition du 9 octobre 1967 sur le psychanalyste de l'Ecole" (commonly known as "Proposition sur la passe").[11]

Hence, what the Rome Report and Vienna conference had been for the SFP, these two new texts were for the EFP:[12] at the same time as they founded an institution, they instituted a break with the past. But the relationship between the two sets of texts is strictly one of analogy, as will be shown in more detail below.

The Subject of Science

In the Rome Report, Lacan wrote: "The unconscious is that chapter of my history that is marked by a blank or occupied by a falsehood: it is the censored chapter. But the truth can be rediscovered."[13] And where is it rediscovered? In formations of the unconscious, insofar as they have been analyzed!

Owing, therefore, to the power of speech, and by means of interpretation, analysis is a truth-speaking, there where it was absent. It is, in other words, the recognition of desire by another desire. As a process by which empty speech is exchanged for full speech and misunderstanding for understanding, analysis would consist in the establishment of an intersubjective continuity, that is, in nothing less than a discourse in which the subject's history is constituted.

Now, what *subject* are we talking about here? The very subject *enunciated* in and through the intersubjective relation. Presupposed—and this is really quite surprising!—is the power of interlocutory speech, a power at once creative and illuminating, the very power of the symbolic order in its *primacy* over the imaginary. The issue: ungluing analytic practice from the imaginary relation in which it has gone astray; an ethics of truth, which would reveal the infinitude of desire, beyond the demand directed to the object of need.

What is the historical context of this issue? It is "the most profound alienation of the subject in our scientific civilization."[14] In the objectifications of discourse (including the discourses of Freud!), the subject loses his meaning. He forgets himself and misrecognizes the specific meaning of his life in false communication. Thus, where the wall of language stands in opposition to speech, analysis allows subjective speech to tear down this wall.

Whence the questions: if psychoanalysis remedies the effects of science on the subject, is it against science? Should we go back to the ancient notion of *episteme* (found in the *Theatetus*), beyond modern science (that of Galileo and Newton)? Finally, what relationship does the symbolic have to the *real*? Questions such as these could not be left hanging much longer: "Psychoanalysis has played a role in the direction of modern subjectivity, and it cannot continue to sustain this role without bringing it into line with the movement in modern *science* that elucidates it."[15]

But once "brought into line," what sort of subjectivity is it? Beginning in 1964, Lacan settles the matter: there is no intersubjective relationship; the subject is not what is presupposed by another subject. Having seen "the relaxation effect" suffered by his own concepts in proportion to their diffusion under the name "Lacanism," he shielded himself with this statement: "The subject we deal with in psychoanalysis can only be the subject of science,"[16] that is, the subject first born in the West in the seventeenth century, in the Cartesian *cogito*. At that moment, an event took place without which no one would speak of Freud. For without the advent of the Cartesian *cogito*, Freud would not have discovered the unconscious, inasmuch as the subject that realizes itself in psychoanalysis is this very *cogito*. It is not the psyche, the soul of an *Innenwelt* that replicates an *Umwelt*. It is not the Jungian subject arising from the depths. It is not the substratum *(hypokeimenon)* of permanent identity. Even more emphatically, it is not the intersubjectivity of a speaking subject. It is, rather, the subject whose historical origin is in the subject of science.

For Descartes, what was at stake was ethical in nature: to acquire practical certainty. He wrote: "I always had an excessive desire to learn to distinguish the true from the false, in order to see clearly in my actions and to walk with confidence in this life."[17] The Freudian precept—*Wo es war, soll Ich werden;* there where it was, there as subject must I come—responds to this precisely. How, then, is the Freudian approach Cartesian? Let us now unfold a single act into its three discursive moments.

a. Dubito

I have received, said Descartes, much knowledge from innumerable sciences, all of it coming from the outside, via custom and the senses, in accordance with corporeal imagination and the symbolic order of language. Therefore, it is sheer probability, mere opinion. If truth is defined as *adequatio rei et intellectus* (a relationship of parity between object and idea) then, indeed, it is impossible to derive knowledge *(savoir)* from these truths.

But what distinguishes man is the power of the *dubito;* through it, he can unglue himself from the merely probable, which leads him to nothing certain. Inhibitions, symptoms, anxiety: some point to the organic, others to a failure of will. I move from the descriptive to the normative: I can doubt, therefore I must. For, from all these truths, no light is shed with respect to the conduct of my life.

b. Dubito, Cogito

However, through doubt I introduce a split between *intellectus* and *rei* and gather up, from their disjunction, a residue: a succession of *Gedanken* (thoughts), according to Freud; a "chain of thoughts," according to Descartes; the defiles of the signifier, according to Lacan. Now, this I cannot doubt. I am assured *that* I doubt, *that* I think. Such is the fundamental rule of analysis: true or false matters little; one expresses one's thoughts as they come. It is sufficient to respect the order of their arrival: the primacy of the ordinal over the cardinal. To be happily duped by them is our lot—and our Archimedean lever. We are each of us responsible for our own thoughts. After all, we have something to do with them. My thoughts belong to me because I belong to them: "*cogito ergo sum*" *ubi cogito, ibi sum:* "I think, therefore I am, there where I think, there I am."[18] The break with the outside establishes an inside, a place that's mine, home.

c. Cogito, Sum

Preliminary doubting of the merely probable made it possible to accept the present *Gedanken;* from these the subject in his or her certitude is produced through a relation of implication. The birth of the subject is *contemporaneous* with his or her certitude: the affirmation "I am" is certain each time I pronounce the "thought" that comes to me. "We must come to the definite conclusion that this proposition: *I am, I exist,* is necessarily true each time that I pronounce it, or that I mentally conceive it."[19]

Lacan, with Freud, echoes the notion: "Thought does not found being except by knotting itself in *speech* where every operation reaches to the essence of language . . . nothing is spoken except by depending on the cause."[20] If through speech I take on my own causality, then the subject and the subject's certitude are born simultaneously: in a single instant, the

I am is the *effect* (Descartes says *ergo*) of the I think. The subject is summoned out of the signifier in its actuality. There is no subject except for the *suppositum,* placed underneath the bar of the signifier:

$$\frac{S}{s}$$

d. Wo Es War

While the Freudian subject is very much a revival of the Cartesian *cogito,* the foundation of its certitude has been revised. Between the subject's birth in the past *(Wo es war)* and the subject's present certitude *(soll Ich werden),* there is a temporal *space.* Freud called it deferred action. In the deferred action of unconscious formations, certitude rests on a subject already born from an "it *(ça)* thinks," before certitude occurs.

Indeed, no present signifier, by itself, can represent the subject. The subject would be petrified in it, as in madness: a king does not consider himself a king, unless he is mad; and Napoleon does not identify himself with Napoleon, unless he is at Sainte-Helene. Why is this so?

Let us consider one formation of the unconscious, the dream. How does the subject grasp himself in it? Choang-tsu dreams he is a butterfly; in the butterfly "he apprehended one of the roots of his identity,"[21] that he is caught. If he isn't mad he can, upon waking, *question himself;* he can *ask himself* why he dreamed that. Of course, he doesn't believe he is, doesn't take himself for . . . a butterfly. How then is the subject's certitude revealed? Of course, Choang-tsu must begin by acknowledging that he was *represented* by the butterfly as signifier. But for the subject to achieve certitude, is it enough to explain what the butterfly, with its show of colors, is in his history?

To answer this, we will need to work out a clear *distinction* between formations of the unconscious and the unconscious itself. The unconscious is not the dream. Let us begin with a dream Freud reported toward the end of the *Traumdeutung.* A father had just witnessed his son's death and was keeping watch over the body, which had been laid out. Seized by fatigue, he entrusted an old man with the task of watching the body and went to sleep. He dreamed that his son was alive and reproaching him: "Father, don't you see I'm burning?"[22]

Where did this text come from? It did not come from the sound of the lighted candle falling on the child's bed. Did it repeat an earlier scene in which the child, burning with fever, had beseeched his father with voice and look? It was certainly this, but not entirely. It is insufficient to say that, in this dream, the father has the satisfaction of seeing and hearing his son alive again.

This repetition of an earlier occurrence of possible paternal failure is merely the staging of something else. The unconscious is *un-bewusst* (Lacan translates it *"une-bévue,"* "one-slip"), with this *un* bearing the stamp of the obstacle generated by the dream's very text: the father *as such* does not see, he is not all-seeing. What repeats itself is not some paternal powerlessness, which is only the underside of power, but the impossible, the encounter, forever missed, between the father (not a father) and the son: the impossible that is the real.

Structurally, radically, no signifier we can remember can represent father-being as father. No signifier can represent this except *for* another signifier (S_2). Father-being is named, of course ("Don't you see?") but is forever absent, unanswering, irreducibly repressed, *urverdrängt*. In Lacan's notation:

$$\frac{S_1}{S} \longrightarrow S_2$$

Now this gap between S_1 and S_2—the gap that causes the subject—also *founds* the subject's certitude. There is *no* possible knowledge *(savoir) of* the subject. (That there is is a pretention common to both madness and psychology.) Rather, the "no" of negation, the bar through the subject (Lacan writes it $), is the subject's certitude, deferred inasmuch as it is born from that very gap.

Two Sub-positions

Beginning in 1964, Lacan turned to the subject of science as the sole subject implicated in the *praxis* of psychoanalysis. Two steps prepared the way:

1. There is a *distinction* between knowledge *(savoir)* and truth. Truth speaks through formations of the unconscious, all of which Freud put under the same heading: dreams, symptoms, parapraxes, and jokes. But

these productions are not the unconscious. The unconscious is knowledge *(savoir)*: an unknown, *sub-posed* knowledge *(savoir)*, which has the *effect* of truth there where it speaks. What is this effect? It is the mark of the subject's effacement, the index of the subject's enigma, the imprint left by the absence of S_2. In it, the interpretation will be found.

Therefore, in the analytic session, interpretation is not translation from one language into another, but authentication of this breaking point, of this boundary sign, by means of a mark that *punctuates* the text: end of session ... period! Whether the session is long or short is not the question!

2. To the sub-position of knowledge *(savoir)* is added that of the *subject*. What subject is it who, through the work of the *soll Ich*, assumes his or her causality? It is not the speaking subject supposed *by* another speaking subject, but the subject of the *cogito*, the one that is the effect of the signifier by the very fact that it represents it.

And so the Freudian subject is the same as that of the Cartesian *cogito*, except that it is otherwise founded in its certitude, insofar as a signifier represents it *for* another signifier forever absent.

The Pivotal Role of the Transference

These advances with respect to the Freudian subject and unconscious knowledge *(savoir)* now permit us to render more precise the definition of the transference as metaphor of love. Its mainspring is the *sub-position* of a subject supposed to know:

$$\frac{\text{supposed}}{\text{subject} \ldots \text{to know}}$$

(a)

Is it supposed *by* a subject? No. The supposition is not an intersubjective one, such as a subject (the analysand) would make in supposing that another subject (the analyst) possessed knowledge *(savoir)*. This would constitute a psychologizing definition of the subject. There is no supposition except by a signifier, and what is supposed is this: a *subject* and with it, at one and the same time, this textual *knowledge (savoir)* that is the unconscious (a chain of signifiers). In keeping with Lacan's algorithm, we write the supposition thus:

$$\frac{S \longrightarrow S_q}{s\,(S_1, S_2, \ldots S_n)}$$

(b)

Now, according to the definition of the subject, S represents the subject supposed to possess knowledge *(savoir)* for another signifier, any signifier at all, S_q. Transference occurs as soon as this signifier, any signifier in its marked place, is inscribed *somewhere* (which does not mean anywhere). This place marked "somewhere" comes, according to Lacan, "from one knows not *where*" (April 15, 1980).[23] Certainly different names have been applied to it, conforming to different cultures and different times. But is it incarnated in the psychoanalyst? The answer, more than being antinomic, belongs to the order of paradox: "The subject supposed to know is not real."[24] For analysis to take place, there is no need at all for the analysand to clothe the analyst in this vestment. What matters is the place marked for a *third*, a third party between two partners. If the analyst (wrongly) identifies himself with this third party, or if the analysand identifies him with it (this happens occasionally, in moments when the unconscious is closed up), then there is no transference properly so called; and to persist in defining it this way is the cause of infinitely many mixups.

On the contrary, what is essential is to see what the desire-of-the-analyst effects through this third party. The analyst's desire is circumscribed by this double choice:

1. Whatever referential knowledge *(savoir)* the analyst already has, *he or she will choose not to know it*. Indeed, such knowledge *(savoir)* has nothing to do with the meaning of the signifiers that belong to each new analysand $(S_1, S_2, \ldots S_n)$. The analyst is a *Laie* (layman), as Freud said in 1926 in *Die Frage der Laienanalyse*. This means he does not rely on the prior learning that earned him certification. On the contrary, the analyst learns to acquire the sort of knowledge *(savoir)* that is embedded in language and flows from the analysand's speech, that is to say, textual knowledge *(savoir)*. Whence the second choice:

2. Whatever the analyst doesn't know of the supposed textual knowledge *(savoir)*, *he will choose to know it*. The willingness not to know of the

first choice begets the path for the second, that is, a framework for what there is to know. Freud's audacity lay in his invention of this fundamental rule: speak . . . something will come out of it.[25] What will it be? A literal knowledge *(savoir littéral)* that dwells in the language that produces it. And the analyst, through the analytic process, may gradually acquire a bit of this knowledge—that is, if the analyst is not merely a "clerk" or a fool but a "layman."

This double choice belongs to the desire-of-the-analyst, as in the case of Socrates who, desiring Alcibiades, said he wished to know "nothing, unless it concerns desire" *(Banquet,* 177d). The operation of the metaphor is shown in the table below, where it is important to note that, at the beginning of analysis, "*s.s.s.*" is read as "subject supposed to know" *("sujet supposé savoir")* whereas later, at the end of analysis, "*s.s.s.*" becomes "knowledge without a subject" *(savior sans sujet),* that is to say, textual knowledge (S_1, S_2 . . . S_n). In effect, the resolution of the transference consists in literal knowledge *(savoir littéral)* of the *Wo es war, from which,* retroactively, the subject comes forth.

Therefore, to the *che vuoi?,* to the question "what does the Other want?" the analysand ceases demanding an answer. There is lack in the Other: S (A̸). Having become desirous because of this lack, he responds by constituting the fantasy, set in the locus of lack in the Other: $ ◊ a.

Now, what this operation has made possible is the transference, that is, a change in the place of inscription, not its liquidation. But the subject supposed to know, supposed there where a known knowledge *(savoir)* is conquered, *where* was he or she *before*? From where does the "somewhere" of his or her place come to us?

The Finitude of Psychoanalysis

To respond to these questions would be to engage in doctrinal research of a theological nature: is the God who founds knowledge *(savoir)* deceitful or worthy of faith, is He to be believed or not? To answer the question, "What does the Other want?" would require an absolute guarantee of my evil or my good. On this crucial point, psychoanalysis must continually find and refind its own limits, lest it itself become theological. "There is nothing doctrinal about our office," wrote Lacan. "We are answerable to no ultimate truth; we are neither for nor against any

THE TRANSFERENCE

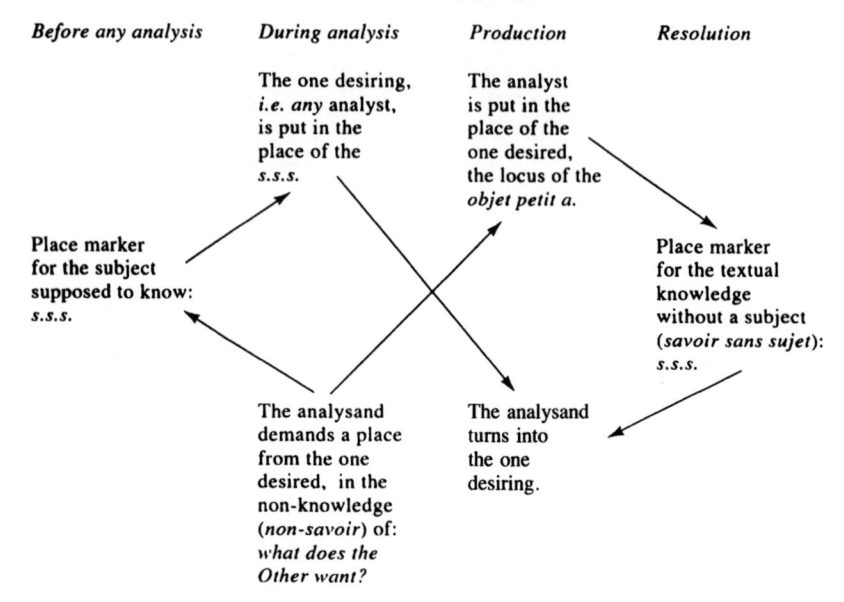

Before any analysis	*During analysis*	*Production*	*Resolution*
Place marker for the subject supposed to know: s.s.s.	The one desiring, i.e. any analyst, is put in the place of the s.s.s.	The analyst is put in the place of the one desired, the locus of the *objet petit a*.	Place marker for the textual knowledge without a subject (*savoir sans sujet*): s.s.s.
	The analysand demands a place from the one desired, in the non-knowledge (*non-savoir*) of: *what does the Other want?*	The analysand turns into the one desiring.	

particular religion."[26] But the primacy everywhere accorded the symbolic makes it difficult for psychoanalysts to resist, on the one hand, antitheism or, on the other, finding parallels between the Bible and the unconscious.

Psychoanalysis establishes its finitude, not by silence, but—in keeping with its own practice—by responding to the following question: where (to what place) does this knowledge *(savoir)* lead us? In order to answer, Lacan christened this "place" with the name of a dimension: the *real*. If this knowledge *(savoir)* leads us to a little more of the real than it does to reality sustained by fantasy, *then* one can and must say: the unconscious knowledge *(savoir)* we are dealing with is a knowledge *(savoir) in* the real and nowhere else. The only way to situate psychoanalysis with respect to science (as opposed to religion) is to put in place—via the symbolic—a *limit* to the symbolic, namely, the real.

Here we find the true practical and theoretical difficulty: unconscious knowledge *(savoir)* is disharmonic. It is given to us, but only insofar as it is not conceptually within our grasp. It falls by the wayside, slips out of reach. Freud calls it *Vergreifen,* something mis-grasped, mis-taken. I want your good as I conceive it, I want my good as I conceive it, but—it fails! The "one-slip" surprises me; like a slap on the face, it wakes me up to the desire of the Other. But on which side of the Other's good or mine will it serve to wake me up? On this side or beyond?

One approach is to refuse the disharmonic knowledge *(savoir)* that the unconscious is, to refuse to admit the *Vergreifen*. At the end of his 1973–1974 seminar entitled "Les non-dupes errent," Lacan would state: "For the first time in history, it is possible for you to wander away, that is, to *refuse* to love your unconscious, since finally you *know* what it is: a knowledge *(savoir)*, a knowledge that mucks us up."[27] In an incomplete, interrupted analysis, don't we encounter that will to refuse that issues from horror briefly glimpsed? It is a knowledge *(savoir)* that mucks us up, because it is not a knowledge *(savoir)* of our good. We would perhaps prefer retiring to our rooms . . . to commit suicide apace or at our leisure.

The other approach is to become the dupe of the unconscious, to love it strongly enough to cross the threshold to which this love leads: "True love ends in hatred," Lacan said.[28] The *love-hate* of the transference: this is the path to take so as not to wander. It is the road to traverse, for it leads us beyond, to the *real*, which sets a *limit* to love-hate and unknots the attachment to our destiny. This is the way to become the dupe of unconscious knowledge *(savoir)*; in return, unconscious knowledge *(savoir)* permits us to laugh about it, in accordance with the structure of witticism.

Thus a new question arises. How is the *symbolic*, as locus of the truth that speaks, linked to the *real*, as locus of knowledge *(savoir)*?

11

A Literal Operation

> Spelling mistake: an infraction of fidelity in love or marriage.
> —Littré

The Real Is Constituted from the Impossible

Truth has an effect on knowledge *(savoir)*. What is this effect? Isn't it that truth, through *speaking* and nothing else, forever leads us by the nose? Therefore, the only way to deal with truth is to *know* how it proceeds, so that analysis may find its end in this knowledge *(savoir)*. Picasso said: "I do not seek, I find." It must be the same for the analysand.

But how? On what *path*? It will not be the path of truth alone, which does nothing but speak. The only path is the path of writing, in other words, whatever of the *letter* there is in speech. Indeed, it is only through the letter that the relationship of the symbolic to the real can finally be posed, as today it is posed in psychoanalysis, inasmuch as this is where we encounter the subject of science.

Taking things step by step, we begin by establishing this landmark: *the institution of the real as the impossible* with the birth of science in the seventeenth century. An historian of scientific thought, Alexandre Koyré beautifully elucidated the ground-breaking steps taken by Galileo and Descartes. For example, to a contemporary of Galileo, the ideas of motion and space—principles of modern mechanics—constituted a paradox. Motion, in Galileo's day, was conceived in accordance with the image of the *physis* of any living being that is born, develops, and dies. Motion was life in its temporal existence. It was a scandal when modern science put forward the following: "To be in motion or at rest makes no difference to a body in motion or at rest, and produces no change in it."[1]

Motion is relative. Moreover, like rest, it is a state: "Both are *persistent states*. The celebrated first law of motion, the law of inertia, teaches us that a body left to itself persists eternally in its state of motion or repose; in order to transform a state of motion into a state of rest and *vice versa*, we must put a force into operation."[2] Agreed. But endless persistence is not characteristic of every motion, "*only* of uniform motion in a straight line."[3] A contemporary of Galileo, influenced by Aristotle, would object that he had never encountered any such motion. Modern physics responds (another scandal!): "Of course! Uniform, rectilinear motion is absolutely *impossible* and can occur only in a vacuum."[4]

Koyré concludes: "It is not surprising that an Aristotelian would be astonished and bewildered by this amazing effort *to explain the real by the impossible* or—what comes to the same thing—by the effort to explain real being by mathematical being. For, as I have already said, bodies that move in straight lines in an infinite, empty space are not *real* bodies moving in *real* space, but *mathematical* bodies moving in *mathematical* space."[5]

Now—and this is the decisive point—there are no mathematical bodies or spaces except *letters*. Hence, it is through the letter that psychoanalysis reproduces, with the subject of science, the ground-breaking steps described above. This time, however, it is not nature that is conquered, but the speaking subject.

A Literal Operation

To consider psychoanalysis a product of speech is to condemn it to being endless, to not having that end implied in the *relationship of symbolic to real through the letter*. For while no metalanguage exists to provide an answer, analysis is not for all that an indefinite process, which can be interrupted only by accident, with no proper end of its own.

Love of knowledge *(savoir)* is born of the way in which truth comes to us. Lacan used to say: "I, truth, will speak,"[6] letting truth speak in his speaking, just as every speaking being does: in spite of himself! Discreet in its luminosity, tenacious in its insistence, truth speaks through the *formations* of the unconscious. And it does so, not for our comfort, but rather for our dis-comfort, as a slip or mis-take. And from this discomfort love of knowledge *(savoir)* is born, or, rather, may be born (since it need not happen). How does one deal with truth that speaks thus? This is an eminently practical question; dealing with it requires a certain know-how.

There are two ways not to deal with this question. One is for the analyst to claim to speak the truth *about* the truth that speaks thus; any collusion with truth on the part of the analyst is a refusal of knowledge *(savoir)*) Another is for the analysand to take the formations of the unconscious as an oracle or divine revelation; to submit to the Other's goodwill is to will to know nothing of this good.

What does the Other want? What does the Other want of *me* . . . by speaking thus? Two tangled questions! In order to answer (and thereby to untangle) them, we seek help in analytic discourse—that link determined by the experience of analysis—for therein is the enactment of unconscious *knowledge (savoir)*.

Now, according to Lacan, the unconscious "reminds us that to the side of meaning that fascinates us in speech—in exchange for which being—this being whose thought is imagined by Parmenides—acts as speech's screen—reminds us, I conclude, that to the side of *meaning* the study of language opposes the side of the *sign*."[7] Through this fascination with meaning in speech, the unconscious wakes us up and focuses attention on what, beyond the disjunction of verbal and nonverbal, has the structure of language: on the side of the sign, this would be the *letter*. Indeed, what Freud taught us was to *read* symptoms, dreams, parapraxes, and jokes "as one deciphers a message in code."[8]

The sign is not to be read in its relationship to what precedes it or to what follows it (the side of meaning). It is to be deciphered as coming in the place *(an Stelle)* of another sign, which it thus renders discernible *(vernehmlich)* by virtue of a process of transference *(Übertragung)* or transposition *(Übersetzung)*: sign *for* sign, letter *for* letter. Such is the work of the unconscious in its formations. To interpret them is to perform the operation in reverse . . . leading to a new obverse.

The "Pas" of Negation

Let us imagine a watermill. What course does the water take? It flows in with the current itself, then ascends little by little into cups and small troughs on the wheel. Finally, it falls in droplets onto the current from which it came. This is how I imaginarize the adventures of a first mark *(trait)* as it returns to its point of departure: transformed by its ascent into the troughs of *speech,* it results in a cascading waterfall of little *letters.*

For return to the point of departure, three stages are required. Three stages are also required to answer this question: how are we to take this first mark, trace, stroke, *litura*? Should we take it as a sign representing a thing for someone, or not? The course it follows will permit us to answer, but first the intuitive support of a watermill must be replaced with one drawn from the linguistic order. This is the way Lacan makes the *"pas"* accomplish its course.[9]

First stage: an outline *(tracé)* in the sand, an outline of a footprint *(trace d'un pas)*. Is it the image of a foot, a figure that has taken on the form of a foot? Or is it a nonfigurative mark *(trait),* a pure indication of the passage of a foot? It will be enough if we call it the inscription and vision of a mark *(trait)*. The question lies elsewhere: should a passerby who sees it take it for the *sign* of a thing, or not?

Second stage: the moment when *"pas"* is pronounced, *read aloud*. In doing this, I forget whatever portion of the outline *(tracé)* represents the object "foot" *(pas)* for me and, through vocalization, raise this mark to phonetic status. Now the syllable *"pas"* can be linked to others: at - least - one other. One syllable can be connected to another, thanks to its disconnection with the signified object. From phonation is born the ambiguity of sound and meaning: *"pa*-taquès."[10] Through homophony, meaning is created: the way of the rebus!

Third stage: I gather up what has fallen and return to the outline *(tracé)* of the print *(trace)*. No longer does the sound *"pas"* represent a footprint *(trace de pas)*. It has transformed *trace de pas* (footprint) into a *letter* that bars and excludes: *pas-de-trace* (no-trace).

This *"pas"* is the *"pas"* of negation *(pas-de-la-négation)*. It negates that portion of the print *(trace)* that could (conditional of possibility) signify an object and turns it into a letter that erases and prohibits: *c'est pas-possible!* (it's not-possible!).

Hence, the three stages: *trace de pas, pataquès, pas-de-trace*. Through the phoneticism of writing, there is a transformation of *trace* into *tracé*, of *sign* into *letter*.

The return of *"tracé"* serves to answer the question posed at the outset: is the outline of a footprint *(tracé qui est trace de pas)* a sign or not? The "pas" of negation comes to bar the signifier from the signified. Certainly the second stage, phoneticism as *effect of meaning*, was necessary. But there is a residue: through negativation of the sign, the function of the letter as bar appears. This *borderline effect*, an effect of non-sense *(pas-de-sens)*, descends from the effect of meaning (that is, from the *"pas"* of meaning in the second stage) to reveal that portion of the outline *(tracé)* that belongs to the order of the letter.

In effect, the *"pas" of* meaning does not lead to the-meaning *(le-sens)* that would create a sexual relationship. Something goes wrong. Is it an accident or not? Is there any hope? Will we remain suspended in indefinite analysis?

Of course not! The second stage of phoneticism is necessary in order to break away from the sign as revelatory. But it is not sufficient, since it doesn't exhaust the function of the outline *(tracé)*. Via the third stage, what has escaped the order of speech appears in the outline *(tracé)*. The letter is not a pure and simple transcription of sound.[11] It has a supplementary aspect: that part of the letter that, in being written, produces a border zone, a littoral, which is not read: "The erasure of any previous trace, this is what makes dry land from littoral. The literal is pure *litura*."[12]

Stated differently, there is lack in the order of *speaking*: endless slip, perpetual *pataquès*. What are we to make of it? Is it impotence? Is it the impossible? What should we finally conclude? The letter *inscribes* this lack, and the letter responds: the real as the impossible!

m.c.l.

How does the unconscious work?

Observing the letter as it functions concretely in a *sequence of dreams*,

A Literal Operation

we shall attempt to answer the following question: is the letter's function to designate sets or to be the operator of those sets?

First dream: I saw a lion in a cage watching a serpent escape through the bars. The manifest content of the dream is so evident in terms of its meaning that it produces an *enigma:* impossible to associate!

Second dream: I see a chameleon biting a serpent. In accordance with the law of *homophony,* the father's first name appears: Camille!

1. Should we now, following Jung, enlist the entire cultural baggage of signifieds that characterize said chameleon (for example, one who turns himself into a reflection of his environment)? That's a lot of baggage to put on the father's back!

No. The letter is that part *of* the signifier that bars it from all preestablished signifieds. It is that part of the signifier that belongs to the phonetic order, insofar as each phoneme is only pure difference from every other: c.h.a.m.e.l.e.o.n. Whence homophony.

The letter, however, is not only what is heard-in-reading but what is outlined-in-writing. What results? A border zone in the locus of the Other, forming a hole in that very place: not-to-be-read *(pas-à-lire)!* Indeed, the transformation from "lion" into "chameleon" is to be taken as the inscription of the proper name "Camille" in the place of the Other, an inscription that bars that part of the common noun "lion" that *could* lend itself to the signifying metaphor.

$$\text{chameleon} \rightarrow \text{camille/lion}$$

There is no negation without a mark. The letter marks the signifer "lion" at the point where it erases whatever appearance of meaning there would be in the signifier. Non-sense *(pas-de-sens)* is the step *(pas)* that meaning accomplishes when it makes itself letter: the step of meaning *(pas-du-sens).*

2. This is not without consequence; thanks to support from the inscribed cut, the *fantasy* can appear.

In the first dream, the serpent escapes between bars right before the lion's eyes. In the second, the *threefold* movement of the drive is accomplished: to bite, be bitten, *get oneself bitten.* What matters here is being able to articulate the fantasy, which earlier had been inscribed on the screen put in the empty place of the Other's desire. To the question, "what does he want of *me?*" the Other had offered no response. It is the fantasy that replies. Without being *objet petit a,* the serpent—bitten object—represents *objet petit a,* which is held *between* subject and Other (its gullet!), as if stuck onto the Other.

But this is not possible *except* through operation of the bar—the bar of the Other—on the subject: $. This bar divides the subject by way of the letter, c.a.m.e(i).l(l).e., which, by inscribing itself in the locus of the Other, creates a border zone and thereby effects what Freud called *ein neues Subjekt.*[13]

In this void created by the cut, the third stage of the drive can occur: a "getting oneself bitten," which is neither a swallowing up nor an escape from the cage (as in the first dream). Once detached from the drive's demand, the inscription of "getting oneself bitten" becomes the *road* to *surplus-enjoyment (plus-de-jouir),* for this is what is at stake in the articulation of the fantasy, there where desire finds its cause: in this case, as oral object.[14]

The cut *effects the subject*. It allows for a place, a space wherein the subject can dwell by representing itself as *object* of the Other's desire.

Surely the serpent is not be taken in its visual aspect, as evoking a phallicized form. It is an oral object. But is it, for all that, a maternal, mammary object? No. It represents the phallus; more specifically, it represents the subject *for,* that is, it stands *in place of,* another signifier: the phallus as signifier lacking in the Other. What is at stake here is being the phallus for the Other. Again it was necessary for the *empty* place in the Other to be established, therefore inscribed. This occurs *through the letter*.

3. By what operation of the letter is this place inscribed? I would answer: through transformation of "Camille" into "chameleon," through the work that converts a *proper* noun into a *common* one. In other words, through *reopening* a lack in the Other.

The condensation of "Camille/lion" into "chameleon" in effect reduces the father's proper name to *just any* signifier (although determined), reduces it to the status of a signifier representing the *subject* for another signifier, forever lacking. Whence the vacillation effect: the reopening of a gap in the Other. What is really at stake is this: if there is a lack in the Other, then I can seek my place there, a place may be found. With a proper name, it is precisely the opposite: there is denomination, an act of founding, which *sutures* the subject to the extent that the proper name is

A Literal Operation

idealized: a herald proclaims it and—voila!—the inscribed *Majuscule* (capital letter) becomes heraldic, a breastplate and shield! The unconscious shakes up the proper name, fragmenting it, breaking it into pieces, disseminating it in letters. Hence the reduction to lower-case letters. Which leads us to this assertion: there are no letters except lower-case letters.

Isn't this the operation that each analysis demonstrates? Does it not accord with what Freud heard from the Wolf Man who, dreaming of a *Wespe* (wasp) and deciphering *espe*, said: " 'But *espe*, why, that's myself: S.P.' (which were his initials)."[15]

Third dream: "I see a man with a blowtorch (chalumeau). Its fire has burned his hands, and he removes the skin from his palms as if it were paper. I experience intense pain; but he, he was feeling nothing." The following memory comes from the dreamer's childhood: his father cut his thumb with a saw, and the child suffered greatly *with* him. Certainly, this transcription of the dream produces *some* meaning through metaphor. In his occupation—writing and publishing—the subject "makes things out of paper." So, too, does the father, in his own way. Manual labor with a pen: here we have a single, *common* stroke from the ego-ideal: *litura*. What is the fate of this mark?[16]

In the dream, the mark made by the pen is erased and replaced by the blowtorch, which *burns*. If there is meaning via metaphor, the meaning of this meaning remains enigma and questioning: why is paper produced by fire? What does this have to do with paternal castration? A burning question, posed from the start—a question whose inscription was permitted by the real childhood episode, following the visible mark on the thumb. A question about paternity and filiation: how *to be of* this father, without reexperiencing the *same* burning sensation whenever paper is produced.

What is *decisive* in this inscription will be found in its operative cause *and* in the response generated.

a. That the sequence *peau-paume-papier* (skin-palm-paper) can lead us back to pa-pa is not decisive: this would only be a matter of assonance. The same may be said for the coincidence of *chalumeau* (blowtorch) and *calamus* (reed pen) as productive tool: a simultaneous juxtaposition of figurative and literal. What really *effects* the inscription is just the letter itself: in this case, the three consonants of the father's first name—c.m.l.—present and active in *chalumeau*.

b. Given this literal operator, what is decisive in the inscription is the *effect* obtained. As we showed above (*peau-papier*/skin-paper), this effect is not simply a production of meaning. Rather, it is the response generated to a question posed since childhood by the subject, a question about the father's *jouissance* and, therefore, about the real of his body. The subject responds with this inscription of the letter, which creates a corresponding border zone. Littoral becomes literal: "I experience intense pain; *but he,* he was feeling nothing."

To the overzealous fusion of two bodies—experienced at the time of the traumatic childhood episode, which created both a reference point and a landmark—the inscription opposes a demarcation and a *frontier:* I, *but not* he. May my father be spared at my expense! This wish is *realized* by the inscription, via the bar of "not he." Moreover, its realization has ordered the subject's existence from childhood even *up to this very moment.* It produces an answer through knowledge (*savoir*) of the Other's *jouissance:* I know he at least does not suffer. Such is the effect of love for the father—more specifically, of love for his first name. Indeed, love cannot make one out of two; there is no love except of the letter.

This sequence of three dreams allows us to answer the question we posed about the work of the unconscious. Its work is the work of the letter, as operator.

In effect, *c.m.l.* functions *at the very interior* of this group: *lion/chameleon/chalumeau.* These letters do not name elements, since $A \neq A$, since the signifier *of* the Other (which names the Other) is not *in* the Other. There is no metalanguage. Rather, these letters constitute the elements as a set, being themselves elements of the set.

Lacan: "Letters *make* collections; letters *are,* and do not *designate,* these collections; they are to be treated as functioning like the collections themselves."[17] Such is the unconscious: not structured by a language but *as* a language. An effect of the signifier, the unconscious functions as a letter, like the collections in set theory.

Names Proper to the Subject

Before going on, let us review the path thus far traveled. The first step was Saussurian, grounded in the duality of sound and meaning. Primacy was given to the signifier in the effect of the signified—a primacy of artifice, since the signifier is constituted of a phoneme, a unity that is nothing but difference from another. Such is spoken language.

During the years 1953–1957, from his seminar on the "Purloined Letter" to his "Agency of the Letter in the Unconscious," Lacan (building on this Saussurian base) emphasized the impact of the signifier on the signified. From a locus that is preestablished with respect to the signified, the signifier operates independently, in virtue of its *place* in the suite of signifiers. But, in this flux, what *fixes* a place, if not whatever of the letter is in the signifier? The letter is the essentially localized structure of the signifier. This is the general principle of the rebus. An *effect of meaning* is thus produced, more through condensation (metaphor), less through displacement (metonomy).

However, this first step left two questions hanging: the question of the subject and the question of the letter, inasmuch as "there is a universe between word and letter."[18] The answer to these two related questions would be found by passing from the first to the second topography, that is, by analyzing the identification process—the sort Freud designated as secondary and described as "a partial and extremely limited one" that "only borrows a single trait *(einen einzigen Zug)* from the person who is its object."[19] Lacan called it "identification with a single mark" *(trait unaire)*.

It is the constellation of these traits/marks that constitutes the ego-ideal for the subject. How can the subject find his or her place, given that the subject is represented solely by a signifier for another signifier forever absent from the field of the Other? How is this void to be recognized if not in the *marks* of the parental response? Indeed, "the first words spoken *(le dit premier)* stand as a decree, a law, an aphorism, an oracle; they confer their obscure authority upon the real other."[20]

Thus these marks, insignia of authority and power, come to *fill up* the original void left by the missing signifier—and the subject *identifies* with them. Their mark *(trait)* alienates the subject and leads to formation of the ego-ideal, a possibility-of-being, a potential for . . . *Ein einziger Zug*: such is the proper name, proper to the subject . . . in the Other. *More than* any other word, the proper name as single stroke will show us what the letter is about, not on the side of meaning but on the side of the sign and of insignia.

Lacan's Hypothesis

1. What is a proper name?[21] Lacan rejects Russell's answer: a word for a particular. This would be to reduce the proper name to a demonstrative pronoun, such as "this" or "that," which designates a particular object. To give a proper name is not the same as simply to designate an object in its particularity. When I call this cat "Pitchounette" or this house "Le Pas-du-Loup," I am not replacing "this" with a proper name, or conversely. Indeed, there is something irreplaceable in the proper name, and we shall see why.

Gardiner, the Egyptologist, points us in a different direction: an astute psychologist, he observed that, when one pronounces a proper name, one is sensitive not only to the signified, as with a common noun, but also to the sounds insofar as they are distinctive. The sonorous material, one might say, is not forgotten or reduced to the rank of a pure instrument of meaning, but remains present to the minds of the interlocutors in its consistency of differentiated modulation. Thus Proust, sensitive to the "heavy syllable" of the name "Parma" wrote:

> The name of Parma, one of the towns that I most longed to visit, after reading the *Chartreuse,* seeming to me compact and glossy, violet-tinted, soft, if anyone were to speak of such or such a house in Parma, in which I should be lodged, he would give me the pleasure of thinking that I was to inhabit a dwelling that was compact and glossy, violet-tinted, soft, and that bore no relation to the houses in any other town in Italy, since I could imagine it only by the aid of that heavy syllable of the name of Parma, in which no breath of air stirred, and of all that I had made it assume of the Stendhalian sweetness and the reflected hue of violets.[22]

But this appeal to the awareness of the psychological subject is insufficient. It makes us miss what is going on with the unconscious subject *properly* so called (something that particularly needs to be said here). On this point, Lacan again took up what he had said on the agency of the letter in the unconscious and advanced from there to break new ground. He proposed the following: a proper name is there wherever a link is established between a vocal emission and something belonging to the order of the letter, there wherever an affinity is created between such denomination and an inscribed mark taken as object. This affinity is recognized in the fact that a proper name as such is nontranslatable from language to language. It resists translation by virtue of its literal mooring, voyaging and transferring just as it is. The phrase "*bâton rouge*" (red stick) forfeits its letters when translated into English, but the name of Louisiana's capital preserves them: Baton Rouge. In spite of slight phonetic modifications, the names "Parma" or "Lacan" are pronounced as such in every language and remain recognizable. What makes a proper name is the connection, not to sound, but to writing.

2. But then the question arises: what is a *letter*? Here it is interesting to examine expert opinion. How do historians of ancient civilizations see the birth of writing? Whether dealing with Mesopotamia, Egypt, or China, they encounter similar data. Yet they diverge on the question of where to situate writing or what criterion to use in calling this or that graphic representation a letter.

The answer depends on the way one views writing and its reading. For some, writing evolved gradually through history, achieving its perfection or maturity only in phonetic writing. Others believe the opposite: there is no progress. Writing is already there before its function in the transcription of a language. Thus Leon Vandermeersch could write about China: "From the point of view of the nature of writing, there is no fundamental difference between pictographic symbolism and the symbolism I would call phoneticographic."[23]

Lacan's conjecture amounted to a position at variance with both points of view outlined above. His purpose was to bring to the fore the nature of the proper name. His position consisted in breaking free of the *evolutionary* idea, according to which writing is first a figure that imitates the object; then, by abstraction and stylization, becomes a pure sign of the object (an ideogram); and finally accedes to the full status of a letter as phonetic support in alphabetic writing. Breaking free means seizing the letter in its radical origin and thereby capturing what in the letter escapes change. To accomplish this, the evolutionary schema must be negated in two ways:

a. First break: at its endpoint, the letter is not pure *notation of the phoneme*. It is not born fresh in order to serve in the transcription of language. Rather, it is found *already there* in its materiality. Only at a second stage, by way of a functional reversal, does it serve to transcribe language. Leon Vandermeersch writes of China: "One of the first means of extending the lexicon, of recording a word, was to borrow the graphic representation of a homophone. For example, the representation of the right hand (𐤉 , pronounced *yu,* or the graphic representation for sacrifice in general (Ψ) also pronounced *yu,* have been *utilized* for the verb 'to have', which is pronounced *yu* as well."[24] In a similar vein, Jean Bottero remarks about Mesopotamia: "Homophony, common in the Sumerian language, must have given the idea of *utilizing* a pictogram to designate, not the *object* it represented, either directly or indirectly, but another object whose *name* was phonetically identical or very close." He adds: "To utilize the pictogram of an arrow *(ti)* to designate something which is also called *ti,* 'life,' was *to cut,* utterly and completely, the original relation of this sign to an *object* (the arrow), so as to fix it to a *phoneme (ti),* which is something that belongs, not to the domain of extramental reality, but strictly to spoken language, something far more universal."[25]

Here then is the first negation: the letter does not come from the phoneme; its material existence does not depend on its function as a phonematic notation.

b. Second break: if we go back to the beginning, we will encounter this question: where does the literal material, which is, so to speak, "waiting"—where does it come from?

It is neither stylization of a design nor abstraction from an originally concrete figure. Rather, it is a negation of these through inscription of the *mark (trait).* The mark is not a reminder of the figure of the object but is instead its effacement by the one countable mark that marks the object's uniqueness. The unary mark destroys and denies everything in the object that is alive to our senses, so as to retain only its uniqueness.

Writing is born with *negation*—this is Lacan's hypothesis. It connects with and makes more precise Freud's definition: "a partial and extremely limited" identification that "only borrows a single trait."[26] Thus the painter, Magritte, wishing to indicate on the canvas what the drawing of a pipe on a surface is all about, wrote: "This is not a pipe."

c. In conclusion, the letter is not born from its function as phonetic support; moreover, it is not the figuration of an object. But it is a distinctive mark. Hence the letter—which is the mark *(trait)* in isolation—is not defined by its pronunciation, its phonic articulation, or its link to sound.

On the other hand, it is *named* as such, just like any other *object.*

Essentially, signs are read in this way: the mark *(trait)* is called by its name. Hence the letter outlined α is *read* "alpha" in Greek, independently of its value as a transcription, when it is pronounced in accordance with the sound "a." A French child learns that the letter *g* is pronounced differently in the words *"girafe"* and *"guenon."* Moreover, he or she learns that the letter *g* is called *"gé"* but that one doesn't say *"gé-irafe."* The name of the letter is not its pronunciation; *c, q,* and *k* are vocalized the same but called by different names. As a function of what? Of their *outline (tracé)*.

All this becomes entirely comprehensible when looked at historically. Isn't this what paleography reveals to us?

Rodlike shapes on Magdalenian cave walls (Portugal to Bavaria);[27] notches carved by hunters on ivory or deer bones; gashes on sticks; quipus (pre-Columbian Peru);[28] divination lines on the fissured backs of turtles (China, second millennium); painted inscriptions on stones (Le Mas d'Azil, 9000 B.C.);[29] hatchings on pottery (predynastic Egypt and neolithic China)—in each case, the stroke denominates the relationship between language and the real. In naming the outline, the subject *already* reads it, well before that outline serves to transcribe spoken language. What does the subject read? Not the stroke that is a unique exemplary but the one that is countable, the one distinct from another one.

3. The proper name clearly reveals this. *More than any other name,* it is bound, before all phonematization, to what language contains of the letter as distinctive mark *(trait)*. Far from being translated, the proper name transfers just as it is, revealing its connection to the mark.

Now this distinctive stroke *is* the proper name in its letters. How is it *linked* to what Freud called *einziger Zug,* the "single trait" of the ego-ideal, with which the subject identifies to the point where he sees himself as being seen in the Other (locus of signifiers), seen as lovable, loved, and thus . . . narcissistically loving insofar as loved? To respond, we will first need to inquire about the subject in his relationship to the name.

Elision of the Subject

Let us listen to what a little girl tells us, as reported by Moustapha Safouan in *L'inconscient et son scribe:*

> A little girl of six had drawn a queen and divided her gown into boxes, putting in each box the name of an object she prized: candy, sugar, rings,

etc. Nor did she forget to add "Me." Asked if she were the queen, she answered, manifestly annoyed by the question: "Of course not. You're stupid! Queens are like that: they have funny names."[30]

In those boxes, we recognize the distinctive mark of the letter as "essentially *localized* structure of the signifier."[31] Moreover, the boxes, in themselves empty of meaning, are then denominated by names ("candy," "sugar," "ring") that do not refer to their official signified but to what is "prized": proper names, traits belonging to the ego-ideal, represented by the queen. Lest we doubt this, the little girl wrote, in addition, "Me." But the decisive element is the position of the child in the Other. Stupidly asked whether she *is* the queen, she answers: "Of course not. You're stupid."

Truth speaks through the mouths of children, without their knowing it. The subject of the enunciation is not the ego or its ideal. Indeed, to the extent that the subject speaks, there is elision of *the name of* the subject of the unconscious, an original signifier, forever *urverdrängt*. The subject, on the other hand, is represented in language that is *already there,* in the *pre*conscious, outside, visible in the real. The proper name is there, already there. We have to *read* it at the level of the little girl's "Me" as that part of language that belongs to the order of the sign, the sign that is the letter. It is there for, in place of . . . the name that is forever absent, elided, the name of the subject of the unconscious: a subject ceaselessly excluded and rejected from the signifying chain. Whence the negation: "Of course not, you're stupid!"

In effect, in the proper names of the ego-ideal, where the subject sees himself or herself being seen by the Other as lovable, the subject is desirable but not *desiring*. How then can desire be born, if not from this empty place (an empty box on the queen's robe!), from this lack that is the subject insofar as the proper name of the ideal *can* be lacking?

Isn't this what formations of the unconscious do, that is, make the proper name fail? The analytic stake is not on the side of the ideal (consolidation of the name) but elsewhere, on the side of desire and of its empty place, there where its cause dwells. We shall see this now, in describing avatars of the proper name, along with the unconscious and its formation. First, forgetting the name; next, the dream.

Forgetting the Name

The relationship between the unconscious and the proper name is established according to the following process: (1) Far from strengthening the ego-ideal, the Freudian *unbewusst* (Lacan termed it the *"une-bévue"* or "one-slip") introduces a fault. (2) To the extent that the proper name functions as an ideal trait, it attempts to ward off the fault by suturing it. (3) But formations of the unconscious cause the suture to fail, not purely and simply, but by fragmenting the letters of the proper name so as to create a specific hole. How?

We begin with the slip of forgetting a name.[32] Traveling with Freyhau, a lawyer from Berlin, Freud conversed with him about the frescoes of the "Four Last Things" at Orvieto. Suddenly, the name of the painter, Signorelli, escaped him. . . . It was, however, not a pure and simple forgetting! The unconscious had in fact generated a *substitute* formation, in which "substitute names . . . were formed . . . like symptoms," as Freud wrote Fliess.[33] "Botticelli," "Boltraffio," . . . *Ersatznamen* that go around the empty place and specify it.

Yet they do not block it, for, without hesitation, without having to ask his companion, Freud *knows* these names are not the ones he seeks. He knows they aren't—which is not nothing. It is a strange substitution that doesn't substitute, since at each go-round, the *Ersatznamen* lead further afield. In other words, if the formula for metaphor is one word for another, what we have here is a nonmetaphorical substitution, a failed metaphor.

In this very precise case of Freud's forgetting, we grasp what limits metaphor: the proper name, *insofar as* it is linked—as it is here—to the ego-ideal. To the extent that it is linked to the ego-ideal, it is not metaphorized. It is irreducible, irreplaceable, written in stone. And, as we saw above, the proper name does not translate; it transfers from place to place by virtue of its unbreakable connection to the letter. In brief, it travels as Freud does with Freyhau: a trans-port, a trans-fer!

What is the nature of this place? We will see as we follow the testimony of Freud himself, in the role of analysand.

First Place

Writing after the fact, Freud reconstructs the temporal sequence of his "series of thoughts" *(Gedankenreihe)*. He is in Herzegovina; the name reminds him of a story told by a colleague about the customs of the inhabitants, known for their confidence in doctors. The relative of an incurably sick person might therefore say to the physician: *"Herr* (Sir), what is there to be said? If he could be saved, I know you would have saved him."[34]

Freud speaks, gives himself free rein. But his thoughts lead back to another story, told by the same colleague about the same inhabitants, this time regarding their attitude toward sexual problems: *"Herr,* you must know that if *that* comes to an end then life is of no value."[35] Here Freud stalls, becomes quiet. This story is linked to a "series of thoughts" that concern him directly: at Trafoi he had received word that "a patient over whom I had taken a great deal of trouble had put an end to his life on account of an incurable sexual disorder."[36] Freud therefore interrupts what he is saying and turns his attention elsewhere, toward another "series," namely the frescoes at Orvieto. What has happened?

Freud has been cut to the quick with respect to his status and stature as a capable, erudite physician. In terms of his ideal ego—his image as a doctor faced with sickness, sexuality, and death—a lack has arisen. At such moments, a trait/mark belonging to the ego-ideal "normally" arrives to suture the lack. But this time, there has been trouble in the identification. Having lost his signature, as it were, Freud is unable to speak. A felicitous fault, which indicates the place of his *desire,* indicates it at the very point where he is *unable* to see himself as medically estimable in the Other's view, because at that point, there is *no* name.

Second Place

Whatever does not surface in the symbolic, whatever passes underneath *(unterdrückt),* reappears elsewhere, not in the real but in another place in the signifying chain or in the thought series. Freud called it displacement, *Verschiebung.* Displacement of what? He doesn't know yet, but he will later. It is a matter of his own name, *Sigmund.* This names voyages, becomes bound up with another name, the name of one who, through an art other than medicine, attempts to master death through frescoes on ultimate ends, through exaltation of the human body and its beauty. Isn't this where the physician fails and the artist triumphs, in the function of the beautiful?

Signorelli! The name that just now failed to suture is displaced and bound up with Signorelli, as it seeks its support. This is the *forgetting!* Sigmund leans on Signorelli and, in the attempt at suture, drags it down into the *Unterdrückung,* permitting a hole to emerge. A specific hole, limited, shaped by the words that bubble up in its place: Botticelli, Boltraffio.... But this failed act is a successful act. For it is here—at the point of lost identification, blindness, and absence of landmarks—at the point from which Freud sees himself in the Other as *Herr* and master of life—that the locus of his desire is found. It is here that the truth of his identification as subject is found, at the point where—outside, in the Other—there is nothing: the name is lost. Hence forgetting "Signorelli" brings Freud back to his desire, in his stumbling up against the limits of narcissistic love, so long as to love and be loved amount to the same thing.

Now, according to Freud, this displacement, this trans-fer has been made thanks to an external association *(eine äusserliche Assoziation),* to be understood as a literal identity. Contrary to Freud's conclusion, this postulate requires, not the series *Herr Signor Signorelli,* which presupposes a translation from German into Italian, but this one: *Sig/mund Sig/norelli.*[37]

Therefore, at a first locus in the signifying chain, the name "Sigmund" sinks below in order, at a second locus, to bind itself up with "Signorelli" and bring this name down in its fall. The three letters, *S-i-g,* of his signature fall away, but not without the resurgence of *-norelli* in the *o* and *elli* of "Botticelli" and "Boltraffio." In their floating function, the three purloined letters remain suspended: mission accomplished! (A successful act, which is really a failed act.) The unconscious has opened up a path. But there is a price: Freud will have to make the *Sig* of his signature fall *some other way,* that is, make it fall into the wastebasket *(à la poubelle)* by publishing *(poubliant)* his book, *Zur Psychopathologie des Alltagslebens.*[38]

And what does he write there? That the *Verschiebung* (displacement) that allowed the *Namenverbindung* (binding up of "Sigmund" and "Signorelli") operates "without consideration for the sense or for the acoustic demarcation of the syllables" *(ohne Rücksicht auf den Sinn und auf die akustische Abgrenzung der Silben zu nehmen.)*[39] In effect, neither the meaning of the word nor its link to the vocal emission is decisive. It is the materiality of the letter that is determining. Freud insists on it: "Thus the names have been treated in this process like the pictograms in a sentence *(die Schriftbilder eines Satzes))* which has had to be converted into a picture-puzzle (or rebus) *(Bilderrätsel)*."[40]

Such insistent clarity allows us to conclude that the subject's own name—understood as a single stroke (in no way reducible to a family name) and as a privileged point in the signifying chain—is distinguished by its direct link to the materiality of the letter.

The Dream

If forgetting a name is always accompanied by substitution of false recollections—which is what the *Ersatznamen* are—what of that other unconscious formation, the dream, in its relation to the proper name?

Earlier, we found that Freud's forgetting indicated the locus of his desire in the Other. Yet he himself told us nothing about it: he had cut and censored his own speaking. The dream goes further. Here again we need to distinguish two stages, two places in the chain. But, unlike forgetting a name, these two places generate only one hole. We will see how.

At the first stage, one of the letters in a proper name is elided, a literal circumcision. A fault opens up in the name, causing its function of suture to fail, insofar as it constitutes a feature of the ideal. This fault is a precondition for a second stage where, in the very place where the letter has fallen, a border zone is outlined, setting up a locus for the cause of desire. Indeed, in the construction of a second dream, a demand is articulated in instinctual terms. Let us examine the series of two dreams.

"I am in my native town. I see inscribed in big letters on the window of a dilapidated building: N E L L Y." In the dreamer's association, this building on this street was the place where the subject went to relax and where, on his fifteenth birthday, he had a decisive encounter with a teacher occupying the position of the father. The teacher's name was Lyonnet, four letters of which *(N-e-ll-y)* made up a part of the dreamer's family name.[41] Thus, through fragmentation and the floating function of proper names, the dreamer's family name had been able to link itself to the teacher's. What then does the dream add?

A Literal Operation

The window constitutes a mirror, in which the image of the body is reversed, the left being seen on the right and the right on the left. To the reverse of the one, there corresponds the obverse of the other, and conversely:

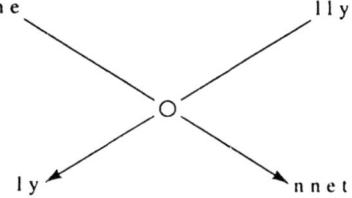

```
    n e              l l y
         \          /
          \        /
           \      /
            . O
           /      \
          /        \
         /          \
    l y              n n e t
```

The letter O has fallen away at the blind spot in any image of one's own body. Indeed, from where I see myself being seen (from the *I* of the Ideal, whence appears the *i* [a] of the self-image), there is a hole: I don't see myself from where you look at me. In the dream-text, doesn't the dilapidation of this place point to the mourning to be accomplished?

Such is the first stage: the letter O is inscribed as fallen; but it is not read.

Second dream: "In my hand I have a half-empty glass of water, and I am asking an old man, older than I am, for water."

The inscription "NELLY" is a border zone delineating the absence of the letter O and thereby making possible the birth of a demand addressed to the A-father. A demand for what? A demand no longer to be that letter that the Other lacks, but to have what the letter O *names* by homophony: *eau* (water). During a momentary vacillation in the reference points indicating what phallic power is (*eau*/spermatic fluid), the subject demands a transmission from father to son. Here the subject's momentum comes from the demand itself, before he later discovers the castrating, desiring father. Indeed, as far as phallic power is concerned, there is no such thing as "full": isn't a "half-empty" glass the same thing as one that is half-full?

But this is to say too little: he will have to discover that there is no half-half, only all or nothing. In effect, what Freud meant by castration was this: if the phallus is transmitted from father to son, it is not by virtue of the activity of the one and the receptivity of the other, as in a trans-fer through siphoning. Rather, this very transmission presupposes a preliminary annulment of the father's phallus, in order that the son may one day be its bearer.

The Named Letter

With the *forgetting* of "Signorelli," there were two stages, two holes in the signifying chain; with the *dream,* two stages and a single hole: from the non-sense of the fallen letter *(O)* there bubbles up the phallic meaning of what is lacking. There where forgetting a name fails, the dream (or witticism) succeeds. In effect, the letter is first inscribed as missing at its place *(O),* then at this very place it is read: *"eau"* (water).

Such is the reading of signs: a naming. This is because to read is to decipher, to turn the outline of the *litura* into a named *littera.* As we have seen, to name is not to pronounce or to phoneticize. Let's take an example to grasp the difference.

One day, a pianist dares to stop being satisfied with playing the works of others. He becomes a composer: themes possess him "in his head." But how is he to transcribe their sounds on a musical score? An inhibition is at work here: he has no way to "hear himself in his head." He needs the "crutch" of a keyboard in order to be able to transcribe. His analysis will allow him take the step of writing at a table and not at the piano, of "hearing himself" in some other way, thanks to the power of *naming* sounds in a notation written directly, without the piano.

This example is not a comparison. It concerns the real itself insofar as it is produced from number, which itself exists only insofar as it is named by the cipher. There is no reading except by deciphering the cipher: a work of the unconscious and of its textual knowledge *(savoir).*

The name is a mark. The name itself, which we have qualified by adjectives and loaded with attributes as signs of something for someone—here we are, elevating it to the status of stroke, to the status of proper name in its pure, symbolic denomination. For example, the utterance, "my mother is my mother!" is not a tautology, but the designation of the word "mother" as such, that is, "that insupportable, devout, infamous middle-class woman, thanks to whom I learned that one arrives at truth solely through the deceit of language; and is yet *the very same one* who, in the official registry, appears in letters as being my father's wife by the symbolic links of marriage, insofar as the act in question has to do precisely with my birth." Thus, "my mother is my mother" is a naming of the letter, not a tautology.[42] Now, this is at the very foundation of what we have discovered:

1. Names proper to the subject do not *translate*. Translating them would mean appealing to the signified; if certain names such as "Baker" or "Miller" do not exclude the signifier, then this is not what specifies the proper name as such. To translate proper names into another language in order to say why they are mute would be to render them mute forever.

2. Proper names are *irreplaceable*, to the very degree that they constitute a single stroke from the ideal. Therefore, they are not metaphorized.

3. On the other hand, they *transfer*. For this they are fragmented into their literal elements so that, when trans-ferring to another name, such and such letter maintains its inscription, an operation Lacan formulates as follows: letters do not designate collections, "letters *make* collections; letters *are*, and do not designate, these collections; they are to be treated as functioning like the collections themselves."[43]

4. However, this operation of fragmenting a proper name is not without loss: it establishes a border zone of lack, from which a demand in *pulsional* terms can arise. Thus, fragmentation of a proper name disconnects it from its function as single mark of the ego-ideal and reduces it to just any signifier, hence . . . metaphorizable.

What is operative in analysis, therefore, is the letter, insofar as its materiality is directly linked to the names proper to the subject. If it happens that they become identified with the symptom, the work of the unconscious and its interpretation dissolves this connection. Indeed, if the transfer leads the demand, as a demand for love, back to identification with a mark/trait of the ideal, the desire-of-the-analyst and what he incarnates through his *imago* will lead that demand away, lead it away so that it comes from the cause of desire, that is, from the *objet petit a*, beyond capital *I*.

12

The Drive at Stake

What Do You Want Me to Say?

In the course of a conversation with Robert Mallet, Jean Paulhan recounted this story from his childhood:

> My grandfather was a terrible tease. He had come up with a game—really a kind of bad joke—that irritated me no end. We would be passing in front of a toy store and he would say to me, for example:
> "Look at that beautiful puppet theater. If you would like me to give it to you, I would give it to you."
> "Yes, I want it, grandfather."
> "Listen, it's not a matter of what you want. Besides, a child never says 'I want' if he is well brought up."
> "I pray you, grandfather."
> "Look, it's not a matter of prayer. I am not the holy God. If you want me to give it to you, I will give it to you."
> "Then give it to me!"
> "What! You're giving orders to me, your grandfather! What are you thinking about? If you want me to give it to you, I will give it to you."
> This was known as a "mocking game." This particular one was called—I don't know why—"white lamb's mocking game." At the end, fed up, I would say:
> "What do you want me to say?"
> To which the obvious reply would be:
> "It's not a matter of what I want you to say. If you wish me to give it to you, I will give it to you."
> Since then, I have thought, more than once, of that atrocious game and others like it.

From this game was born Jean Paulhan's fascination with language, a fascination that later led him to conclude: "I could not get used to the idea (however simple) that there might be no word for this difficulty nor any answer one would not immediately render ridiculous precisely by treating it as an answer."[1]

The Real and Language

The goal of analysis is not exhaustion of the subject's history in the symbolic. Why? Because the Freudian unconscious is not reducible to the repressed. If it were, given there is no repression without return of the repressed, a totalization of the subject's history could be accomplished through speech that names. But nothing of the sort happens. The unconscious, in its initial structure, is altogether different. This is how Lacan opened his seminar on *The Four Fundamental Concepts of Psycho-Analysis* in January 1964.

1. What does the unconscious introduce with its formations (symptoms, dreams, parapraxes, jokes)? First of all, not meaning but rather an obstacle, failure, a rupture that produces non-sense. It *(ça)* skids. And where it *(ça)* skids—in the elaboration that is the series of dream-thoughts—this is where interpretation must take place. For this is the one-slip *(l'une-bévue)*. Whence the question: does the rift arise on a foundation of unity, continuity, and harmony? Does the one-slip, which is the non-relation of lock and key, break away from some perfectly successful relation, somewhere inscribed? Here Freud answers "no" to Jung. But the *un* of the *unbewusst*, the *un* of the fissure and of the negative mark that produces a cut—should we then say that it arises on a foundation of absence? Here, too, we should not presuppose some original "here" *(en-deçà)*. The *un* makes absence arise, just as the musical note, far from originating in silence, creates it.

Hence, in the suite of signifiers that constitutes my history, a master signifier is missing: effaced, submerged (as Freud said of the dream's umbilicus) by reason of the *urverdrängt*, a hole in the symbolic order.

2. But what analysis shows is that this *Vergreifen*, this mis-take, repeats itself . . . in the same place. Freud called it the automatism of repetition (compulsion to repeat), an *automaton* in the structure of the signifying network. What is at stake here? *Beyond* the symbolic of the *automaton*, there is the *real* as failed encounter: the real that insists and returns to the

same place, a place where the subject, led by his or her *Gedanken* (thoughts), does not encounter it.

Why this repetition? The answer comes from Freudian experience, which *coordinates* the *urverdrängt,* the hole in the symbolic, *with the real.* Now, on the basis of repetition (repetition even of deception, repetition of the one of the one-slip), Freud coordinates the hole in the symbolic "with a real that will henceforth be situated in the field of science, situated as that which the subject is condemned to miss, but even this miss is *revelatory.*"[2] How does this miss reveal the real? That is our question.

In the previous chapter, we have seen with Alexandre Koyré how the real, situated in the field of science, is "explained by the impossible." But what about the subject? How does the impossible reveal the subject?

A Father's Dream

To address this question, Lacan, four times in the course of the *Four Fundamental Concepts,* took up the dream presented by Freud in chapter 7 of the *Traumdeutung.*

A father has just lost his ailing son. Having spent many long hours by the child's sickbed, he goes to an adjacent room to rest a little. He entrusts the task of watching the body to "an old man." Will he be up to the paternal task? Will he stay awake? The father asks himself these questions and falls asleep exhausted, to produce this dream: *"His child was standing beside his bed, caught him by the arm and whispered to him reproachfully: 'Father, don't you see I'm burning?'"*[3] Is this the fulfillment of a wish to see his son alive? If so, why does he see him distressed and demanding?

Through the half-open door, the light of a flame appears. A candle has fallen on the child's bed. The old man keeping vigil has not been able to maintain his watch, having fallen asleep as well. What is repeated in the dream via this index of reality?

1. Is it, as Freud writes, the memory of an earlier episode in which the child, burning with fever, called out to his father? Or is it, correlatively, the father's remorse at not having been up to the task, or at not having known how to intervene effectively in or on behalf of his child's life? Certainly, this is part of it. But the reproach does not have to do solely with the father's *incapacity* to act in the real. Doesn't the father's impo-

tence, by maintaining narcissistic excuses and endless remorse, serve as an alibi for something else?

2. Beyond these demands and responses belonging to the order of need and vital protection, what is repeated concerns the irreducible misunderstanding between father and son: a non-transmission that can only be said otherwise, that is, via the staging of the dream. Indeed, in its *automatism*, the compulsion to repeat returns beyond itself to the *impossible:* to the *real* of an encounter, forever missed, between *the* father as such and *the* son: "Father, don't you see I'm burning?" The father as father is *he who does not see.*

Hence the question posed by the dream is not "what does it want to say?" but "in saying this, what does it *(ça)* want?" Through the dream, the unconscious constructs a phrase where meaning matters less than the point where things go wrong: in the father's case, the rift or fault where the child burns, desire *from which* another desire catches fire, "some secret or other shared by the father and the son," according to Lacan.[4] What does it *(ça)* want when it stamps the dream: "outside meaning/encounter blocked"?

3. The reply belongs to the order of the *drive*. According to Lacan, what we call it is the "*Trieb* to come."[5] The imagery of the dream is made only from *Vorstellungsrepräsentanz*.[6] Hence, what the dream designates by the rift is something beyond the representations it gives us through its apparatus. Is it only the lack of *Vorstellung*, for which there is nothing but *Repräsentanz*, nothing but a representative? Not at all. What "it *(ça)* wants by saying this," what the dream points us toward, is behind the drive's lack of representation: the *Trieb* to come. Indeed—and here we find Freud's originality—the real as missed encounter "finds itself ... to a very great degree the accomplice of the drive,"[7] of the *Trieb* to come.

In the case of the scopic drive, "to come" does not refer to seeing or to being seen. Rather, for the father, it means *making himself seen* by his son. At the level of the Other, the son's look is the object of the father's drive to *make himself seen*, an object that the drive aims at and misses. To direct the look there, it will *first* have been necessary to establish an empty place in the field of the Other ... a place fantasy can occupy. In effect, "it is only with its appearance at the level of the Other that what there is of the function of the drive may be realized."[8]

4. To summarize: there is a lack in the *symbolic* order; no signifier bespeaks father-being. "For no one can say what the death of a child is,

except the father *qua* father, that is to say, no conscious being."[9] Indeed, if Freud speaks of *Urverdrängung*, if there is an irreducible repressed, this is because of the paternal function. Because it is transbiological, paternity "has something that is originally repressed there, and which always re-emerges in the ambiguity of lameness, the impediment and the symptom, of non-encounter, *dustuchia*, with the meaning that remains hidden."[10]

From this impossible (which is not an inability that might possibly be overcome) *the real* emerges, beyond our *Gedanken*, as missed encounter. What is at stake belongs to the order of the drive: the *Trieb* to come and the *fantasy* that supports it, that is, sexual reality.

This is how things stood with Lacan in 1964. This is not to say that no new questions were being introduced, questions not only about the father's dream, which Freud had left unanalyzed, but also more radical questions:

Can the real be said to belong to the order of the drive? Isn't the order of the drive linked instead to the imaginary, that is to say, to the image of the body and its orifices?

If it is linked to the imaginary, on what *condition* will the "*Trieb* to come" manifest itself, with a view toward *ein neues Subjekt,* a new subject?

The Covering Up of Two Holes

Only gradually would Lacan reveal the condition for the advent of the *Trieb* and the constitution of its underlying *fantasy*. It would take time, time to situate—beyond the father's dream—the structure of the relationship between the Other and the subject.[11] Therein lay the novelty of his 1964 seminar, which introduced the relationship *between the symbolic and the real,* at the risk of leaving aside the imaginary, to be taken up later ... and in a different form.

Lacan presented this relation as a bet (placed in advance of any analysis): two holes would be covered up, one by the other, through the addition of a second operation to a first.

1. First Operation: Passive Addition

Even before his or her birth, the human being has been assimilated into the symbolic order. *Alienation* is primordial, insofar as there is no subject except as an effect of discourse in the Other, locus of signifiers. Man or woman, the subject is not constituted by biological life alone, but only insofar as this life exists in language. In other words, the unconscious is the discourse of the Other.

From this primordial situation in language, there is immediately born a question about the desire of the Other, posed as follows: *By telling me this, what does the Other want?* The question is posed indirectly, in connection with anything at all, for example, why is the moon round? The issue lies beyond: *to know* what the relationship between Other and subject is about. This is why I ask you what I am . . . for you! Ultimately, I ask this question to find out what you are . . . for me!

Indeed, if the Other interests me, it is not alone for his capacity to satisfy my vital needs. Rather, it is through them (by anaclisis) that I learn what the Other lacks and what the Other's desire is. I question at the level of what the Other lacks because I have *no other way* to find out what I lack as cause of my desire. In Lacan's formula: the desire of the subject is the desire of the Other.

Now—and this is either tragic or comic—once I enter the defiles of the signifier, I find there is no end to it. I bump up against the limits of language in its incompleteness: in it, there is no *final* word that would constitute a reply to my question. What about the lack in the Other? Can I find my place, my being, my love there? The enigma of the Other's desire persists: too many words turn around it; not one of them speaks it. It remains unknown: either beyond or on this side of what is said.

This obstacle is neither an accidental contingency nor a temporary impuissance. The lack in the Other—which is what desire is—escapes by reason of the symbolic order *itself.* Freud called this reason *urverdrängt,* the irreducible repressed, and Lacan writes it S(A̸). It is the very limit of identification, inasmuch as this is always mediated: the subject is never represented except by another signifier, hence only in the field of the Other. Represented thus—in the signifier—the subject is frozen in it.[12] But the signifier only represents the subject for (in place of) another signifier that, as signifier of the Other's desire, gives it value. Now, this signifier is outside any system. By designating the Other, it distinguishes itself from the Other. Signifier *of* the Other, it is not *in* the Other: A ≠ A.

The subject is thus divided: one foot inside, one foot out. The subject is split because it is excentric to the signifiers that nevertheless constitute it. Squaring the circle of the Other is impossible, according to Lacan, because "the subject is constituted only by subtracting himself from it and by decompleting it essentially in order, at one and the same time, to have to depend on it and to make it function as a lack."[13] Whence the second operation.

2. Second Operation: Active Subtraction

If the symbolic fails to answer me, shall I just stand there, mouth agape? No. For it is there—at the point of the unknown, which is the desire of the Other—there, in the specific locus of the barred $S(\bcancel{A})$, that the subject's desire is constituted. How is it to be specified? Far from waiting for an answer, I generate one by subtracting myself from the *symbolic* order through an operation of *real* separation. I respond by causing my real lack to be juxtaposed to the lack—in the symbolic—of the Other. It is an attempt to *cover two holes,* one by the other, since the subject "effectively encounters the desire of the Other, before he can even name desire, let alone imagine its object."[14]

There where the symbolic order fails, "what the subject will put is his own lack, in the form of the lack he *would produce* in the Other by his own disappearance."[15] Here we simply note the conditional, *"would produce."* We shall return to it later.

What is involved here is an active operation: the subject *produces* the determinate form of the border zone, the specific delineation of the lack in the Other, *through* his own "real lack,"[16] his *real* loss as a *living* being with a beginning and an end. The subject subtracts himself by bringing about his own disappearance, that is, by reverting to a state that *precedes* his own existence. There are a thousand ways to do this.

For example, there is the way of the failed suicide who, with the scene he or she creates, puts his or her signature on this conclusive message: "you have finally lost me!" The failed suicide is attempting to know what lack his or her death would engender in the Other. Or there is the way of the jealous husband who, having despaired of obtaining his wife's admission that in fact she has rejected him, rejects himself and provokes the rupture. There is the adolescent girl's flight from home, either by sudden entry into a convent or precipitous marriage to the first suitor who comes calling. In either case, she is making a "vengeful" response to the absence, in her father, of a signifying lack with respect to herself. There is the way of the anorexic who wants to fulfill her mother's demand to nourish her but finally gives up trying to know whether she is eating too much or too little; she lets herself die by eating "nothing," since for her there is "nothing" in her mother except a demand to eat "this." And there is the boy at bedtime who constructs melodramatic scenes of his own death so he may enjoy the pleasure of imagining his parents' mournful faces at his funeral; in this fashion he demonstrates to himself that his parents will love him forever.

There are more radical solutions: that of Empedocles, who threw himself into Mount Etna (invoked by Lacan at the end of his Rome Discourse); or, today, the Roman death of a Montherlant—the only act of mastery that cannot fail to succeed.[17]

In each case, what we have is a reply to the question, Is she able, is he able, to lose me? The reply is *made* through a kind of active inertia, by producing the lack antecedent to the moment when the subject did not exist. The wish is that the shape of my absent body be drawn in the Other—creating a hole!

Such is the nature of what Freud called *Versagung*—not frustration but refusal: no-saying, *per-di(c)tion*.[18] From this subtraction, the subject of the unconscious is born, born at the place where the said originates as signifier of *negation*, permitting the subject to refuse the symbolic order.

It is the *"me"* of *"me phunai,"* spoken by Oedipus at Colonus: "Would that I had not been born!" Similarly, at the end of Claudel's *L'otage*, it is the head movement (left to right) that Sygne de Coûfontaine makes on her deathbed: the sign of *no*.[19] By marrying Turelure, the man who murdered her family, she had already given everything that, within her tradition, constituted her being. At stake, according to the abbot Badilon, was saving the Heavenly Father, represented in the person of the hostage pope. Thus did Sygne de Coûfontaine say "yes" to the social order to come, in which Christendom and revolution would be reconciled. But at the end, after having willingly received the bullet meant for her husband, she sought the impossible: the impossible of seeing her son, heir to this reconciliation, and of forgiving her husband for having killed the brother she loved. She said "no" with her head; and from this "no" was born the subject of the enunciation—a subject, from the outset, outside the symbolic order that she herself had supported through marriage to a man she didn't love. When Turelure bellowed an enormous, mocking: "Coûfontaine *adsum!*" ("Coûfontaine, present!"), she could only subtract herself. Sygne chooses to be lacking to the Other via a *real* lack, refuses simply to give her death. This is what the abbot Badilon really hears when, in the first version of the final scene, Sygne says: "Too good a thing for me to have given him" (act 3, scene 4). In a variant, Turelure understands the same thing from his wife's "no": "Death was too good a thing for her to give me." Isn't the "no" already there in her name, Coûfontaine, with its unaccustomed circumflex marking the subject's excentricity from the symbolic order?

A Death That Gives Life?

But does this real lack really produce the form of the lack in the Other? If everything gets totally screwed up, is the Other's desire truly met? Is the wish to make oneself the response at the very place where the symbolic fails—is this wish realized? Of course not! It is a moment of crucial importance in the analytic process. Indeed, if the holes in the symbolic and in the real are to be covered, isn't another dimension necessary to serve as a *link*? From now on, this will be the question. "Two true holes make a *false* hole. This is really why 'two' is such a suspect personage, and why it is necessary to move from it to 'three' for it *(ça)* to hold."[20]

To the extent that it was a matter of arguing with the post-Freudians, it was sound strategy to assert the primacy of the *symbolic* over the *imaginary*. But when his own followers insisted he continue his teaching, Lacan encountered—in them—the effect of his polemic: "an effect of laxity, sustained by our thematic to an extent that its diffusion surprised us."[21] The primacy of the symbolic had become a Lacanism, that is to say, a *broken record*.

In 1964, it became necessary to institute a "correction" and to approach at last the relationship between *symbolic* and *real*. From this, another thematic was born: a confrontation with the necessity of covering two lacks, symbolic and real. Lacan now stumbled up against the question of how to accomplish this covering for a "true hole." Finding an answer was mandatory, and it required a new step forward. At stake was the *drive* itself. Psychoanalysis offered something new, a new *path*, so that failure of the link between symbolic and real not result in barren loss, a pure and endless repetition of a failed encounter—failed by refusal of suicide! It was the path of separation and subtraction achieved at last. But for that, *imagination* of the hole would be necessary. Later, when Lacan had accomplished this step, he would write: "Imagination of the hole certainly has consequences: do we need to evoke its 'pulsional' function or, to put it better, what is derived from it (the *Trieb*)? The victory of analysis is that it made a matheme out of this, when before the mystic gave no testimony of his trials other than to make it the *ineffable*. But if one stays at that hole, it is fascination that is reproduced."[22]

Indeed, in turning around the hole of the symbolic [$S(\bar{A})$], analysis turns toward the indefinite, toward the interminable. Beginning in 1964, the project will be to ward off the mystical effects (effects that could not have been predicted from the Rome Report of 1953) of a certain practice of analysis. This practice took the imaginary for "caca, booboo, something bad"[23] and the symbolic for something good—a practice that made one forget the drive and what it imposes: the finitude of desire.[24] The project was not based in an antimystical a priori, but in an ethical exigency that—by taking into account the specificity, internal limit, and end of the analytical process—determines the *place* of the analyst (as we shall see).

V
ANOTHER IMAGINARY

13

A Hole in the Imaginary

Introduction of -ϕ

If there is failure to cover the symbolic lack with a real lack (i.e., if this is not accomplished by means of suicide), then psychoanalysis will seek to accomplish it by grasping the imaginary through the body image. How?

The imaginary was what Lacan first read in Freud, first in the narcissistic investment of the object, then in the specular image, whose constitution in the mirror stage he invented. Advancing along a path that specified immersion and "transfusion of the body's libido towards the object,"[1] he added: "But even though part of it remains preserved from this immersion, concentrating within it the most intimate aspect of auto-eroticism, its position at the 'tip' of the form predisposes it to the phantasy of decrepitude in which is completed its *exclusion* from the specular image and from the prototype that it constitutes for the world of objects."[2] And furthermore: "The phallus, that is, the image of the penis, is *negativity* in its place in the specular image."[3]

In effect, in the constitution of the ego as narcissistic, there is a limit to the body's libidinal investment in the image of the other; hence, the libido does *not pass in its entirety* onto the specular image. There is a blind spot, a part that is lacking in the image: the minus small phi (-ϕ).

This is what explains the fact that the little boy—*seeing* the absence of a penis in the little girl—imagines what could happen to him; while the little girl—seeing what is present in the little boy—imagines what she could have lost. This *not yet* in the one and this *already there* in the other refer back to the *same* -ϕ in the image (and later on to the same refusal of this lack, as exemplified in the female's "penis envy" *[Penisneid]* and the male's "rejection *[Ablehnung]* of femininity," to use Freud's terminology.

In the image of one's own body, the phallus appears *as a minus,* a blank, a blind spot. The phallus is a libidinal reserve, not represented in the image. But it is delineated there as cut from the image—and not without carving out a border zone by its absence.

At the place of this precisely determined hole, which just is the -ϕ, the *objet petit a,* cause of desire, is posed. The *objet petit a cannot* join with the phallus (nor precede it as pregenital stage!) except when the phallus is, according to Lacan's gorgeous expression, *"flappi"* ("dead-beat"). In speaking of the Oedipus complex (really not a complex at all!), Freud never ceased stating that, since phallic *jouissance* is forbidden, a *substitute* takes its place, namely the function of surplus-enjoyment *(plus-de-jouir)* through pulsional objects. This is the b-a, which Freud spelled "ba." What consequences did Lacan draw from this in his 1964 seminar on *The Four Fundamental Concepts of Psycho-Analysis?*

The Imaginary and the Gaze

In a careful reading of this Lacanian discourse, is one not struck by the insistence on the *gaze?* The insistence is underscored by the father's dream ("Father, can't you see I'm burning?"); by the recitation—not once but twice—of Aragon's poem *Contre-chant* (the other is my reflection, yet there is no look);[4] by the introduction of Merleau-Ponty's posthumous book on visibility, as well as references to the work of Roger Caillois on the *ocelli* of mimicry; and, finally, by analysis of the painter's gesture in presenting a picture to our gaze. In conclusion, the analyst is defined as one whose gaze is hypnotized *by* the analysand, a sort of reverse hypnosis.

From all these threads, what is woven? In presenting the list of drives, Lacan counts out four: to stuff one's mouth, to make oneself shit, to make oneself see, to make oneself hear—in each case, the object of the drive is posed in the field of the Other. *However,* with respect to the third, that is, the scopic drive, Lacan remarks: "Freud . . . shows that it is not homologous with the others."[5] "Its privilege . . . derives from its very structure."[6] Indeed, the gaze is "the most characteristic term for apprehending the proper function of the *objet a,*" cause of desire, insofar as it "is presented precisely, in the field of the mirage of the narcissistic function of desire, as the object that cannot be swallowed."[7] We would add: as the irreducibly external object, *beyond* the image of the narcissistic object I am

A Hole in the Imaginary

able to see (beyond Freud's *narzisstliche Objektwahl*). Freud, in his famous schema, clearly indicates this beyond-the-object in the field of identification that founds narcissism:[8]

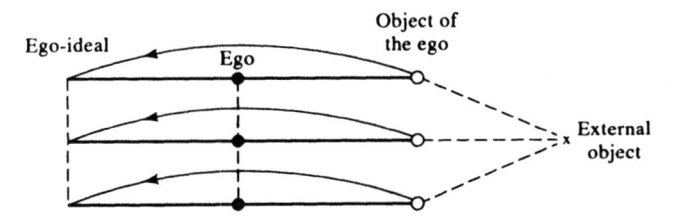

In Lacan's notation, the ego-ideal is designated with a capital *I*, the narcissistic object of the ego with an *i* (*a*), and the object *beyond* with a small *a*. The curved arrows indicate the possible confusion by the subject who attempts to return the *objet petit a* to an idealizing identification in *I* and thereby elude castration.[9]

More precision is required, but for the moment let us note that, among the objects of the drive, Lacan chose the object of the scopic drive, that is to say, the *gaze*, in order to show the relationship of junction/disjunction between drive and corporeal imaginary. For the gaze, more than any other object, necessitates a *subversion* of the presentation of the imaginary itself. How so?

We begin with what we already know of the visual. Lacan gave it a privileged introduction in the mirror stage. Through vision of the image of the other's body, I anticipate my own mastery and totalize my specular image: therein lies the origin of the ego's narcissistic satisfaction. But, before this origin, that is to say, primordially, what am I? A being that is *looked at*, looked at from everywhere, handed over, un-covered, ex-posed. I am *in* the world's spectacle even before I constitute the other as a specular object. The posthumous publication of Merleau-Ponty's work, *The Visible and the Invisible*, gave Lacan an opportunity to insist on this originary state. Below, one of the most characteristic passages from that book:

> We have to ask ourselves what exactly we have found with this strange adhesion of the seer and the visible. There is vision, touch, when a certain visible, a certain tangible, turns back upon the whole of the visible, the whole of the tangible, of which it is a part, or when suddenly it finds itself *surrounded* by them, or when between it and them, and through their commerce, is formed a Visibility, a Tangible in itself, which belong properly

neither to the body qua fact nor to the world qua fact—as upon two mirrors facing one another where two indefinite series of images set in one another arise which belong really to neither of the two surfaces, since each is only the rejoinder of the other, and which therefore form a couple, a couple more real than either of them. Thus since the seer is caught up in what he sees, it is still himself he sees: there is a fundamental narcissism of all vision. And thus, for the same reason, the vision he exercises, he also undergoes from the things, such that, as many painters have said, I feel myself looked at by the things, my activity is equally passivity—which is the second and more profound sense of the narcissism: not to see in the outside, as the others see it, the contour of a body one inhabits, but especially to be seen by the outside, to exist within it, to emigrate into it, to be seduced, captivated, alienated by the phantom, so that the seer and the visible reciprocate one another and we no longer know which sees and which is seen. It is this Visibility, this generality of the Sensible in itself, this anonymity innate to Myself that we have previously called flesh, and one knows there is no name in traditional philosophy to designate it.[10]

Now, this primordial state on this side of the mirror stage is neither reduced nor erased by it. It remains beyond it, calling into question the mirage of narcissistic satisfaction. If I am a being who is looked at, what then is the look? It is not the eye, organ of vision, but the gaze, whose function is to articulate in "its fundamental relations to the *ink-blot* . . . the fact that there is *already* in the world something that looks before there is a view for it to see, that the ocellus of animal mimicry is indispensible as a *presupposition* to the fact that a subject may see and be fascinated, that the fascination of the ink-blot is anterior to the view that discovers it."[11]

The gaze is not the eye. If the ocelli make an impression it is not because they "resemble eyes," writes Caillois. On the contrary, "eyes intimidate because they resemble ocelli. The important thing here is the *circular* form, *fixed* and *brilliant*, a typical instrument of fascination."[12] The three functions of mimicry described by Caillois—travesty, camouflage, and intimidation—activate the conditions of a fascination that precedes any effective presence of the other's eye.

A human being knows how to play with this material from the animal kingdom. He or she transforms it into something *given-to-be seen:* a mask, a stand-in for himself or herself. With a flourish, the painter lays down *spots* of color on the canvas so that there I may lay down . . . my eye. *"You want to see? Well, take a look at this!"* (Lacan paraphrasing the painter)[13]

... "*those little blues, those little browns, those little whites,*" as Cezanne himself called them.[14]

The gaze in the field of the Other is therefore a spot, a touch, a ray, a line, meant for my eye's vision. The split between eye and gaze has the effect of a failed encounter: "*What I look at is never what I wish to see*" in the Other, from the Other.[15] What I am presented with is a screen, that is to say, something beyond what I demand to see.

Thus the real is an effect of the split between eye and gaze. Moreover, this *same* split is found when eye and gaze are reversed. Looked at primordially from every corner, I in turn enter the game: make myself a gaze, provocatively display myself. I constitute myself as a *spot* given-to-see on the tableau that I am in my image. Once again, I do this in order to establish a lack in the field of the Other: "*You never look at me from the place from which I see you.*"[16] From this split between subject and Other comes castration as phallic lack: recognition of the impossibility of mastering that point in the Other from which what the subject gives to be seen is looked at.

Apropos of this, Lacan recounts a story from his twenties. Young, bourgeois, Parisian, he wanted the experience of manual labor and so joined a family of fishermen in a port city in Brittany. A noble intention in a period when Maoism had not yet been born! One day, before pulling in the nets, a man named Petit-Jean pointed to a sardine can floating on the water in the sunlight. He said to Lacan: "*You see that can? Do you see it? Well, it doesn't see you!*"[17]

Forty years later, Lacan analyzed the incident. Not for nothing did it reappear in memory: "*Wo es war, soll Ich werden.*" For, if Petit-Jean had found it funny, Lacan had found it less so. Why had Petit-Jean spoken thus? Those words—to the effect that the glittering can didn't see him—those words in no way made Lacan forget these words: *elle te regarde!* (It [does] see you!).[18] No metaphor is involved in understanding this by way of "*ça me regarde,*" "that concerns me, summons me, is required of me." In other words: "This is my affair; I can't wash my hands of it!" How, then, is it my affair?

The luminous point is there, outside, where everything is that looks at/concerns me. It is not something I objectify by standing back and getting it in perspective. It is what I am as a spot *in* and *on* the tableau of this world, a being-that-is-looked-at from birth (and even before birth, with the invention of sonography!). I am there, captured in space, inscribed in a specular function—just as every subject is, from the start, spatially inserted and presented as other than he or she is.

Thus the point of gaze interrogates Lacan. This young intellectual, as a being-that-is-looked-at, produced a stain on, a screen over this Breton landscape, composed as it was of rough-hewn workers "earning their livings with great difficulty."[19] The triple function of travesty, camouflage, and intimidation, through mimicry of the "fishing" situation, in no way impressed Petit-Jean. He found it all rather ridiculous, a mere game, and indicated as much by pointing out the sardine can. A brilliant flash of wit, an evanescent treasure *(agalma),* the can showed Lacan what he was missing, namely the point *from which* Petit-Jean was looking at him.

This schism between eye and gaze—where does it lead? To a hole in the imaginary, a hole in the image of the Other, -ϕ, where the *objet petit a* is situated.

A Third Presentation of the Mirror Stage

Important consequences would follow from Lacan's introduction of the gaze as *objet petit a* in the field of the Other. As we have seen, the scopic object, more than any other object of a drive, has a direct relationship to narcissism and, thereby, to the mirror stage. Hence Lacan would need to modify his presentation of the *mirror stage,* which he did in 1966, with the publication of the *Ecrits*. Among the chronologically arranged communications making up the *Ecrits,* five prefaces are sprinkled in: "Ouverture de ce recueil," "De nos antécédents," "Du sujet enfin en question," "D'un dessein," "D'un syllabaire après-coup." Here Lacan puts his pioneering work and his "finds" into perspective, explains his reasons for delaying such an advance, and offers a pedagogical justification: a sense that what he had to say might earlier have fallen on deaf ears. With deferred vision, he throws new light on his early writings. Thus, in "De nos antécédents," he gives a wholly different presentation of the mirror stage, one that takes into account the long path traveled since his first intervention. This perspective makes it possible to distinguish three stages of the mirror stage: before 1953, after 1953, and after 1966 (publication date of the *Ecrits*).

First Stage

Before 1953, Lacan disengaged a pure imaginary, whose purity affirmed the primacy of the visual. Through this imaginary, the child constituted his or her ego on the basis of the other's bodily image, insofar as this was *seen* in its totality. Basic principles from *Gestalttheorie*, animal ethology (Harrison and Chauvin), and phenomenology were adopted to establish the impact of *invidia*[20] at the source of the fraternal complex and aggressivity.

From the beginning, human space has a geometric structure, which Lacan called "kal-eido-scopic."[21] A "beautiful form" in the field of the other fascinates me and structures my own field. In return, my own field is later projected into the other's field during comparison, competition, and warlike conquest of the other's space. The primary impact is from the image of the unified form. "Container" geometry determines complete totalities, with surfaces seen as frontiers of a volume. It also sustains the hypothesis of *sub*stance *(upokeimenon)*, turning volume into a permanent unity on this side of changing appearances.

Finally, this ego space determines thought as *intuitus*,[22] ordering the world as a sphere[23] and limiting grasp of the concept to two dimensions—extension and comprehension—conforming to the grasp of a hand.

Hence, on every level—material objects, limits of territory (room, apartment, car), cognitive theory, organization of political and religious actions—there reigns a corporeal imaginary, in accord with the "geometry" of the ego and of its specular image. Mastery, unity, and stability here find their *Euclidean* foundation.

Second Stage

From 1953 on, Lacan doubles this primary alienation, in which the image of one's own body is in the image of the other—doubles it by means of another order, the symbolic, in which the unconscious is the discourse of the Other.

However, it is not a matter of a simple doublet, where each relation functions according to its own plan. The symbolic *determines* the imaginary, renders it impure, nonabsolute, connected. Connected to what? To illustrate, Lacan struggles (from 1953 until 1960)[24] with the optical schema of the inverted bouquet. The schema was precisely that—*optical*. It founded a geometry of straight lines, based on the process by which light rays are refracted on two mirrors. It was an optical metaphor for the introduction of the symbolic *into* the imaginary, insofar as the ego-ideal of Freud's second topography determines the ideal ego. Put another way, Lacan was again approaching the process of identification. Such a reprise was needed to solve the problem posed by the Aimée case and the mirror stage: that of aggressivity. The imaginary, dual relationship is one of exclusion: either I or the other; either I kill the other in order to shatter this insupportable image or the other kills me by robbing me of myself. Is there no solution other than perpetual oscillation between ego and ideal ego (i-i')?

The signifier is located in the field of the Other. The child at the mirror remains unsatisfied. He awaits confirmation, a sign from the one occupying the place of the Other: the mother. He demands from her a word, a testimony to temper and stabilize the imaginary tension and unlock the future—some sign of assent, some sign of the love demanded: let the third respond! Here Lacan situates the second type of identification noted by Freud in *Group Psychology and the Analysis of the Ego*, chapter 7. Here, in this place *from which* the subject sees himself or herself as lovable or not, desirable or not, the ego-ideal is constituted, insofar as there is identification with a trait *(Zug)*. Here the subject finds a response to his or her demand. But what should this trait be called?

Lacan begins by speaking of the "sign, image of *petit a*." The subject interiorizes *"einen einzigen Zug,"* a *single* mark/trait, as sign.[25] But can one speak of a sign here—a sign that represents something for someone—if what is at stake is identification? A dog may see nothing but signs. Still, what are signs to a dog in terms of its own representation? A dog is fixed in the image.[26]

This is why Lacan specifically says that the mark/trait does not belong to the order of *mimesis* or to the order of the sign as figurative resemblance, but to the pure signifier as such, which represents a subject in his or her trace, in his or her letter.[27] He therefore translates *"einziger Zug"* as *"trait unaire,"* designating the *"un"* ("one") as a counter of marks. In this denomination, no preestablished attribute or quality intrinsic to the name is implied. Its difference from the imaginary is irreconcilable. Constituted of single marks/traits, the ego-ideal is a symbolic introjection that transcends the imaginary projection onto the ideal ego. Moreover, by transcending this imaginary projection, the ego-ideal thereby determines and supports it. Yet some questions remain unanswered: the Other's response—does it come from love or desire? And what about the imaginary lack itself, denoted $-\phi$?

Third Stage

Offering a new version of the mirror stage, "De nos antécédents" (1966) broke with the first presentation, in which a *biological* cause—delayed coordination of the nervous system linked to prematurity at birth—made it necessary for the *infans* to go beyond its present insufficiency by means of the image of the other (matrix of the specular image). The infant is jubilant because, in imagination, it anticipates overcoming its biological insufficiency. But in "De nos antécédents," Lacan dissociates himself from this: the causal lack does not result from a physical deficit. For that would be to presuppose a harmony in animals between *Innenwelt* and *Umwelt*, which the human child rejoins by way of a detour through the imaginary. In addition, it would lead to the belief that harmony is in the other, and that I anticipate it in the other's image.

Jubilation does not come from resolution of an organic or motor lack, but from elsewhere: "What is operating in the triumphant assumption of the body image in the mirror is the most evanescent of all objects, [so evanescent] as to appear only in the margins: the exchange of looks, manifest in the child's turning toward the one who, in some way or another, is helping him, even if he is merely there at his game."[28]

The significance of this: the child not only sees but also knows it is seen, knows it is the object of the Other's look. Lacan's 1964 teaching had already dealt with this. The stake was not mastery through vision, but the scopic object as *objet petit a*, which may be *lacking* from the field of the Other. What sort of lack would this be? Not the symbolic lack $[S(\mathcal{A})]$, but a lack in the imaginary: $-\phi$. Here in this empty place, in this blindspot, the *objet petit a*, the gaze, can situate itself. Lacan continues: "Let us add to this what one day a film, made in a completely different context than ours, revealed to us of a little girl confronting herself nude in the mirror: in a flash her hand, in a leftward movement, crossing the phallic lack."[29] Jubilation is born from the intersection of looks that comes to cover the phallic lack. But this intersection is only a point, reaching only the most evanescent of objects: the gaze as object of the scopic drive. Indeed, as we have seen, there is a split *between* the eye (organ of vision) and the gaze: the field of the Other, which is where the subject sees himself seen as lovable, *is not* the point from which the subject sees himself.

Such then is the nonorganic cause of the mirror stage: "the alienation, which *already* situates desire in the field of the Other."[30] The causal gap is not the inertia inherent in our biology but the phallic lack in the specular image. What is at stake here is a reversal of perspective, the very thing at stake in this chapter: imagination of the hole *for* the *Trieb* to come. But how can one imagine this, if not *with* the imaginary itself? But, then, what imaginary?

Reversal of a Surface

We need to assess this third presentation of the mirror stage. Vision of the image in the other is by itself not enough to constitute the image of one's own body. Does a blind person have no ego? Identification is effected by the gaze from the field of the Other: "even the blind person is a subject."[31] But what *imaginary* does this imply? That is our question.

As we already know, in the first version of the mirror stage, constitution of the specular image depended "on connection to the quality of seeing"[32] in the subject. This connection permitted us to believe in an imaginary that imbues the ego with characteristics of a bodily surface: "substantial," with a full, closed shape, since it had been constituted by the mirror that just is the other, just is the figure of the counterpart. But if instead the Other's look founds this constitution, then the other's image has a hole in it: the *objet petit a* comes from the field of the Other to the locus of this hole that is $-\phi$ in the image. Whence Lacan's (belated!) statement: "The ego is nothing but a hole."[33] There is no underlying substance! This is why our most reliable definition of *objet petit a* is this: *objet petit a* is that which makes the image *hold;* or, because the image has a hole in it, it *holds* only the *objet a*.[34]

But, is this imaginable? Certainly not, unless "*another* mode of imaginarization"[35] is established in the dwelling place of the said, in the "dit-mension."[36] In other words, we need a new way of naming by imaginary nomination. We are not to imagine the hole as cropping up later in an already constituted totality so as to rend its surface. On the contrary, it engenders the figure: its structure as border zone is *operative*. Now presentation of this imaginary requires abandoning the metric properties of classical geometry (e.g., height, measure), in favor of a *topology* where the qualitative properties of boundary are conserved after transformation. This presentation would account for properties of a "figure" that remain invariant after a transformation that neither lacerates nor covers up, but is continuous in nature. Such is the imaginary of the mirror stage in its new presentation. As we shall see, this other imaginary is not linked to narcissism or to the ego.

This is why a new presentation was required, presentation of a continuous transformation of an image into its reverse, *starting from* $-\phi$. To illustrate briefly what is at stake, we begin with the objection Kant rightly made to himself in his transcendental aesthetic:

> What can be more similar in every respect and in every part more alike to my hand and to my ear than their images in a mirror? And yet I cannot put such a hand as is seen in the glass in the place of its original; for if this is a right hand, that in the glass is a left one, and the image or reflection of the right ear is a left one, which never can take the place of the other. There are in this case no internal differences which our understanding could determine by thinking alone. Yet the differences are internal as the senses teach, for, notwithstanding their complete equality and similarity, the left hand cannot be enclosed in the same bounds as the right one (they are not congruent); the glove of one hand cannot be used for the other. What is the solution?[37]

Indeed there is no solution if one starts from the intuition that is ocular vision, a light cast over object-substances. And yet identification succeeds: *E pur, si muove!*[38] How to imaginarize this? Lacan takes up the gauntlet (i.e., the objection) that Kant has thrown down—and reverses it!

If I reverse this figure, this left-handed glove of the other's body, then it will be able to outline the surface of my right hand. There is a right-left inversion (that is, an inversion of whatever pertains to imaginary nomination and its impact). And it operates via *reversal*. But only on one condition: the glove must be a surface with a hole; there must be an opening.

Let us now consider the body in its *Gestalt*. Imagine a one-piece garment (e.g., the pyjamas babies wear or the jumpsuits worn by athletes and astronauts), and what you have is identification via continuous transformation of a figure, a transformation from other into ego, defined as "not merely a surface entity, but . . . itself the projection of a surface."[39] Now what engenders the ego is the cut: the zipper or the neckband, which is nothing but a *hole*. This imaginary is different from the one we have demonstrated until now, different from the imaginary linked to narcissism. But if this is so, won't this change the *relationship* between the imaginary and the symbolic, between the imaginary and the real?

14

Imagination of a Triple Hole

The introduction, in the preceding chapter, of the idea of the hole in the imaginary will now permit us to answer a number of questions posed but left hanging: how are the symbolic and the real to be linked? How is the symbolic lack to be covered by the real lack? What are we to create out of the failed encounter that is the real? How can the real be an accomplice of the *Trieb* in the pulsional order?

Psychoanalysis offers this possibility: production of a *true* hole by adding the hole in the imaginary (-ϕ in Lacan's notation) to holes in the symbolic and real. Hence a *triple* hole. *If there is no relationship between symbolic and real, then the imaginary is required*. This is Lacan's discovery, inseparable from that of the *objet petit a*.

What is at stake belongs to the order of the *drive,* along with fantasy, inasmuch as a reply must be made to the lack in the Other. What is desire in the Other? The symbolic fails to answer this question, responding only to demands for this or that. Therefore, I answer the question, "Can he lose me?" with the *real* lack of my existence. Yet, for all that, I don't die: what is really involved is the realm of the comic and "dying from laughter." In this way, pulsional objects become the cause of desire and form a *link* between the subject's desire and the desire of the Other.

However, they can't do this except through the *inter-mediary* of the imaginary and its gaps, operative in the body image insofar as it has a hole. Fantasy, by means of its role as support for desire, responds to the fundamental lack in the symbolic, in the Other, locus of signifiers. In fantasy, the subject's desire for the Other becomes *knotted*. How is this possible? At the point where the symbolic falters—the point of failed encounter that is the real—*how is it possible* for *objet petit a* in the fantasy to become the support that the subject gives himself? *How* can he find this support in the very vacillation of his certitude as subject, there where the symbolic fails him in the Other? *It can appear only in the imaginary:* it is a question of the *place* (topos) of revelation and presentation.

Topology and the Imaginary

May 7, 1969. Rereading a passage from a clinical description by Helene Deutsch (1930), Lacan demonstrated the necessity of the imaginary. In the course of a seminar aptly titled *D'un Autre à l'autre,* he used the passage to exhibit the importance of the "turn" from the symbolic to the imaginary so that the *objet petit a* may appear.

Helene Deutsch recounts the history of a childhood phobia as told to her by a twenty-year-old man who came for analysis on account of his homosexuality. She writes:

> One hot summer day the little seven-year-old boy was playing with his grown-up brother in the farmyard of the house where he had been born and brought up. He was playing at something on the ground in a squatting, stooping position, when his big brother suddenly leaped on him from behind, held him fast round the middle, and shouted out, "I'm the cock and you're the hen."
>
> It was clearly a case of a playful sexual attack on the part of the brother. It developed into a tussle between them, for our little friend refused to be a hen at any price. Nevertheless, he had to give way to the stronger brother, who went on holding him clasped in the same position, and in a paroxysm of rage and tears he screamed out: "But I won't be a hen!"[1]

From that moment on, the boy had a hen phobia, rather inconvenient when one lives on a farm. Deutsch added that the phobia decreased, even disappeared, when his brother was absent, "only he lost all interest in the female sex and developed . . . into a manifest homosexual."[2] Thus, at the age of twenty, he came for analysis. Helene Deutsch observed: "It turned out that hens had already played an important part in his fantasies long before the experience with his brother. His mother used to pay particular attention to the henhouse, and the little boy took a lively share in these activities, was delighted at every newly laid egg, and used to be particularly interested in the way his mother felt the hens to see whether they were laying properly. He himself loved to be felt over by the mother, and would often ask her in fun when he was being washed, etc., whether she would feel him with her finger to see if he was going to lay an egg."[3]

This passage makes it clear *in what sense* the episode with his brother, ten years his senior, was revealing: it made the subject *know*—through nomination of the signifier "hen"—what he *was* before without knowing it. A wild interpretation, but correct. Whence its effect, which Helene Deutsch called "traumatizing." With respect to these two moments (before/after seven years), let us, with Freud, distinguish the two sorts of relationship in which a human being is caught: anaclitic and narcissistic, to use his own terms.

1. First there is the *relationship* of the subject, in his real body, to the *symbolic:* a relationship of dependence on the Other, locus of signifiers. For the subject of whom Helene Deutsch speaks, this is where the mother assumed her place. She is an expert in raising hens and gathering eggs in the *"bon endroit."*[4] Thus the child finds his place *in* and *for* the *jouissance* of the Other: his place is that of a "hen," not only fondled by the mother like the others and among the others, but particularly *active* in furnishing fecal eggs.

This is the first stage of the child's "polymorphous" perversion in his relationship to the Other (mother, father, institution, whatever). Anaclisis and perversion are but *one* stage. In Lacan's words, *"poule de luxe!"*[5] The boy devotes himself, sacrifices himself, as a crusader for the mother's *jouissance*. He completes the Other by masking that aspect of the Other that belongs to the order of lack. In this way, the *"un"* of the mark/trait is inscribed in the symbolic: *une poule* (a hen).

Let us summarize the anaclitic relation: the subject *can* operate effectively, but he *doesn't know* by what right or on the basis of which mark/trait of his being he can do so. It is power without knowledge *(savoir)*, because it is without revelation or presentation of what he is.

2. *But, at age seven,* one has one's precious self-esteem: one is a little man facing the mirror of other little men, experiencing love within the narcissistic relation. Indeed, *love-hate* of the counterpart has long ago been added to the primary, anaclitic relation of dependence. This is the imaginary dimension, in accordance with which the ego is constituted on the basis of the other's image. To the real of the bodily organism is added the specular image. Face to face with his brother, older by ten years and stronger, the little boy has a competitive relationship of little cock to big cock.

But is that all there is to the imaginary dimension? No—and therein lies the novelty of Lacan's final position: the imaginary is the *only* place where one day the symbolic can be revealed to the subject, that is to say, it is the only place where the subject can learn what he or she counts for in the field of the Other.

Often on the farm, the older brother had seen a cock mounting a hen. He mimicked this attack on his brother, *linking* it to the nomination: "I'm the cock and you, you are the hen." This could have been a simple game— it would have been for other boys. But in this case it carried great weight: for the younger brother, it had the effect of a revelation of what he had been for a long time without knowing it. Now he *knows* it. Immobilizing his brother's body, the older sibling hit the bull's eye in linking this nomination to mastery of mobility. Thus it is in the imaginary, dual relationship that the effect of the symbolic *in* and *on* the subject's imaginary appears. A link is established *between* the subject's specular image of boy-hen [i(a)] and what makes it hold. What makes the image [i(a)] hold is the *objet petit a,* in this case, the egg as *objet petit a,* as the mother's surplus-enjoyment *(plus-de-jouir)*.

Now this relationship between i(a) and *a* is intolerable. The boy screams: "No! No!" The negation signals his impotence: not a hen! No longer can he be one. Reversal of the situation: power without knowledge *(savoir)* has become knowledge *(savoir)* without power.

From this new disjunction, anxiety is born: on the one hand, he knows now what he has been; but on the other hand, he doesn't know how to deal with the desire of the mother. Having been in the past imprisoned in her *jouissance,* he has been closed to the question of his desire, of the desire of the mother. Confronted with the insufferable void of a question without answer, he fortifies himself with a hen phobia: the signifier turned devouring (like the horse's mouth drawn in black in the case of little Hans). When all is said and done, fear of *something* is ultimately less uncomfortable than the anxiety of the *nothing* of the nonresponse; with something, one at least knows what to do!

But the important thing to see is this, inasmuch as it dictates the direction of the cure: through the brother, therefore in the *field* of narcissism, a question is born: that of knowing *how to be lacking* to the mother. In effect, the *objet petit a,* that is, what can be missing in the field of the Other, is revealed as the subject's very *stake* in the field of narcissism. But *only* in the field of the Other can this stake find a solution other than *only* in the field of the Other can this stake find a solution other than phobia, a solution that answers the question, "how to be missing to him?" and then the question, "can he lose me?" Before indicating the route to such a solution, let us retrace, using Lacan's schemas, the path we have followed.

First Period

In the primary, anaclitic relation, the real of the bodily organism is dependent on the symbolic, that is, on the field of counting in accordance with the numerical *"un"* ("one") of the unary mark/trait (what Freud called *einziger Zug*). What is inscribed is unknown to the subject.

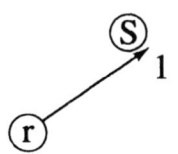

$$\begin{matrix} & Ⓢ \\ & \nearrow 1 \\ ⓡ & \end{matrix}$$

Second Period

The real has a relationship not only to the symbolic but also to the imaginary, insofar as the real of the body is added to a specular image *i(a)* coming from the other, the little other. *But,* the specular image is not constituted solely on the basis of the image of the other; we have seen this in the new version of the mirror stage. Indeed, "the imaginary is the place where every truth is enunciated"[6] because the *"un"* of the symbolic counting *reveals* its effects *in* the imaginary (I).

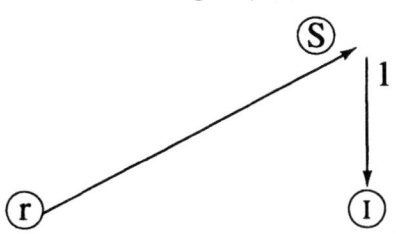

$$\begin{matrix} & Ⓢ & \\ & \nearrow & \downarrow 1 \\ ⓡ & & Ⓘ \end{matrix}$$

How? by making the perverse game of the *objet petit a* appear in the field of narcissism. The *objet petit a* is what the subject has at stake, for it makes the subject's specular image *i(a)* hold:

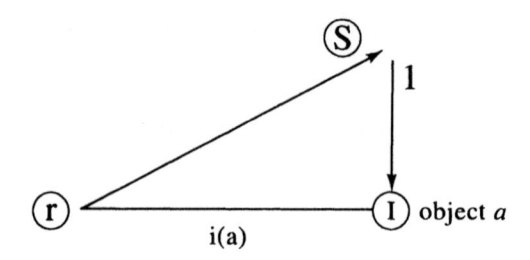

Third Period: A Nonnarcissistic Imaginary

Can one stop with this? What contribution does the analytic process make? Helene Deutsch tells us nothing of the process by which *"this analysis ended with the patient's becoming heterosexual."*[7]

And yet, what the analysis establishes is not ineffable. What in the second period is revealed as effect in the field of the imaginary must be *returned* to its cause. That is to say, it must be restored to the field of the Other. It is a matter of putting a hole in the Other—a specific hole, unique to each case, a hole that encircles the lack in the Other of *objet petit a*. Analysis terminates when the structure of capital *A* is *reduced* to what it is: a lack in the *form of petit a*. By its very fall, it makes a hole in the structure of *A* (we shall see how the analyst contributes to this by his or her presence). Whence the title Lacan gave his seminar: *D'un Autre à l'autre* ("From an Other to the other").

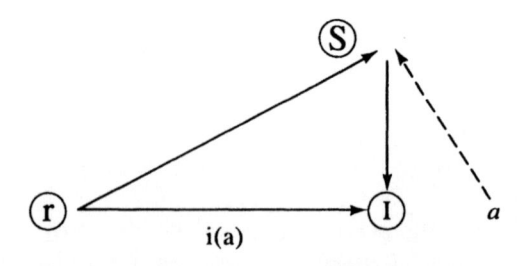

All that is impossible without a return of the imaginary into the symbolic.

But this return is not pure repetition. For that would be again to give primacy to the symbolic. This return is the establishment of *another* imaginary: a nonnarcissistic one. In effect, the stake is *to imaginarize* this hole starting from what encircles it; the fall of *objet petit a* just *is* the imaginary figuration of the *border zone* left by this very fall. We now present this figuration.

15

An Imaginary with Consistency

> Man, whose appetite outside imagination insulates itself by a ceaseless provisioning, shall deliver himself by his own hands, suddenly swollen rivers.
> —René Char, "L'homme fuit l'asphyxie"

Imagination of a triple hole—this is what Lacan glimpsed in February 1972. He returned to it on May 15, 1973, at the end of his seminar *Encore*.[1] From then on, in each of the seminars that followed (1973–1980), he was dedicated to it, presenting it in the transition from a topology of surfaces and border zones (rims) to one of knots: a knot that creates a hole by knotting three holes into one.

But to get from 1953 to this point required a long evolution. Faced with the confusion of terms in analytic literature, Lacan worked, in the first years of his teaching, to "put things in order." This meant eliminating false questions whose useless and discouraging complexities had been brought in more to satisfy the narcissism of the so-called analyst-theoretician (a narcissism based on "little differences") than to permit a reading of Freud. In the "after-Freud," Lacan accomplished the cleanup by means of a *distinction*, implementing (from 1953 on) a triple terminology: symbolic, imaginary, and real. These three terms apply to what Lacan called order, function, register, category, dimension,[2] and even relationship.

This triplicity allows for a more precise definition of castration (as distinguished from frustration and privation), paternity (symbolic father, imaginary father, real father), the phallus, the transference, the analytic relation, etc. This ground-breaking work came to a head in Lacan's statement of April 13, 1975: "If there is no hole, I don't see very well what we should do as analysts, and if this hole is not at least a triple one, I don't see how we can support our technique, which gets its bearings essentially from something that is triple, and that suggests a triple hole."[3] Put differently, the stake now was to forge a *link* between three proper names, the symbolic, the imaginary, and the real ("proper names" understood in Frege's sense). Success would depend on first distinguishing three lacks: a hole in *each* of the three dimensions, such that—from three holes constituting only *one*—a conjunction might be established between the three dimensions, that is, a *knot-hole*.

Thus, between 1953 and 1975, a great deal of ground had to be covered in order to respond to the question: what does it mean to name a hole?

The first advance concerned the symbolic. With Freud, Lacan termed the hole in the symbolic *urverdrängt*. There is an irreducible repressed, such that there is no possibility of exhausting the subject's complete history in the symbolic. Lacan found this hole to be analogous to the body, inasmuch as the body has holes or orifices. Freud called them oral and anal. Lacan added the vocal and the scopic. From them the drive is born. These orifices have something in common with the gap in the unconscious (the hole in the symbolic). Thus, in 1964, Lacan wrote: "It is insofar as something in the apparatus of the body is structured in the same way, it is because of the topological unity of the gaps in play, that the drive assumes its role in the functioning of the unconscious."[4]

But, is it a matter of analogy between symbolic and real, between symbolic and corporeal imaginary? If the real is apprehended as a failed encounter, is it not "through this that the real finds itself . . . to a very great degree the accomplice of the drive"?[5] Couldn't one *then* speak of a *pulsional real*? This is what Lacan let us think until 1975, when he settled the matter with a clear-cut distinction.[6]

The Three Impossibles

What enabled Lacan to settle the matter was his designation of the link between symbolic, imaginary, and real as a triple hole: a hole that closes itself up and squeezes itself into a knot *à trois*.[7] But before we show how this happens, let us identify each impossible that makes a hole in each of the three dimensions:

1. The Symbolic

There is a limit in the symbolic: the limit of the impossible to say. Freud called it the *urverdrängt*, and it is not unrelated to what he named "the umbilicus of the dream," the *unerkannt*, the impossible to recognize. Lacan formulated it thus: there is no metalanguage, no Other of the Other; and he notes it with the formula S($\bcancel{A}$), to be read "signifier of the barred Other."

This hole is not solely a limit or stumbling block. It is an operator, in the sense that it is at the root of language. From the ex nihilo, the signifying chain is born. From unpoiesis, poiesis is produced.

Where does this come into analytic experience? With the *paternal* function. To read analytically the two Freudian myths on the Father (Oedipus and *Totem and Taboo*) is to understand the following: if the paternal function is operative of metaphors belonging to the signifier of the desire of the Mother, it is because no one can say *what* father-being is. The appeal to the biological or the juridical changes nothing: "The fundamental transbiological character of paternity, introduced by the tradition of the destiny of the chosen people, has something that is *originally* repressed there, and which always re-emerges in the ambiguity of lameness, the impediment and the symptom, of non-encounter, *dustuchia*, with the meaning that remains *hidden*."[8]

It is *from* this originally repressed, primary signifier that the subject is constituted; later, endless, diverse significations from the subject's history will be inscribed in its place.

2. The Real

The real is specified by this impossible: there is no sexual relationship. Between an X and a Y, it is impossible to inscribe an R, which would produce relationship. There is, of course, relationship to the phallus, but it itself does not create relationship. This impossible is revealed in the fact that what remains, secondarily and for want of something better, is merely identification to traits/marks of the ego-ideal: each man and each woman on his or her own side. These traits/marks are mere comic masks that cannot mask the *real hole* between the two sexes. There is no knowledge *(savoir)* of the *jouissance* of the Other (subjective genitive): phallic *jouissance*, insofar as it is sexual, does not relate to the Other as such, in the heterogeneity of the Other's place, in the Other's hetereity. There is no answer to the question: *does the Other enjoy what I enjoy?*

Hence, what constitutes encounter is this: a woman is a symptom for a man and vice versa. There is no sexual relationship except the inter-symptomatic. We must learn to manage, for even now there is nothing else on the horizon.

Lacan remarked in 1972: "There was no need for analytic discourse except—and here is the nuance—to announce, as *truth,* that there is no sexual relation."[9]

Making reference to Saint Paul, Lacan added that the import of the Message was that men and women should remain apart—and with what repercussions across the ages! In the "true" religion, there is no sacralization of sex nor sacred prostitution: the divine is separated from the cosmo-biological.

But "the nuance" is not a delicate one. It is announced "as truth." Analysis has no "good tidings" to proclaim. It aims at the real and its knowledge *(savoir),* which, however, is not without the effect of truth. What effect, if not the introduction of what is outside-meaning? The real is strictly that which has no meaning, a meaning born *of* nonmeaning.

3. *The Imaginary*

The body of the speaking being does not exist for him or her except in the form of images. That is to say, it is altogether imaginary. How, then, does this imaginary take on the *consistency* of a unit? Freud's metaphor notwithstanding, this does not occur through the image of a "sack" but, on the contrary, via a hole in the corporeal image. The imaginary has consistency to the extent that castration is operating, together with $-\phi$ of the phallic image. Boy or girl, it doesn't matter! For each, the phallus is elided in the image. *Starting from* this visual impossible, various objects of the *drive*—supposedly pregenital, but they aren't—become the everyday support for human behavior.

But—as another Jacques, Jacques Maritain said—one must take apart in order to combine. Earlier, Lacan had seen fit to account for analytic experience, its process, and its end. Now he suggested the necessity of their coincidence: a knotting of these three holes into one true hole.

An Imaginary with Consistency

Imagination of this triple hole is shown with a Borromean knot:

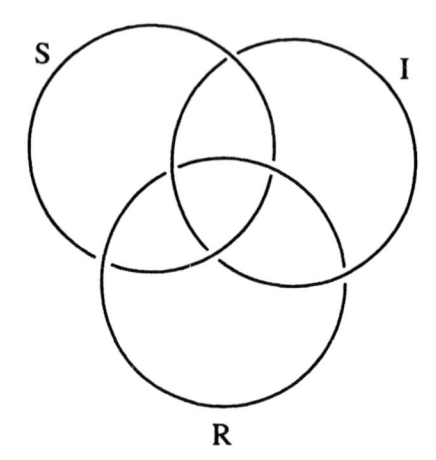

The knot is "Borromean" for this reason: if any one of the three rings is cut, the other two also come undone. Moreover, each ring is linked to another by a third. The term "Borromean," as used in topology, derives from the Milanese family Borromeo (or: Buono Romeo), whose fifteenth-century coat of arms bore, at the bottom left, three rings knotted in this fashion.[10]

In other words: there is an *equivalence* between the real, the symbolic, and the imaginary in their fundamental circularity. There is no primacy of one over the other. Each knots the other two. But what is most remarkable about the Borromean knot is this: the *homogenization* of the three elements, such that the distinction flowing from their names matters little, since they are equivalent. What remains is 3, the number three. Thus the meaning-effect that comes from the three names (symbolic, imaginary, real) is erased and falls outside the knot itself. A strange consequence ensues, one that is foreign to our mental habits: "The Borromean knot, insofar as it is supported by the number three, belongs to the register of the *imaginary*."[11]

What imaginary are we talking about? Not the all-too-familiar corporeal imaginary that, because of its dependence on the mirror stage and specular image, gives us only *re*presentations situated more easily in flat *space,* in *two* dimensions. (This is why it can be visualized when flattened on a blackboard or on paper.) The Borromean knot is different. To help us grasp its novelty, Lacan formulated the term "consistency." Its consistency lies in its oneness: the one keeps it together; the one gives it body. Now, with the Borromean knot, consistency is neither symbolic nor real, but imaginary. It is not symbolic because its meaning (as we have seen) is external to the knot itself, by virtue of the homogenization of the three elements.

Is consistency something real? This would make the Borromean knot an imaged *re*presentation (hence in two dimensions) *of* the real conceived as sub-stance (what is below). It would then be substance that makes the knot hold and gives it a third dimension. Consistency would derive from subsistence, the "con" from the "sub." But the Borromean knot is not the outside of an inside, nor is it the manifestation of an essence. In brief, it is not a theoretical *model* to be applied to analytic practice, not an ideal schema whose function is to clarify and illuminate (this was the ethical function of *theoria* in antiquity: one sees before one acts). Nor is it something the analyst, in the role of "good student," uses to reduce asymptotically the "distance between" analytic practice and "lived experience."[12]

The Borromean knot belongs to the register of the imaginary, because there is no consistency elsewhere, inasmuch as each element is *not, except* in relation to the other two. What the symbolic, imaginary, and real have in common is that they form a knot with the others. Nothing more, nothing less. Thus the Borromean knot does not *consist* except insofar as it is supported by the number three: desire has no substance other than what is secured by the knot itself. In it, all substance evaporates, since the outside is not that of a not-inside. It is a *presentation* that is neither representation nor analogy. But there is one condition: that this imaginary *itself* belong to a three-dimensional *space,* where under and over are respected for each intersection of lines. Indeed, the flattening . . . serves only to accommodate the centuries-old deficiency of our thought, whose spatial intuition is more comfortable in two rather than three dimensions: a cross the worthy pedagogue has to bear!

Therefore, the imaginary that gives body and space to the Borromean knot via three is an imaginary of manipulation, of braiding by hand. It gives consistency to a fabric through a tightening of knots. We need to *show* it, for, as Freud said, *Darstellbarkeit* (presentability) is a necessary requirement, given our inability to think and therefore to grasp the real. The analyst, like everyone else, suffers from this disability.

Theological Theoria

What is the status of this topological writing? If the Borromean knot is not a theoretical model—a model to be read in order to illuminate analytic practice—if it is not the foundation that validates the truth of the analyst's words, what is it then?

In seeking to answer these questions, we are led to ask about the relationship of *truth* to the *real*. We shall examine this by exploring the path historically taken by Christian theology in our culture. Indeed, Christian theology came to draw a Borromean knot well before the Borromeo family, who appear simply to have borrowed it from theology for their own armorial bearings.

Before the 1944 fire at the municipal library of Chartres, one could see a manuscript on which were drawn four figures, each representing three circles intertwined in such a way that if any one among them were broken, it would be enough to free the other two. The manuscript dated from 1355. Happily, a century before its destruction, the first figure had been reproduced in a work of iconography:[13]

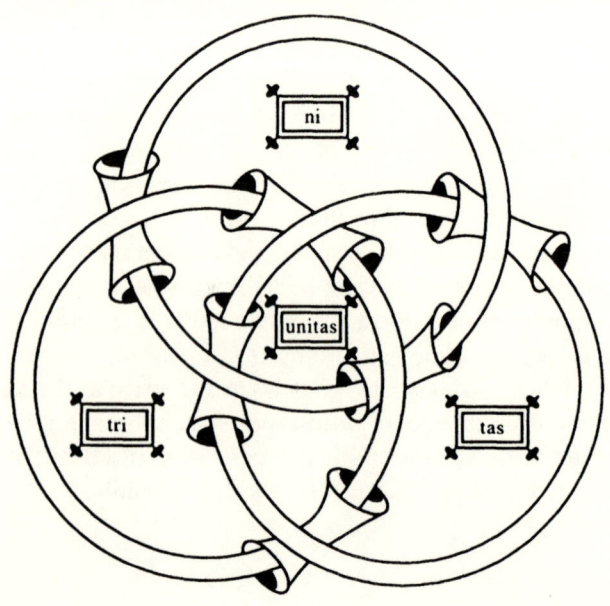

But what is most remarkable is the incription that was added to this drawing: in the center is the word *unitas,* and set into the interior of each of the three circles are the three syllables *tri-ni-tas.* The words are there to give a theological *meaning* to the figure.

Without them, there is the enigma's excess-meaning. With them, the figure becomes a theoretical *model*. There is something *to read*, something to decipher, a knowledge *(savoir)* already there. And where is this knowledge, if not in that being who is the subject supposed to know? It is no longer the God who speaks to you and names you in the words of the teaching, but the Other, from the other extremity, which Lacan describes in these terms:

> The subject supposed to know, God himself, to call Him by the name given Him by Pascal, it is more precise to say what he is not: not the God of Abraham, Isaac or Jacob, but the God of the philosophers, ousted here from His latency in any theory. *Theôria*, is this the place of theology in the world?
>
> Surely, [it is the place] of Christian theology since it began; this is why the atheist seems to us to be the one who is most attached to it.[14]

Indeed, this *trinitarian knot* is a representation that figures the relation of the One and the Three and does so as the *result* of long theological elaboration. It is interesting to see why, over the centuries, theologians found they needed to provide this interpretation, a necessary interpretation, endlessly rewritten, *beginning from* the "Christic revelation,"[15] that is, from the word of the Holy Scriptures. Let us start, therefore, from this primal word, in order to examine the *status* of the trinitarian (Borromean) knot it engendered.

Lacan was aware of this theology, having had a presentiment of what was at stake, namely the relationship of psychoanalysis to "true" religion. The issue could not be avoided, unless of course one was content with facile formulas regarding the atheism of psychoanalysis:

> It is necessary to see what truth is capable of making you do. The truth, my friends, leads to religion. You never understand anything of what I say about this stuff, because I seem to be sneering when I talk about religion. But I am not sneering, I am grinding my teeth! It leads to religion, true religion, as I have already said. And as it is true religion, this is precisely why there would be something to extract from it in terms of *knowledge (savoir)*, in other words, something to invent. The path to follow is to return to it. *If you do not examine the truth of the Trinity*, you become like rats, like the Rat Man.[16]

Christianity is the true religion insofar as it is the culmination of all religions, the truth spoken at last. For better or worse, this is where truth leads ... to the end![17] This is why one must not reject it but add to it, keep going to the point of a stumbling block and from this stumbling block extract knowledge *(savoir)*, a knowledge *(savoir)* of what is beyond belief: God in Three Persons: God the Father, God the Son, God the Holy Spirit. *And yet* there is only one God. But can one be satisfied with this "and yet"?

To examine the truth of the trinity is first of all to see what happens in the *passage* from the words of Christic revelation to their consideration in theology.

Scripture shows the following:

1. *An* Ordinal *of Revelation*

The order of divine missions outside human history conforms to an historical economy (οἰχονομία): God the Father sends *His* Son who sends *His* Spirit. These envoys divide time into a first, second, and third, an irreversible *progression* of visible manifestation.

2. The One *as* Exclusive

Only one Father, only one Son, only one Spirit.

—From Jewish monotheism, Christianity receives a single Father. It is not that no other gods exist. But for His people, *there where* He speaks, only He is to be heard, only His word holds good.

—The second one is equally exclusive. When the messianic promise is at last accomplished, it is accomplished with *this* Son. There is *no other* messiah to be awaited.

—The third one: a single Spirit founds the unity of the institutional body, of the *ecclesia*. It defines the exclusivity of orthodoxy.

Three exclusive ones. Three times "no." No duality. No more-than-one.

3. *The Designation of First* Names

The three ones are called by their *proper* names: Father, Son, Holy Spirit. It is a monarchy of the Father, who subordinates the Son, who subordinates the Spirit. But, in return, no prayer is addressed *to* the Father except through the Son in the Holy Spirit.

What changes occur with the passage from God's authoritative word to theological reason, from a God who speaks to a God of whom one speaks and who is reduced to silence? Or, with the passage from true-speaking to knowledge *(savoir)* of the truth?

Over the centuries, a writing *other* than that of the Holy Scriptures is established, established through conceptual battles, through physical and verbal violence, to the very point of massacring the adversary branded a heretic by the councils. Truth demands it . . . in the name of safeguarding its disciples!

With a rationality inherited from pagan cultures (first Greek, then Latin), theology installs this *theoria: temporal* manifestation of the revelation has its demonstration and foundation in its cause, that is to say, the *eternal* nature of God Himself. The *ex*tension of the historical for-us derives from an *in*tension of the nontemporal for-itself. This is not the place to describe the different moments of this elaboration.[18] The result suffices, that is, the transformation of the three statements cited below.

1. *The Cardinal of* Conumeration

The cardinal of conumeration is substituted for the ordinal of subnumeration, thanks to an *ontology* in which the Father is dethroned for the sake of *equality* in the being of the three. For, from the beginning, the Son is God and the Spirit is God: each is cosubstantial with the other two. Indeed, there is no link between the Father and the Son without the Spirit (contra Arius); there is no link between the Father and the Spirit without the son (contra the East-West Schism, also known as the Schism of 1054); there is no link between the Son and the Spirit without the Father (contra the pneumatists). Philosophical terms imported from the pagans are thus an invaluable aid in the approach to a rigorous, precise univocity in a new, ontological language.

2. *The One of* Union

To point up their unity of substance, the one of union is substituted for the first three ones. Lacan calls it οὐσία: an ontology of love, in which being and love are conjoined. There is no love except of being, in order *to be* more and better, there where being and goodness (and truth) are identical. There is no being other than love, inasmuch as being is *"diffusivum sui"*: the gift of being.

3. The Reduction of the Proper Name to a Common Name

Father, Son, Spirit. For the original sufficiency of nomination, a question is substituted: *what* is father-being, son-being, spirit-being? In order to answer, the path of metaphysical analogy opens up . . . and leads to a fastening of determinations of an *ontological* order, whence flows by deduction a definition of the nature of the paternity of the 1, of the engendering of the 2, and of the procession of the 3: $1 + (1 + (1))$.

What, then, is the final result of this theological travail? An unveiling: according to Lacan, the contingent word of the Christic revelation is *nothing but* the temporal expression of an eternal being, at once One and Three, in whom being and love are conjoined. It is a return of the pagans, a triumph over Judaism via onto-theology. The word of the scriptures is not true by virtue of Jesus' enunciation of it, but the opposite. He says it *because* it is true, a truth that is eternal, necessary, and ontological, according to which one is in three and three in one. This "because" founds the word of Jesus in its cause: a *theoria*.

A Mode of Nomination

Thanks to this historical detour into the truth of religion and the theological knowledge *(savoir)* it engenders, we are ready to tackle the question of the status of the Borromean knot. Is it a *theoretical* model of analytic practice? To answer "yes" would be to forget the speaking that constitutes analytic discourse: "That one speaks remains forgotten behind what is said in what one hears."[19] A forgetting for the sake of ontologizing the topology of the Borromean knot, a forgetting that would make its presentation a representation of being, as if there were a substance that supports the symbolic, the imaginary, and the real. It would be enough to really-read *(unitas, tri-ni-tas)* to use this support to clarify what is to be said. Psychoanalysis would then be today's new theology: a psychology, a discourse on the soul.

But psychoanalysis does not deny theology in order to replace it with another theoretical model. It is the negative of theology, disclosing its underside.

1. Psychoanalysis only exists because a *saying* exists and creates the connection analyst-analysand: a saying that is completely contingent, resting on neither a model nor a metalanguage. This saying names the symbolic, the imaginary, and the real. Hence analytic interpretation "carries weight in a way that goes much further than speech."[20]

2. Indeed, this saying has the *effect* of writing: it leaves a trace where an effect of language can be read. It is through this literal trace that the symbolic reaches the *real*. How? Through inscription of the one. Already in a phrase, each word is linked to another to create a chain; but if a link is missing, the one is no longer. Moreover, in the mathematical language that reaches a real, it is enough for a single letter to be missing—it doesn't matter which—for all the others to become un-linked. This one has nothing to do with being: mathematization has brought about its uncoupling from truth, "and this is why," Lacan says, "it is compatible with our discourse, analytic discourse."[21]

The topology of knots is a writing of the real: one and three in one fell swoop. Symbolic, imaginary, real fall in like proper names, to be written "three," since they are equivalent. It is a three that makes one; the two without the three cannot make one. Now this must hold *by itself*, with neither universe nor ontology to support it: "What bothers me in the Borromean knot," Lacan said, "is a mathematical question, and it is *mathematically* that I intend to handle it."[22] If it were not handled mathematically, the Borromean knot would be a metaphor, "an abuse of metaphor."[23]

3. But this knot is a hole. It cannot be revealed without being shown: it is a question of space, of look, of braiding. It requires an *imaginary* nomination in order to have the consistency of one, mathematically . . . on the blackboard or with strings that are manipulated. This is a new imaginary, no longer specular, no longer founded on the narcissism of the ego: an imaginary of *one* knot-hole engendering a space.

To summarize: analytic interpretation is a saying that makes a knot, or else it is a bla-bla-bla with no relation to the real. It is constantly being written. Now, there is no way to account for this *effect* without *imaginarization* of its presentation: a path that is possible at last, since it takes its consistency from the imaginary alone. Hence, the Borromean knot is figured as the mode in which the *real* effect of the *symbolic* is *imagined*. If the analyst tries to avoid this topological imaginary, he will not be able to account for his practice; from this impotence is born an obstinate attempt to convince through speech.

This is what is at stake for analytic practice: an unsticking of ontology from love and from trinitarian theology in order to reveal the negative, that is, the knot-hole that comes to be substituted for the Other, and to stick there the cause, not of love, but of desire: the *objet petit a*. Thus, when a woman "encounters a man who speaks to her in accordance with her own fundamental fantasy, she will draw an effect of love from it sometimes, [an effect] of desire always."[24] You have the analyst's word on it.

Conclusion: The Psychoanalyst Applied to the Mirror

> Socrates leaves Alcibiades suffering from I know not what strange wound.
> —Lacan, *Le transfert,* December 14, 1960

From start to finish, Lacan's teaching was a debate with the imaginary. Linked first to the narcissism of the ego, the imaginary as such was next subjugated to the primacy of the symbolic, to reemerge in different form when Lacan finally tackled the relationship of the symbolic to the real.

As we shall see, each of these three moments in Lacan's teaching involved a certain analytic practice, and this practice in turn determined the analyst's place. The analyst's place? Indeed, for what each moment is really about is a place to be occupied and maintained.

1. Before 1953. In 1936, Lacan did not submit a written text on the mirror stage. Rather, he published, in *Evolution Psychiatric,* an article entitled "Au-delà du principe de réalité,"[1] three pages of which are devoted to the most exquisite description (exquisite from a literary point of view) of the process of an analysis.[2] The aim of analysis: to have the subject *reconstruct the unity* of the image that activates him and explains his conduct and symptoms. How? Through the analyst who, through his or her word, communicates the design and portrait of this image: a word-mirror shown to the gaze, where the subject can recognize himself in his being.

But this is possible only if the analyst's very *person* is a blank screen on which the subject can "print" an outline of the *imago,* of which as yet the subject is ignorant. Hence, Lacan describes the person of the analyst in terms of "immobility" and "depersonalization." He comes back to this in 1948: "The concern is to provide the dialogue with a participant as devoid as possible of individual characteristics; we efface ourselves, we deprive the speaker of those expressions of interest, sympathy, and reaction that he expects to find on the face of the listener, we avoid all expression of personal taste, we conceal whatever might betray them, we become depersonalized, and try to represent for the other an ideal of impassibility."[3]

Given the paranoiac structure of the ego, the process of analysis (described in detail in part 1, chapter 3 above) involves "inducing in the subject a controlled paranoia,"[4] a paranoia that is directed *onto* the person of the analyst, if only to be stanched in due course. Now, in order that the subject find no support for his or her paranoia in the analyst's image, the latter must reduce this image to "the pure mirror of an unruffled surface."[5] Let us note that Lacan is speaking in terms of a two-dimensional surface: the analyst's ego is a mirror that reveals a surface wherein nothing is reflected.

2. *Beginning in 1953,* this blank statue would, bit by bit, come to lose its comic immobility (comic in Freud's sense!). In 1955, Lacan dealt with the matter in a commentary on Sandor Ferenczi's 1928 article entitled "Elasticity of the Psycho-Analytic Technique."[6] In effect, the stoic apathy and the immutability characteristic of benevolent neutrality determine a distance that is always *the same* in the relation between analyst and analysand: supreme mastery! But, Lacan says, "it is enough for the distance to be fixed in order for the subject to know how to find it."[7] Indeed, what counts in the saying of the interpretation is not its content alone but the place *from which* it is delivered. Such radical complicity in dependence, in keeping the analyst bolted down to a *fixed place*—is this not the ideal of the "good mother" (so dear to Balint), always there when needed, faithful at her post? Is the analyst supposed to satisfy Baden-Powell's maxim: "be prepared"?[8]

Certainly not, says Ferenczi, recommending a pendular oscillation between the empathic warmth of *Einfühlung* and a cold evaluation of the situation, between a smile and being tough-minded. But a practical question arises: what is to condition the movement of this elastic line?

One answer is based on a strategy of changing at will one mask (persona) for another: calculated mobility, the actor's dramaturgical game! To excel at it and assure his or her ultimate mastery, the analyst proceeds in three stages: the analyst demands to be demanded; the analyst remains silent when the demand is made; and finally the analyst permits the intuition of a "no" that is a "yes" and a "yes" that is a "no." Such coquetry (not reserved to women!) becomes a matter of honor for the analyst in this sport of always being somewhere other than where he or she is expected. Social pretense of the purest kind!

But for himself Ferenczi chooses an altogether different path: an "exhaustive" preliminary analysis, during which the future analyst will seek to acquire "a mobility of his libido." Ferenczi does not go into detail on this point, and this is what riles Freud in his letter-response to Ferenczi's article.[9] Thus it is precisely here—at this Ferenczian limit—that Lacan begins with the question: how does the mobility of the place occupied by the analyst depend on the mobility of the analyst's libido? To answer, he returns to the very *origin* of what the ego's mirages cover: the reality of death, original dereliction. The analyst is the one who, through his or her analysis, has effected a subjectification of his or her being-for-death, death as a possibility at once certain and indeterminate—certain in the symbolic, indeterminate in the imaginary. (Like everyone else who will become Other, the analyst cannot picture the face death will have for him or her at that moment.) Now, *from* this subjectification is born the possibility of his or her being in the locus of the Other, there where surprises happen and things unfold one step at a time. The analyst can occupy a place without knowing in advance which one it will be; in brief, the analyst has a mobility that is unmasterable, uncontrollable. Indeed, the analyst's place depends not on himself but on the analysand's *speech:* the analysand's speech is in the locus of the Other.

Lacan concludes: "The analyst can now answer the subject from a place he wants, but he no longer wants anything that determines this place."[10] A condition for this and a requirement for any didactic analysis is "that there are subjects in whom the ego is absent,"[11] owing to the primacy of the symbolic.

3. Has the ego then evaporated, gone up in smoke, thanks to the symbolic? *In 1964,* Lacan sounded a wake-up call for anyone still caught up in this daydream. He ended his seminar of June 24 by speaking directly about the drive: "It is not enough that the analyst should support the

function of Tiresias," that is to say, the symbolic. "He must also, as Apollinaire tells us, have breasts."[12] In other words, the analyst must make himself the support of the oral object, not to speak of the other three!

Support supposes presence—corporeal presence. It is precisely through this that analytic experience becomes possible: through his presence, the analyst assumes the burden of lending himself to the analysand's imaginary and to his specular image. This is a necessary point of support, specific to the analytic path. For, within analysis, the imaginary (and not the imagination) is the *locus* of love. If there is a reflorescence of love from analysis, then it will be via the inter-mediary of the imaginary as locus of love.[13] To help us grasp the point, Lacan recounts the following: "I can tell you a little story, the one about the parakeet who loved Picasso. How could he tell? From the way she nibbled at the collar of his shirt and at his vest lapels. In effect, this parakeet loved what is essential to man, that is, his accoutrements. . . . The parakeet identified with Picasso clothed. It is the same with everything associated with love."[14]

In effect, the lover identifies with the image of the other, such that two make one. The lover sees himself as loved in this image and believes he will obtain what he wants: narcissistic reciprocity. But, if a "costume" loves the one who loves it, it remains no less a "costume." Nothing less, nothing more; and these are equivalent, in that what the image *promises* beyond itself is what makes it hold: a body. Lacan concludes: "What *we* call the body is perhaps nothing other than this *residue* I call the *objet petit a*."[15]

As we saw in the new version of the mirror stage, what makes the image *hold* is a residue. This residue creates a hole in the image, a border zone in the form of *objet petit a*, which can be missing from the field of the Other. Moment of reversal: love is the path that leads beyond narcissism, inasmuch as the loving-beloved image of the specular other consists, in its presentation, only of what is lacking to it, that is, the cause and support of desire. This semblance of being is the costume of the self-image. To it, love is addressed. And why not? Why should we be offended by the servitude of love, *since* there is an "affinity between a and its envelope" ($i(a)$, in Lacan's notation)?[16]

This question finds its answer in analysis. But is the condition that the analyst occupy the place of semblance? No—this would be saying too much. Rather, the analysand puts the analyst in this place, affixes the analyst there; and *correlatively,* the analyst consents to it and allows himself or herself *to be applied.*

Now the analysand will be able to make something of the image at this place of semblance. The analysand will concentrate his or her *acting-out on* the image, work on it, forge a hole in it for the *objet petit a,* such that a *distinction* between i(a) and *a* becomes operative: journey's end. What, then, remains of the analyst? In accordance with the list of objects of the drive, "an insensible piece is to be derived from him, such as voice or gaze, edible flesh or even his excrement; this is what comes *from him* to cause desire, which is our being without essence."[17] Indeed, the analyst responds to the voice created *in* the Other by saying nothing; to the gaze solicited *from* the Other, by seeing nothing; to oral and anal demands to be satisfied *by* the Other, by hearing nothing. Whence Lacan's ultimate advance: the ego is not absent, but it "is only a hole,"[18] because the mirror is a hole. The analysand does not know this, but in due time he or she recognizes it in the analyst, who was a hole from the beginning.

Reversal of the Image

We come to this question: how does it happen one day that an analysand can in turn be applied to the mirror *by* another analysand, thus putting him or her in the position of analyst? Certainly, it is by virtue of his or her analysis, but we need to be more precise. Lacan said: "Knowing how to deal with one's symptom, this is the end of analysis."[19] This is *minimal* definition: rather than disappearance of the symptom, there is modification of its effect, because in identifying himself or herself with it, the subject "knows" it. Lacan repeats this: "To know *(connaître)* one's symptom means to know *(savoir)* how to deal with it, how to manage it, how to handle it."[20] Certainly this is the least we can expect from an analysis carried out far enough. For example, the obsessional who hides himself, the hysteric who reveals herself, both accede to their being-looked-at, without seeking to know *(savoir)* what is seen. They "feel better," which is not the same thing as "feeling well." There is an experience of pleasure or displeasure where previously there was none: an-aesthesia.

1. Yet, in spite of everything, knowing one's symptom leads nowhere, if the *imaginary*—which corresponds to knowing how to manage—is not added to it. This is why Lacan goes on to say: "What man does with

his image corresponds in some way to that, and permits him *to imagine* the way in which one manages with the symptom."[21] This is the crucial part: knowing how to imaginarize *with* one's specular image. This path will lead us beyond preliminary answers to the question: how can the analysand effect a passage to the position of analyst?

At a certain final moment of *mobility* in the specular image—and this does not happen without depersonalization—a new path opens up for reversal of the image. Lacan had a premonition of this when he described man as having a toric self-image. It was foreshadowed, as well, in his endless returns to the last seminars, where there is a reversal of the torus following a *cut* made in it. It was an insistent, constraining intuition, in which the topological imaginary progressed by groping about, in advance of thought.

2. *But how is this reshaping of the image effected?* First of all, at the end of an analysis, a depersonalization occurs, not in the sense of a deficit but in the sense of going beyond a limit. (The various spatio-temporal problems that may accompany this are transitory and have no diagnostic value.) The avatars of the case, the events that crystallize in points of glory or shame, are effaced as carriers of meaning, of elevation or fall. *Ne-uter,* neither one nor the other: the traits/marks of the ideal-ego are neutralized in the im-personal "it" of "it's raining" or "it's beautiful." Analytic interpretation says "you are that," where the "you" becomes a "that." The unconscious is an Other who has no Other, either good or bad. Thus depersonalization decomposes the "paranoic structure of the ego."

From this de-personalization[22] is born *mobility* of the specular image. The former rigid dependence of the specular image on *such and such* other, which Lacan notes as i'(a), dissolves not into egotistic withdrawal but into successive, momentary support by an-other, and an-other, and an-other . . . *any* other.

3. Now, thanks to this availability, the analysand one day imaginarizes a *specific* way of dealing with the mobility of his or her specular image: it becomes the locus for this *anyone who is the other;* moreover, it becomes this *for* an eventual analysand and *through* him. In this way a reversal of the image in the field of the Other is effected, in the locus of that symbolic pact that is the analytic relation.[23]

How is this imaginarization possible? Not by institutional authorization or a personal, voluntary decree, but through a *cut* in the specular image that, if one may say so, serves as a pivot for reversal of the image.

Conclusion

How does this happen? In various ways, of course. One way among others is seen in the following case.

During the period of about a year, certain words heard by the subject in a waking state or read in a dream-text began to take on a peculiar intensity.[24] Far from becoming relativized through placement in a meaningful context, they rose to the status of signifiers: irreducible, unlinked. Thus absolute, they spawned enigma from their excess-meaning and demanded a locus of truth, wherein meaning, through the trans-port of meta-phor, could be engendered.

For a time, the subject experienced uncertainty and intellectual inhibition with respect to these words. However, several weeks later, on three separate occasions, he became convinced that a text could be found in a certain book (a collection of poems, a dictionary), a text that would give these words a meaning hitherto unknown. In addition, the subject was convinced he had *already* read the text, and he would see the passage in memory with particularly clear vision,[25] since the text concerned him. And finally, when he would get to the point of actually looking for the text in a book he had on hand, he would discover his mistake: *Vergreifen* (mistaking) of the seen-before-read-before! This phenomenon is an unconscious formation; Freud used the term *Erinnerungstäuschung* (an error in recollection) to describe it.[26]

The real is what returns to the same place. Three times, a complete text is established in the locus of the Other, where knowledge *(savoir)* of truth would *already* be inscribed. Each time, through *Wiederholung* (repetition), a fault opens up at the point where the text is missing in the book: this is the real as missed encounter. Indefinite research into the perceptible reality that is this book or that dictionary comes to a halt, and the books fall from his hands!

But this loss at the junction of symbolic and real does not occur without inscription of a border zone, the border of the cut that this very loss has engendered. Indeed, what is positioned at this junction is the hole in the *body image;* it is named "blind spot, sore, fracture." But these nominations do not refer to any signified; rather they delineate the minus phi ($-\phi$). They imaginarize the trait/mark of the *cut* at the missed encounter of symbolic and real, there where the text is lacking. What is accomplished: a writing of the impossible that puts an end to the expectation of meaning.

Now, this cut is the pivot on which the specular image *can* be reversed.

The possible (you can, therefore you must, contrary to the Kantian precept) defines the *position* of the analyst. The uncompleted text in the locus of the Other is no longer there, before the analyst, outside the analyst: the analyst occupies the place by reversal of his specular image; hence the analysand can apply him to this very place.

Speaking of his mother, Roland Barthes wrote that she "lent herself" to photography. She did not resist it. She neither retreated out of fear nor assumed the self-conscious, self-imposing aspect of one embarrassed by her *imago*. Barthes concludes: "She did not struggle with her image: she did not *suppose* herself."[27] This word precisely defines the modification in one's own body image that one day gives birth to an analyst: the attitude of one who supposes himself has fallen way, *allowing him to be supposed* . . . by whomever!

The Mistake

What is one to do with one's image? That is the question posed to the speaking being that is man. Animals do not have this problem: via the intermediary of the image of one of its own species, *Innenwelt* and *Umwelt* are brought together in reciprocal relationship. For man, there is no such adaptation. Language (not to be identified with speech: animals speak!) introduces a fault, whence our discomfort *(mal-à-l'aise)*.

In this regard, Jean Paulhan in his *Entretien avec Robert Mallet* (1952), recounts the story of Mina: "Mina is a king's daughter. And badly brought up, of course, as are all daughters of kings. She is given everything she wants. As a result, there is never a time when she is unhappy. Or happy, for that matter. But one day, through the bars, she sees a peasant girl laughing with the man she loves. She is very surprised. The next day, the same peasant girl is crying: the man she loves has wronged her. Mina is even more surprised. Then and there she jumps over the bars and goes out into the world. She observes, she takes notes, she comes to know a little better when to cry and when to laugh. But it is too late. She is never quite sure that sometimes she isn't mistaken and laughs when she should be crying. This makes her life very difficult. I love true stories, where the hero does exactly the opposite of what one would have expected."[28]

Conclusion

Paulhan concludes: "One sometimes says that a man is capable of anything. Yes. One couldn't put it better: Anyone is capable of anything."[29] Mina knows neither joy nor pain: she experiences nothing because she feels nothing. What she needs is an image of herself. This came to her one day from the sight of another, a peasant girl. Surprise: a revelation of opposites, of the alternation of extremes, of laughing and crying. Thus the desire to know *(savoir)* is born in her: she notices everything. But it is "too late." She is deceived and will always deceive her world.

An exemplary story! Who is not Mina? Capable of anything! She believes the peasant girl knows when to cry and when to laugh: a young woman who has applied herself well! That's what Mina believes. In similar fashion, the little girl taken to London admires the fact that children there *already* know how to speak English. "How well they have applied themselves!" she says (Jean Paulhan, *Les Fleurs de Tarbes*). But Mina is mistaken, like the teacher who writes on the report card: "a student who applies herself" *(élève appliquée)* . . . to what? To the notebook? To the writing? To the blackboard?

It is "too late" for Mina to apply herself. But isn't this true for each of us, always? This results from a discordance of the imaginary, original and incurable, owing to which one is never there where one is expected.

Mina is Jean Paulhan himself, a French Baltasar Gracián. Paulhan wrote that, during his military service,

> at the end of the maneuvers, our captain gave the student officers this theme for homework: "Recount the grand maneuvers, emphasizing the organizational mistakes you believe you have noticed and the improvements it would be necessary to make." I wrote the essay explaining that I found the grand maneuvers extremely interesting, that in no way had I come to the barracks to improve the army and that everything had seemed to me to be perfectly organized. . . . My essay was seen as a manifestation of antimilitarism. . . . I never became an officer.[30]

The student Jean Paulhan is "applied" *by* . . . the army . . . *to* the maneuvers. Neither for nor against the army, neither accepting nor refusing it, he allows himself to be applied. He, in return, astonishes.

In 1914, Paulhan went to war, was wounded, and from his hospital bed wrote *Le guerrier appliqué* (The Applied Warrior).[31] The first edition appeared in 1919, to applause from the anarchists. A second edition appeared in 1930; this time, it was the turn of the staunchest patriots to recognize themselves in it. This warrior does not apply himself, he is applied *by* each reader; he is "one traumatized by misunderstanding."[32]

What is an appliqué? It could be a set of shelves, a console, or a candelabrum that is put *onto* the wall. But this "onto" is also an "against." The human being, because maladjusted, does not apply himself or herself to this or that. The human being is plastered by the Other *against* an image, as Eve is for Adam, in the words of the Bible: a helpmeet over against him . . . in *otherness!*

Such is the psychoanalyst: he or she is applied to the mirror by an analysand; in response, from this collage à la Matisse, the figure of an outline is traced onto a canvas, an outline "of the absence of you which makes its blindness" (Aragon, *Contre-chant*).[33]

Notes

Introduction

1. Jacques Lacan, *Scilicet* 2/3 (Paris: Seuil, 1970), 399.
2. Lacan, *The Seminar of Jacques Lacan. Book II: The Ego in Freud's Theory and in the Technique of Psychoanalysis, 1954–1955,* ed. Jacques-Alain Miller, trans. Sylvana Tomaselli (New York: Norton, 1988), 203.
3. At a lecture delivered by M. Foucault at the Société Française de Philosophie, February 22, 1969, entitled "What Is an Author?" Lacan made the following remark: "The return to Freud is something I have taken up as a kind of flag." The text of the session's proceedings may be found in *Littoral* 9, "La Discursivité."
4. Lacan, *Ecrits: A Selection,* trans. Alan Sheridan (New York: Norton, 1981), 115.
5. Lacan, *Ecrits: A Selection,* 115.
6. Ibid., 116.
7. Lacan, *Ecrits* (Paris: Seuil, 1966), 404.
8. *Ex-egesis:* Freud uses the term *Auslegung,* to set forth by means of an extraction. There can be no *Deutung* (interpretation) without *Auslegung* (ex-egesis).
9. Lacan, *Ecrits,* 364.
10. Lacan, *Le séminaire. Livre XI: Les quatre concepts fondamentaux de la psychanalyse* (Paris: Seuil, 1973), 115–16.
11. Ibid., 116.
12. Ibid., 117.
13. Here and throughout the book, the word *savoir* (knowledge) is used in a special sense, based on Lacan's strict distinction between *"savoir"* and *"connaissance,"* each of which might be translated into English simply as "knowledge." For both Lacan and Julien, *"connaissance"* implies a seeing with the mind and entails having an intuitive representation of the object. In contrast, *"savoir"* implies a discursive acquisition and presupposes a set of logically ordered elements. Thus, whenever Lacan or Julien uses the word "savoir" to mean knowledge, the reader will find this indicated in parentheses. —TRANS.
14. Lacan, *Ecrits,* 366.

1. The Pain of Being Two

1. Lacan, *De la psychose paranoïaque dans ses rapports avec la personnalité* (Paris: Seuil, 1975). The thesis was initially published in 1932 by Le François.

2. Lacan's article "Motifs du crime paranoïaque: Le crime des soeurs Papin" first appeared in *Le Minotaure* 3 (1933). It was republished by Seuil in 1975 as an appendix to *De la psychose*.

3. Lacan, *Ecrits*, 178.
4. Ibid., 114.
5. Ibid., 109.

6. Lacan, "La famille," in the *Encyclopédie française*, ed. A. de Monzie (Paris: Larousse, 1938), vol. 8, sec. 40 (La Vie Mentale), 3–16. The article was reissued in book form as *Les complexes familiaux* (Paris: Navarin, 1984).

7. Whence the quotation from Spinoza on "discrepancy," which Lacan used as the motto for his thesis: "Quilibet unius cujusque individui affectus ab affectu alterius tantum *discrepat*, quantum essentia unius ab essentia alterius differt." ("Any affect of one individual is unlike the affect of another inasmuch as the essence of one differs from the essence of the other.") Spinoza, *Ethics* 3, prop. 57.

8. Lacan, *De la psychose*, 401.
9. Ibid., 187.
10. Lacan, *Ecrits*, 168.

11. The French high school degree, sometimes considered equivalent to having one year of college in the United States. —TRANS.

12. Lacan, *De la psychose*, 231.
13. Ibid., 233.
14. Ibid., 232.
15. Ibid., 234.
16. Ibid., 39.
17. Ibid., 400.
18. Ibid., 393.

19. Translated into French by E. Pichon, this article appeared in the *Revue Française de Psychanalyse* in 1928.

20. Sigmund Freud, "The Economic Problem of Masochism" (1924), in *The Standard Edition of the Complete Psychological Works of Sigmund Freud*, ed. James Strachey (London: Hogarth, 1962), vol. 19, 166.

21. Freud, "A Case of Paranoia Running Counter to the Psycho-Analytic Theory of the Disease" (1915), *S.E.* 14, 265.

22. Lacan, *De la psychose*, 395–96.

23. Freud, "Some Neurotic Mechanisms in Jealousy, Paranoia and Homosexuality" (1922), *S.E.* 18, 231–32.

24. Freud, "Group Psychology and the Analysis of the Ego" (1921), *S.E.* 18, 121.

25. Lacan, *Ecrits*, 170–71.

26. Freud, "Some Neurotic Mechanisms," 232. (Emphasis and parenthetical note added by the author.)
27. Ibid.
28. Lacan, *De la psychose,* 396.
29. Ibid., 365.
30. Ibid., 349.
31. Ibid., 321.
32. Cf. an essential passage in the thesis, 234.
33. Lacan, *De la psychose,* 321.
34. Ibid., 322.
35. Ibid., 392.
36. Ibid., 280.
37. Ibid., 269.
38. Ibid., 277.
39. Ibid., 278–79. During this period, Charles Maurras offered identical suggestions, of course from an altogether different perspective.

2. My Dearest Counterpart, My Mirror

1. This description is based on the mirror stage. Only much later, with the introduction of the primacy of the symbolic, will Lacan be able to reveal the truth of this process: that denial of the stranger unites those who look alike; that segregation shapes fraternity. We shall see how.
2. See Jean-Marie Brohm, *Jeux olympiques à Berlin* (Brussels: Complexe, 1983).
3. In France, Montherlant published *Les Olympiques* (1924), as well as *Paysage des Olympiques* (1938), an album of photos of adolescent athletes, taken by a former scout, Egermeier.
4. Henri Wallon, *Les origines du charactère chez l'enfant* (Paris: Boivin, 1934), 197–98.
5. Lacan, *Ecrits: A Selection,* 4.
6. Is this organic lack an explanatory cause? To those who took it as such, Lacan responded, in 1966 in the *Ecrits* (69–70), by affirming the primacy of the Other, the locus of the symbolic, thereby relativizing this lack.
7. Wallon, 198.
8. Lacan, *Ecrits,* 181.
9. Lacan, "Some Reflections on the Ego," *International Journal of Psycho-Analysis* 34 (1953): 15.
10. Gaston Bachelard, *L'Air et les songes* (Paris: Corti, 1943), 7.
11. We shall see how, thirty years later, Lacan gave the imaginary the status of a topological dimension.
12. Lacan, "Some Reflections on the Ego," 13.
13. In "Group Psychology and the Analysis of the Ego" (S.E. 18, 141), Freud

asked himself what creates a group's social bond *(Massebildung)*. He spoke of a libido that was neither homosexual nor heterosexual, "for it is not differentiated according to sex." In effect, he was readopting Aristotle's notion of friendship *(philia)*, defined as the foundation of society and described—remarkably—as a mirroring: "Direct contemplation of ourselves is moreover impossible.... And so, just as when wishing to behold our own faces, we have seen them by looking upon a mirror, whenever we wish to know our characters and personalities, we can recognize them by looking upon a friend, since *the friend* is, as we say, our 'second self.'" *Magna Moralia* 2. 15, 6–7. In *Aristotle*, vol. 18, Loeb Classical Library, trans. G. Cyril Armstrong (Cambridge: Harvard University Press, 1990), 683. Emphasis added by the author. It was not without irony that Lacan characterized Judge Schreber's relationship with his wife as friendship.

14. Lacan, *Ecrits: A Selection*, 4–5.

3. Paranoic Knowledge

1. Lacan, *Ecrits*, 180.
2. Roland Barthes, *La chambre claire* (Paris: Gallimard-Seuil, 1980), 142–43.
3. Lacan, *Ecrits*, 172.
4. Ibid., 170.
5. Ibid., 175.
6. Ibid.
7. Around the age of six or eight months, the infant may have nightmares. More open than ever to others, it tolerates poorly the brutal changes of place and incessant novelty of faces: it needs the oneness of an other who returns to the *same* place to serve as mirror.
8. Lacan, *Ecrits: A Selection*, 15.
9. Lacan, *Ecrits*, 188. Emphasis added by the author.
10. Ibid., 85.
11. Lacan, *Ecrits: A Selection*, 15.
12. Lacan, *Ecrits*, 85.
13. Lacan, *Ecrits: A Selection*, 15.
14. Ibid., 13.
15. Lacan, *Ecrits*, 83–85.
16. Ibid., 84.
17. The descriptive presentation of a portrait is certainly one of the modes of analytic interpretation. But does it bring about an acceptable narcissism? This is a question we must take up again.
18. Lacan, *Ecrits*, 185.
19. Ibid.
20. Elements of the mirror stage were first published in 1938. Cf. "La famille," 6–11.

4. The Lacanian Thing

1. Lacan, *Ecrits*, 179.
2. Freud, "Negation" (1925), *S.E.* 19.
3. Lacan, *The Seminar of Jacques Lacan. Book I: Freud's Papers on Technique, 1953–1954*, ed. Jacques-Alain Miller, trans. Sylvana Tomaselli (New York: Norton, 1988), 55.
4. Lacan, *Ecrits*, 381.
5. Lacan, *The Seminar of Jacques Lacan. Book II*, 326.
6. Michel Foucault, *L'ordre du discours* (Paris: Gallimard, 1971), 27.
7. Lacan, "Some Reflections on the Ego," 11–17.
8. With lowercase letters. Indeed, what would be the point of raising their status to uppercase?
9. From Seminar XXIV, 1976–1977, "L'insu que sait de l'une-bévue s'aile à mourre." Unpublished, but parts of the seminar appeared in *Ornicar?* between 1977 and 1979.
10. In English, see Gottlob Frege, "On Sense and Reference," in *Philosophical Writings*, ed. Peter Geach and Max Black (Oxford: Blackwell, 1952).
11. Lacan, *Ecrits: A Selection*, 119.
12. From Seminar XXII, 1974–1975, "RSI," January 13, 1975 session. Published in *Ornicar?* 2–5 (1975–1976).
13. From Lacan's statement, October 9, 1967, on the psychoanalyst of the Ecole freudienne de Paris, in *Scilicet* 1 (Paris: Seuil, 1968).
14. From Seminar XXIV.
15. July 1980 at Caracas, where he presented Freud's schema, known as the ovum, from chapter 2 of "The Ego and the Id" (1923), *S.E.* 19.
16. In the same place as the optical schemata. See *Ecrits*, 674 and 680.
17. Ibid., 85.
18. Ibid., 107.
19. Freud, "The Ego and the Id" (1923), *S.E.* 19, 26.
20. Lacan, *The Seminar of Jacques Lacan. Book I*, 283.
21. Ibid., 284.
22. The *symbolon* is the tessera, an object cut in two pieces, to be reassembled as a sign of recognition between two partners.
23. Cf. Lacan, *Le séminaire. Livre VIII: Le transfert* (1960–1961), text established by Jacques-Alain Miller (Paris: Seuil, 1991), 397.
24. Freud, *Studienausgabe*, vol. 9, *Fragen der Gesellschaft Ursprünge der Religion* (Frankfurt: S. Fischer, 1974), 100.
25. Freud, "Group Psychology," 107.
26. Lacan, *The Seminar of Jacques Lacan. Book I*, 158.
27. Lacan, *Ecrits: A Selection*, 256.
28. Lacan, *Le séminaire. Livre III: Les psychoses* (1955–1956), text established by Jacques-Alain Miller (Paris: Seuil, 1981), 23.

29. Lacan, *The Seminar of Jacques Lacan. Book I*, 232. Also see *Ecrits*, 680. We will come back to this later.
30. As Lacan has affirmed elsewhere. See *Ecrits: A Selection*, 14.
31. Lacan, *The Seminar of Jacques Lacan. Book I*, 109.
32. *En Panta:* Heraclitus's formula, meaning "one-in-many [beings]." Cf. William J. Richardson, *Heidegger: Through Phenomenology to Thought* (The Hague: Nijhoff, 1974), 11, 492. —TRANS.

5. Exhaustion in the Symbolic

1. Lacan, *Ecrits: A Selection*, 68. (Emphasis added by the author.)
2. Ibid.
3. Here we have a restatement of an observation Lacan made, in his 1932 thesis, on the utility of institutions with strict rules and elevated ideals.
4. Lacan, *Ecrits: A Selection*, 85.
5. Lacan, *The Seminar of Jacques Lacan. Book II*, 243.
6. Ibid., 244.
7. Ibid. Isn't this the sort of language Lacan advocated prior to 1953 and afterwards attributed to Balint? Its function was to create a unified image.
8. Ibid.
9. Lacan, *The Seminar of Jacques Lacan. Book II*, 20.
10. Lacan, *Le séminaire. Livre III*, 307ff.
11. Lacan, *Ecrits: A Selection*, 71.
12. Ibid., 72.
13. *Ornicar?* 17–18: 293.
14. A remark reported by Moustapha Safouan in *Jacques Lacan et la question de la formation des analystes* (Paris: Seuil, 1983), 44.
15. Freud, "Analysis Terminable and Interminable" (1937), S.E. 23, 217.
16. Arthur Rimbaud, *A Season in Hell/The Illuminations,* trans. Enid Rhodes Peschel (New York: Oxford University Press, 1974), 127. (Emphasis added by the author.)
17. "Dit-mension." A play on the word "dimension," which in French sounds like a combination of the words *"dit"* (says) and *"mansion"* (mansion, large house). Speech is a dit-mension of truth, a house for truth. —TRANS.
18. Lacan, *Le séminaire. Livre XX: Encore* (1972–1973), text established by Jacques-Alain Miller (Paris: Seuil, 1975), 88.
19. Lacan, *The Seminar of Jacques Lacan. Book II*, 313.
20. Lacan, *Ecrits: A Selection*, 49. (Emphasis added by the author.)
21. Ibid.
22. Ibid.
23. Lacan, *The Seminar of Jacques Lacan. Book II*, 308.
24. Lacan, *Ecrits: A Selection*, 52. (Emphasis added by the author.)
25. Ibid., 103. (Emphasis added by the author.)

26. Ibid., 104.
27. Ibid.
28. Lacan, "L'étourdit," in *Scilicet* 4 (Paris: Seuil, 1973), 18.
29. Lacan, *The Four Fundamental Concepts of Psycho-Analysis,* ed. Jacques-Alain Miller, trans. Alan Sheridan (New York: Norton, 1981), 83.
30. From Seminar XXII, "RSI" (1974–1975), session of April 15, 1975.
31. Ibid.
32. From Seminar XXIV (1976–1977), session of December 14, 1976. In German, the unconscious is *das Unbewusste.* Compare Lacan's *l'une-bévue.* —TRANS.
33. Ibid.
34. Lacan, *The Seminar of Jacques Lacan. Book II,* 243.
35. Lacan, *Le séminaire. Livre XVII: L'envers de la psychanalyse* (1969–1970), text established by Jacques-Alain Miller (Paris: Seuil, 1991), 159.
36. Ibid., 239.

6. *The Making of a Case of Acting-Out*

1. Lacan, *Ecrits: A Selection,* 240.
2. Ibid.
3. Ernst Kris, "Ego Psychology and Interpretation in Psychoanalytic Therapy," *Psychoanalytic Quarterly* 20 (1951): 15–30.
4. Here the author plays on the fact that "oc-cas-ion" contains within itself, and in that sense generates, the word "cas." —TRANS.
5. Cf. *Ecrits: A Selection,* 239, where Lacan recounts the incident.
6. In 1936, no German Jewish athlete had the right to prepare for or participate in the games. In France, Pierre Mendès-France, alone among the deputies, voted against appropriating funds for the games.
7. Société psychanalytique de Paris.
8. Lacan, *The Seminar of Jacques Lacan. Book I,* 60.
9. Lacan, *Le séminaire. Livre III,* 92–93.
10. Both articles were republished in 1966 in the *Ecrits,* 369 and 381 respectively.
11. Lacan, *Ecrits: A Selection,* 226–80.
12. Ibid., 238.
13. English in the original.
14. Kris, "Ego Psychology and Interpretation," 22.
15. Ibid.
16. Ibid.
17. Ibid., 23. (Emphasis added by the author.)
18. Ibid. (Emphasis added by the author.)
19. Ibid., 24.
20. Freud, "Negation," S.E. 19, 239.
21. Ibid. Here "judgement" is judgment of existence.

22. Kris, "Ego Psychology and Interpretation," 23.
23. Lacan, *Le séminaire. Livre XX,* 114.
24. From Seminar XIV (1966–1967), "La logique du fantasme," session of March 8, 1967. Unpublished.
25. Lacan, *Ecrits,* 388.
26. Ibid., 393. In English in the original.
27. From Seminar XXII, "RSI" (1974–1975), session of March 18, 1975. (Emphasis added by the author.)

7. A Change of Place

1. Lacan, *Ecrits,* 88.
2. Freud, "Beyond the Pleasure Principle" (1920), *S.E.* 18, 18.
3. Ibid., 19.
4. Lacan, *Ecrits,* 83–85.
5. Lacan, *Ecrits: A Selection,* 14.
6. Lacan, *Ecrits,* 215–26.
7. Lacan, *The Seminar of Jacques Lacan. Book I,* 109. (Emphasis added by the author.)
8. Freud, "Moses and Monotheism" (1939), *S.E.* 23, 92–102.
9. Lacan, *Ecrits: A Selection,* 153. (Emphasis added by the author.)
10. Sigmund Freud and Lou Andreas-Salomé, *Letters,* ed. Ernest Pfeiffer, trans. William Robson-Scott and Elaine Robson-Scott (New York: Harcourt Brace Jovanovich, 1972), 120. (Emphasis added by the author.)
11. Ibid., 121–22.
12. Freud, "Remembering, Repeating and Working-Through" (1914), *S.E.* 12, 150.
13. Ibid., 151–52.
14. Lacan, *Le séminaire. Livre VIII.*

8. An Ethical Question

1. Lacan, *Le séminaire. Livre VIII.*
2. Lacan, *The Seminar of Jacques Lacan. Book VII: The Ethics of Psychoanalysis, 1959–1960,* ed. Jacques-Alain Miller, trans. with notes by Dennis Porter (New York: Norton, 1992).
3. Ibid., 321.
4. Lacan, *Ecrits,* 766.
5. Aristotle, *Nichomachean Ethics* (Book I, 1, 1094a) in *The Basic Works of Aristotle,* ed. with an introduction by Richard McKeon (New York: Random House, 1971), 935.
6. Michel Foucault's last two books, *L'usage des plaisirs* and *Le souci de soi,*

admirable in their precision and clarity, bear witness to a strange fascination with this ethics of self-control.

7. In *autruiche*, Lacan combines *autruche*, the bird that attempts to avoid danger by hiding its head in the sand, with *autrui*, others or neighbor. —TRANS.

8. Freud, *The Origins of Psycho-Analysis: Letters to Wilhelm Fliess, Drafts and Notes: 1897–1902*, ed. Marie Bonaparte, Anna Freud, and Ernst Kris, trans. Eric Mosbacher and James Strachey (New York: Basic, 1954), 393.

9. Ibid., 393–94. (Emphasis on "thing" added by the author.)

10. Martin Heidegger, *Poetry, Language, Thought*, trans. Albert Hofstadter (New York: Harper Colophon Books, 1971), 169.

11. According to Aristotle (*Poetics* 6.1449b28), tragedy requires the portrayal of situations arousing pity and fear in the spectator, precisely so as to accomplish a catharsis of these emotions. —TRANS.

12. Lacan, *Ecrits*, 776.

13. In fact, courtly love is not a desexualization, witness the Cornilh affair in the troubadours Arnaud Daniel, Raimon de Durfort, and Truc Malec. Can one really play a horn in a lady's behind? See Pierre Bec, *Burlesque et obscénité chez les troubadours* (Paris: Stock, 1984); and René Nelli, *Ecrivains anticonformistes du Moyen Age occitan*, vol. 1 (Paris: Phébus, 1977).

14. Lacan, *The Four Fundamental Concepts of Psycho-Analysis*, 275–76.

15. Ibid., 276.

9. A Metaphor of Love

1. Lacan, *Le séminaire. Livre VIII*.
2. Also called *Symposium*. —TRANS.
3. Lacan, *Ecrits: A Selection*, 323.
4. See K. J. Dover, *Greek Homosexuality* (Cambridge: Harvard University Press, 1978). (Michel Foucault made judicious use of this book.)
5. See *The Confessions of St. Augustine*, trans. John K. Ryan (Garden City, N.Y.: Image, 1960), 175 (Book 7) and especially 221–23 (Book 9, "The Vision at Ostia").
6. "Boaz knew not that a woman was there, Ruth knew not what God wanted of her." Victor Hugo, *La légende des siècles*, vol. 1 (Paris: GF-Flammarion, 1979), 98.
7. *Phaedrus* 251b. In *Plato*, vol. 1, Loeb Classical Library, trans. Harold North Fowler (Cambridge: Harvard University Press, 1982), 487.
8. *Phaedrus* 255c–d. In *Plato*, vol. 1, 449–501.
9. Lacan, *Le séminaire. Livre VIII*, 83.
10. *Symposium* 218d. In *Plato*, vol. 3, Loeb Classical Library, trans. W. R. M. Lamb (Cambridge: Harvard University Press, 1983), 229–31.
11. Four years later, upon reading *Le ravissement de Lol V. Stein* (in which the triangular relationship of Lol, Tatiana, and Jacques Hold is constitutive for the lover), Lacan again took up the theme of triangulation. See his "Hommage fait

à Marguerite Duras" in *Cahiers Renaud-Barrault* 52 (December 1965): 7–15. Reprinted in *Marguerite Duras* (Paris: Albatros, 1979), 131–38.

12. Lacan, *Ecrits: A Selection*, 15.

13. Here Lacan is referring to the optical schemata that picture the body. See *Ecrits*, 674 and 680.

14. Ibid., 682. (Emphasis added by the author, except for "is-it," italicized in the original.)

15. Ibid. (Emphasis added by the author.)

16. Ibid. (Emphasis on "know" added by the author; "wanted" and "unwanted" in English in the original.)

10. A Cartesian Approach

1. Lacan, "Introduction to the Names-of-the-Father Seminar," in the double volume *Television* and *A Challenge to the Psychoanalytic Establishment*, ed. Joan Copjec, trans. Denis Hollier, Rosalind Kraus, Annette Michelson, and Jeffrey Mehlman (New York: Norton, 1990), 95. This first and only session of Lacan's 1963–1964 seminar originally appeared in *L'Excommunication*, 110–11, a supplement to *Ornicar?* 8 (1977). The English translation is by Jeffrey Mehlman.

2. Lacan, "Introduction to the Names-of-the-Father Seminar," 87. (Emphasis added by the author.)

3. Ibid., 89. (Emphasis added by the author.) I address the question of the paternal function in my book, *Le Manteau de Noé: Essai sur la paternité* (Paris: Brouwer, 1991). Also see my article "L'amour du père chez Freud," *Littoral* 11/12 (February 1984): 153–68.

4. Ibid., 84.

5. Ibid., 92.

6. "Thou shalt not do so unto the Lord thy God; for every abomination to the Lord, which He hateth, have they done unto their gods; for even their sons and their daughters do they burn in the fire to their gods." This text (Deut. 12:31), like Lev. 18:21, reminds us of how interdiction was transgressed in Israel. Cf. 2 Kings 17:17; Jer. 18:21. King Ahaz burned his own son in the fire (2 Kings 16:3), as did King Manasseh (2 Kings 21:6).

7. For the difference between subjective genitive and objective genitive see Lacan, *Ecrits*, 814. In English, *Ecrits: A Selection*, 312.

8. Lacan, "Introduction to the Names-of-the-Father Seminar," 94.

9. Ibid., 95.

10. Lacan, *The Four Fundamental Concepts of Psycho-Analysis*, 53.

11. "La passe" refers to the controversial procedure by which a member of the EFP became an official "analyst of the School." —TRANS.

12. "For" the EFP indicates a relation. The dissolution of the EFP on January 5, 1980, permitted each person to dissolve that relation. Once again, institutional statutes were not sufficient.

13. Lacan, *Ecrits: A Selection*, 50.

14. Ibid., 70.
15. Ibid., 72. (Emphasis added by the author.)
16. Lacan, *Ecrits*, 858.
17. René Descartes, "Discourse on Method," in *The Philosophical Works of Descartes*, vol. 1, trans. Elizabeth S. Haldane and G. R. T. Ross (Cambridge: Cambridge University Press, 1972), 87.
18. Lacan, *Ecrits: A Selection*, 165.
19. Descartes, "Meditation II," in *The Philosophical Works of Descartes*, vol. 1, 150. (Emphasis added by the author.)
20. Lacan, *Ecrits*, 865. (Emphasis added by the author.)
21. Lacan, *The Four Fundamental Concepts of Psycho-Analysis*, 76.
22. Freud, "The Interpretation of Dreams" (1900), *S.E.* 5, 509.
23. From Seminar XXVII, "Dissolution" (1980), session of April 15, 1980. Seminar published in *Ornicar?* during 1980 and 1981. The French text reads "d'on ne sait *zou*," wordplay meant to emphasize what is heard in speaking. —Trans.
24. Lacan, "Proposition du 9 octobre 1967 sur le psychanalyste de l'Ecole," in *Scilicet* 1 (Paris: Seuil, 1968), 20.
25. In French, this recalls the words of Beaumarchais: "Calomniez . . . il en restera toujours quelque chose." ("Slander . . . something will always be left of it"). —Trans.
26. Lacan, *Ecrits: A Selection*, 316.
27. From Lacan, Seminar XXI, "Les non-dupes errent" (1973–1974), session of June 11, 1974. Unpublished. The title of this seminar is meant to recall, via homophony, Lacan's 1963 seminar, "Les Noms-du-Père," which he had been forced to cut short precisely ten years before. —Trans.
28. Lacan, *Le séminaire. Livre XX*, 133.

11. A Literal Operation

1. Alexandre Koyré, *Etudes d'histoire de la pensée scientifique* (Paris: Gall, 1973), 185.
2. Ibid.
3. Ibid. (Emphasis added by the author.)
4. Ibid. (Emphasis added by the author.)
5. Ibid. (Emphasis on "to explain the real by the impossible" added by the author.)
6. Lacan, *Ecrits: A Selection*, 121.
7. Lacan, *Television*, 8. (Emphasis added by the author.)
8. Ibid.
9. See Seminar IX, "L'Identification" (1961–1962), session of January 24, 1962. Unpublished. In this section, the author plays on the homophony of "pas" meaning "step" or "foot" and "pas" meaning "no." —Trans.
10. The word "*pataquès*" means a mistake in pronunciation or liaison. It

comes from the riduculous phrase "je ne sais pas-t-à qu'est-ce." Here we see an example of what happens when "pas" is vocalized and linked to new syllables: letters fall away and new meaning is created. —TRANS.

11. The child learns this very quickly and asks himself: why am I called "Philip" and my brother "Peter"—so different to my ear—when I see they are written with the same first letter?

12. Lacan, "Lituraterre," *Littérature* 3 (October 1971): 7. The Latin word *litura* means "erasure" or "wrinkle."

13. With respect to this *neues Subjekt*, Lacan commented as follows: "This subject, which is properly the other, appears insofar as the drive has been able to show its circular course. It is only with its appearance at the level of the other that what there is of the function of the drive may be realized." Lacan, *The Four Fundamental Concepts of Psycho-Analysis*, 178–79.

14. In German, the Lacanian expression *"plus-de-jouir"* is *"mehr-Lust."* This points to its origin in the German term *"mehr-Wert"* ("surplus value"), found in economists studied by Marx. *"Plus-de-jouir"* is what is "beyond" the pleasure-displeasure principle, the "more" that is the real stake in the encounter between two bodies.

15. Freud, "From the History of an Infantile Neurosis" (1918), *S.E.* 17, 94. At his seminar on February 10, 1976, Lacan indicated the end of the session with remarks along similar lines: "Well now, just look where I have got to at this hour! You must have had your fill ('Vous devez en avoir votre *claque*') and even your *jacquelac* [Jacques Lac], to which I might as well add an *han* [an], to express the relief I feel at having traversed this route today. I have thus reduced my proper name to the most common noun." From Seminar XXIII (1975–1976), "Le Sinthome." Parts published in *Ornicar?* during 1976 and 1977.

16. In these two sentences, the author plays on the fact that *trait* can mean both "trait" (as in "character trait") and "mark." —TRANS.

17. Lacan, *Le séminaire. Livre XX*, 46.

18. Lacan at Yale University. See *Scilicet* 6/7 (Paris: Seuil, 1976), 31.

19. Freud, "Group Psychology and the Analysis of the Ego," 107. The German text reads: "eine partielle, höchst beschränkte ist, nur einen *einzigen* Zug."

20. Lacan, *Ecrits: A Selection*, 306.

21. Seminar IX, sessions of December 20, January 10, 17, 24. Unpublished.

22. Marcel Proust, *Remembrance of Things Past*, vol. 1, trans. C. K. Scott Moncrieff (New York: Random House, 1934), 296. The *Chartreuse* is Stendhal's *Charterhouse of Parma*. —TRANS.

23. Léon Vandermeersch, "Ecriture et langue écrite," in *Ecritures: Systèmes idéographiques et pratiques expressives* (Paris: Sycomore, 1982), 266.

24. Ibid., 265.

25. Jean Bottero, "De l'aide-mémoire à l'écriture," in *Ecritures*, 27–28.

26. Freud, "Group Psychology," 107.

27. See Maxime Gorce, *Les pré-écritures et l'évolution des civilisations* (Paris: Klincksieck, 1974).

28. A device used by the ancient Peruvians for calculating and record keeping, the quipu consisted in a main cord, with various smaller cords of different colors attached. —TRANS.

29. A famous cave in the Pyrenees, where vestiges of prehistoric life have been found. —TRANS.

30. Moustapha Safouan, *L'inconscient et son scribe* (Paris: Seuil, 1982), 35.

31. Lacan, *Ecrits,* 501.

32. Freud, "The Psychopathology of Everyday Life" (1901), S.E. 6, 2–7.

33. Letter of August 26, 1898. See Freud, *The Complete Letters of Sigmund Freud to Wilhelm Fliess* (1887–1904), trans. and ed. Jeffrey Moussaieff Masson (Cambridge: Belknap Press of Harvard University Press, 1985), 324.

34. Freud, "The Psychopathology of Everyday Life," 3.

35. Ibid.

36. Ibid.

37. From Seminar XII (1964–1965), "Problèmes cruciaux pour la psychanalyse." Unpublished.

38. Lacan referred to publication as "poubellication," a play on the word "*poubelle*" (wastebasket).

39. Freud, "The Psychopathology of Everyday Life," 5.

40. Ibid. In typography, *Schriftbilder* refers to the "typeface" or style of type. It is the way the letter looks, its specific form or design.

41. The four letters are N, E, L, and Υ, with L taken twice. —TRANS.

42. It is in this sense that Lacan stated: "The signifier with which one designates the same signifier is evidently not the same signifier as the one with which one designates the other—this is obvious enough. The word *obsolete,* in so far as it may signify that the word *obsolete* is itself an *obsolete* word, is not the same word *obsolete* in each case." *The Four Fundamental Concepts of Psycho-Analysis,* 210.

43. Lacan, *Le séminaire. Livre XX,* 46–47.

12. The Drive at Stake

1. Jean Paulhan, *Oeuvres complètes,* vol. 4 (Paris: Cercle du livres précieux, 1966), 470–71.

2. Lacan, *The Four Fundamental Concepts of Psycho-Analysis,* 39.

3. Freud, "The Interpretation of Dreams," 509.

4. Lacan, *The Four Fundamental Concepts of Psycho-Analysis,* 34.

5. Ibid., 60.

6. "*Vorstellungsrepräsentanz* . . . means not, as it has been mistranslated, the representative representative *(le représentant représentatif)* but that which takes the place of the representation *(le tenant-lieu de la représentation.")* The Four Fundamental Concepts of Psycho-Analysis,* 60.

7. Ibid., 69.

8. Ibid., 178–79.

9. Ibid., 59.

10. Ibid., 248.

11. A structure presented as well in "Position de l'inconscient" (*Ecrits*, 829–50), pages written in 1964, in other words, at the same time Lacan was conducting his seminar on *The Four Fundamental Concepts of Psycho-Analysis*.

12. This is madness: the passion of *being*, because of which a man believes himself a man and an analyst an analyst!

13. Lacan, *Ecrits: A Selection*, 304–5.

14. Lacan, *Ecrits*, 844.

15. Ibid.

16. Lacan, *The Four Fundamental Concepts of Psycho-Analysis*, 205.

17. Lacan, *Television*, 42.

18. Here the author blends *diction* (saying) with *perdition* (destruction) to yield a kind of destruction *through* no-saying.

19. Lacan, *Le séminaire. Livre VIII*, sessions of May 3 and May 17, 1961.

20. November 2, 1976. See *Lettre de l'Ecole freudienne*, no. 21, 474.

21. From Lacan's summary of his 1964 seminar for the *Annuaire de l'Ecole Pratique des Hautes Etudes* (1964–1965), 249–51.

22. Lacan, "L'étourdit," in *Scilicet* 4 (Paris: Seuil, 1973), 42.

23. From Seminar XXI.

24. And thereby distinguishes it from the infiniteness of the subject.

13. A Hole in the Imaginary

1. Lacan, *Ecrits: A Selection*, 319. This first advance comes from Lacan's article, "The subversion of the subject and the dialectic of desire" (September 1960). He would repeat it two years later (November 28, 1962), in his seminar entitled "L'Angoisse." Unpublished.

2. Ibid. (Emphasis added by the author.)

3. Ibid. (Emphasis added by the author.)

4. Lacan, *The Four Fundamental Concepts of Psycho-Analysis*, 17 and 79.

5. Ibid., 78.

6. Ibid., 83.

7. Ibid., 270.

8. Freud, "Group Psychology and the Analysis of the Ego" (1921), S.E. 18, 116. The schema is reproduced on p. 272 of *The Four Fundamental Concepts of Psycho-Analysis*.

9. This clearly shows that Lacan's invention of the *objet petit a* is based on the second topography.

10. Maurice Merleau-Ponty, *The Visible and the Invisible*, ed. Claude Lefort, trans. Alphonso Lingis (Evanston: Northwestern University Press, 1968), 138–39.

11. Lacan, *The Four Fundamental Concepts of Psycho-Analysis*, 273. (Emphasis added by the author.)

12. Roger Caillois, *Méduse et Compagnie* (Paris: Gallimard, 1960), 118.
13. Lacan, *The Four Fundamental Concepts of Psycho-Analysis*, 101.
14. Ibid., 110.
15. Ibid., 103.
16. Ibid.
17. Ibid., 95.
18. Here Lacan is playing on the fact that *"elle te regarde"* can mean either "it sees you" or "it concerns you." —TRANS.
19. Ibid., 96.
20. "Envy" or "jealousy." The word comes from *videre*, "to see."
21. Lacan, *Ecrits: A Selection*, 27.
22. Cf. Merleau-Ponty's valuable study "L'oeil et l'esprit." The study, which first appeared in *Art de France* (January 1961), was reprinted in *Les Temps Modernes* (nos. 184–85), a special issue devoted to Merleau-Ponty soon after his death. Among the contributors to this special issue, Lacan wrote a response to "L'oeil et l'esprit." An English translation is available in *The Primacy of Perception*, edited with an introduction by James M. Edie (Evanston: Northwestern University Press, 1964).
23. See G. Poulet, *Les métamorphoses du cercle* (Paris: Flammarion, 1979).
24. Date of the redaction of his "Remarque sur le rapport de Daniel Lagache: 'Psychanalyse et structure de la personnalité,'" *Ecrits*, 647–84.
25. Lacan, *Le séminaire. Livre VIII*, 411–14.
26. Whence the calming effect on people of animal companionship, which excludes the equivocity of the signifier.
27. See Lacan, Seminar IX (1961–1962), "Identification," session of December 6, 1961. Unpublished.
28. Lacan, *Ecrits*, 70. Also see Seminar XII, "Problèmes cruciaux pour la psychanalyse" (1964–1965), session of February 3, 1965. Unpublished.
29. Ibid., 70.
30. Ibid. Note that Lacan says "desire" and not "love."
31. Ibid., 71.
32. Ibid.
33. Lacan, Seminar XXII, "RSI" (1974–1975). Session of December 17, 1974.
34. As we shall see later, this same definition applies to the position of the analyst.
35. From Seminar X (1962–1963), "L'Angoisse" (session of November 28, 1962). Unpublished.
36. A play on words: "Dit-mansion," mansion of the said. —TRANS.
37. Immanuel Kant, *Prolegomena to Any Future Metaphysics*, ed. Lewis White Beck (Indianapolis and New York: Liberal Arts Press, Bobbs-Merrill, 1950), 33.
38. "And yet, it moves!" (Galileo). —TRANS.
39. Freud, "The Ego and the Id" (1923), *S.E.* 19, 26.

14. Imagination of a Triple Hole

1. Helene Deutsch, *Neuroses and Character Types: Clinical Psychoanalytic Studies* (New York: International Universities Press, 1965), 85–86.
2. Ibid., 87.
3. Ibid.
4. Literally, *"bon endroit"* means "good place." In slang (and here) *"le bon endroit"* refers to the buttocks. —TRANS.
5. Seminar XVI, "D'un Autre à l'autre" (1968–1969), session of May 7, 1969. Unpublished. A *"poule de luxe"* is a high-class prostitute. —TRANS.
6. Lacan, Seminar XXII, "RSI" (1974–1975), session of March 18, 1975.
7. Deutsch, *Neuroses and Character Types,* 93.

15. An Imaginary with Consistency

1. Lacan, *Le séminaire. Livre XX,* 112.
2. At least until 1972, when Lacan began to write it as "dit-mension."
3. Lacan, *Lettres de l'Ecole freudienne,* no. 18 (April 1976): 265.
4. Lacan, *The Four Fundamental Concepts of Psycho-Analysis,* 181.
5. Ibid., 69.
6. He clarified the matter at Strasbourg, January 26, 1975. See *Lettres de l'Ecole freudienne,* no. 18 (April 1976): 7–12.
7. With respect to this ground-breaking step, see *Lettres de l'Ecole freudienne,* no. 18 (April 1976): 263–70 (address of April 13, 1975), as well as Seminar XXII, "RSI" (session of December 17, 1974).
8. Lacan, *The Four Fundamental Concepts of Psycho-Analysis,* 248. (Emphasis added by the author.)
9. Lacan, *Le séminaire. Livre XX,* 17. For example, Gerhard von Rad wrote in *Theology of the Old Testament,* vol. 1 (Geneva: Labor & Fides, 1962), 34: "What is most extraordinary in the eyes of the historian of religions is the manner in which the cult of Yahweh is carried out in the face of all sexual mythology. In the Canaanite cults, intercourse and generation were envisaged mythically as divine events; there resulted a religious atmosphere saturated with mythical sexual images. But Israel did not participate in the 'deification' of sex. Yahweh holds himself totally beyond sexual polarity, which means that Israel never considered sexuality as a sacral mystery." And on page 132: "Yahweh himself is represented as a male, but Israel always completely eliminated any idea of sexuality, of creative sexual function, in him. In view of the religious world that surrounded it, this is an astonishing thing, for the Canaanite cult of Baal was a fertility cult that celebrated the *hieros gamos* as the divine, creative mystery par excellence. But for Israel, sexual polarity belonged to the order of creation, not to divinity." There is no sacred marriage in Israel that could produce a *sexual relation.*

This rupture effected by Israel is not unrelated to the one Freud introduced with respect to Jungianism. It is striking to observe how Christians, relying on Jung in order to better refuse Freud, denied the Judaic origin of their Christianity; paganism returns in them with Jung. L. Poliakov has demonstrated this well in *Le mythe arien* (Paris: Calmann-Levy, 1971), 298–304.

10. Best known of the family was Cardinal Carlo Borromeo, an important promoter of the Counter-Reformation.

11. From Seminar XXII, 1974–1975, "RSI," session of December 10, 1974.

12. See *Ecrits*, 649.

13. Yves Delaporte, *Les manuscrits enluminés de la Bibliothèque de Chartres*, Chartres, 1929, Ms. 233, p. 115; and M. Didron, *Iconographie chrétienne* (Paris: Imprimerie Royale, 1843), 569. See Lacan, *Lettres de l'Ecole freudienne*, no. 18 (April 1976): 265.

14. Lacan, "La méprise du suject supposé savoir," in *Scilicet* 1 (Paris: Seuil, 1968), 39.

15. Lacan, *Le séminaire. Livre XX*, 98.

16. From Seminar XXI, 1973–1974, "Les non-dupes errent," session of April 8, 1974. Unpublished.

17. "That it is the true religion, as it asserts, is not an excessive claim, all the more as when the true is closely examined, this is the worst one can say of it." Lacan, *Le séminaire. Livre XX*, 98.

18. I have done so in "Note sur la Trinité," *Littoral* 5, Topological Approaches, 32–44.

19. Lacan, "L'étourdit," *Scilicet* 4 (Paris: Seuil, 1973), 5.

20. From Seminar XXII, 1974–1975, "RSI," session of February 11, 1975.

21. Lacan, *Le séminaire. Livre XX*, 118.

22. From Seminar XXVI, 1978–1979, "La Topologie et le temps," session of February 20, 1979. Unpublished.

23. Ibid., session of January 9, 1979.

24. From Seminar XXVII, 1980, "Dissolution," session of March 11, 1980. Published in *Ornicar?* during 1980 and 1981.

Conclusion

1. The article is reprinted in Lacan, *Ecrits*, 73–92.
2. Ibid., 83–85.
3. Lacan, *Ecrits: A Selection*, 13.
4. Ibid., 15.
5. Ibid.
6. Lacan's commentary is "Variantes de la cure-type," reprinted in *Ecrits*, 323–62. "The Elasticity of Psycho-Analytic Technique" appears in Sandor Ferenczi, *Final Contributions to the Problems and Methods of Psycho-Analysis*, ed. Michael Balint, trans. Eric Mosbacher, et al. (New York: Brunner/Mazel, 1980), 87–101.
7. Lacan, *Ecrits*, 347.
8. Robert Baden-Powell founded Girl Guides in Great Britain in 1910.

9. Freud's letter-response to Ferenczi's paper may be found in Ernest Jones, *The Life and Work of Sigmund Freud*, vol. 2, *Years of Maturity, 1901–1919* (New York: Basic Books, 1955), 241. Curiously, Ferenczi leaves out Freud's name whenever he cites the letter. Each time this happens, it is because his analyst's name, although determined, has not been reduced to just any signifier.

10. Lacan, *Ecrits*, 349.

11. Lacan, *The Seminar of Jacques Lacan. Book II*, 246.

12. Lacan, *The Four Fundamental Concepts of Psycho-Analysis*, 270.

13. In this and only this—but this is by no means negligible—does psychoanalysis differ from religion, where (divine) love belongs to the symbolic order. This is why the symbolic can link the imaginary of the body to the real of death. Cf. Seminar XXI (1973–1974), "Les non-dupes errent" (session of December 18, 1973).

14. Lacan, *Le séminaire. Livre XX*, 12.

15. Ibid., 85. (Emphasis added by the author.)

16. Ibid.

17. Lacan, "De la psychanalyse dans ses rapports avec la realité," in *Scilicet* 1 (Paris: Seuil, 1968), 58.

18. From Seminar XXII (1974–1975), "RSI" (session of December 17, 1974).

19. From Seminar XXIV (1976–1977), "L'insu que sait de l'une bévue s'aile à mourre" (session of November 16, 1976).

20. Ibid.

21. Ibid.

22. Here the French text does not read *"dépersonnalisation"* (depersonalization) but rather *"dé-personnaison,"* which contains the same sound as "naît" (he, she, it is born). Thus from dé-person*naison* is *born* mobility of the specular image. —TRANS.

23. This modification of the specular image is an effect of the symbolic in this way: the analysand-become-analyst reduces what is proper to his or her own case to something common, and his/her proper name to one signifier among others. Literally, he or she has been given a discharge, a discharge not to nothing but to a "whatever" or a "whoever." The nomination "psychoanalyst," which he or she does not refuse, does not produce a trait/mark in the ego-ideal.

24. The three expressions were: *point aveugle* (blind spot); *c'est la plaie!* (what a pain!); *fracture d'un membre* (fracture of a limb). The literal meaning of *plaie* is "sore" or "wound." —TRANS.

25. Freud called it *Überdeutlich* (over-clear). In "The Psychopathology of Everyday Life," he used the term three times to describe the type of vision that is characteristic of the phenomenon of belief in "déjà vu."

26. See chapter 1 of "The Psychopathology of Everyday Life" (1901) *S.E.* 6, where Freud describes his forgetting of the name "Signorelli."

27. Roland Barthes, *La chambre claire* (Paris: Seuil, 1980), 105.

28. Jean Paulhan, *Oeuvres complètes,* vol. 4 (Paris: Cercle du livres précieux, 1966), 474.
29. Ibid.
30. Ibid., vol. 1, 306.
31. Reissued by Gallimard as part of the collection "Imaginaire."
32. As Lacan said of himself on June 10, 1980.
33. The last line of Aragon's poem "Contre-chant," quoted in *The Four Fundamental Concepts of Psycho-Analysis*.

Index

acting out *(agieren)*, 10, 66, 71–73, 81–82, 95, 189
after-Lacan, 2–3, 10–11
aggressivity, 21–23, 34, 39, 159–60
Aimée, xvi, 16–21, 24–25, 27, 35–36, 38, 160
Alcibiades, 92–93, 95–99, 185
alienation: imaginary, 50; primordial, 37–38, 49, 144, 159; symbolic, 50
analysand, 68, 73, 77, 80, 98–100, 114–16, 118, 154, 189–90, 192, 194, 212 n. 23
analysis. *See* psychoanalysis
analyst. *See* psychoanalyst
Andreas-Salomé, Lou, 80–81
Antigone, 27, 85, 88, 90, 92
Apollinaire, Guillaume, 188
aporia(s), 9, 46, 83
Aristotle, 59, 63, 84, 87, 118; on form, 34; on friendship, 198 n. 13; on tragedy, 203 n. 11
Auf-hebung, 5
Augustine, Saint, 84

Bachelard, Gaston, 33
Balint, Michael, 48, 54
Banquet (Plato), 92–99
Barthes, Roland, 192
Bentham, Jeremy, 85
body, 30–32, 34, 101, 137, 167, 168, 175; fragmented, 35, 39; of the mother, 128; and *objet petit a*, 188; of the other, 28, 30–31, 163; real of, 126, 167, 169

body image, 137, 153–54, 156, 162, 165, 191–92
border zone, 122–24, 126, 137, 139, 154, 163, 171, 191
Borromean knot, 176–79, 182–83; as belonging to the imaginary, xvii; as handled mathematically, 183; and metaphor, 183; as triplex unity of holes, xvii
butcher's wife, dream of, 64

Caillois, Roger, 154, 156
castration, 137, 155, 175; symbolic, 99
Claudel, Paul: *L'otage*, 147–48
cogito, 70, 109–10, 113
consistency, 177, 183
cut, 124, 141, 190–91

death, 148, 187
death drive, 55, 88–89, 91
demand, 72, 80, 96, 98–99, 108, 116, 136–37, 139, 187
depersonalization, 54, 190, 212 n. 22
Descartes, René, 109–11, 118
desire, 72, 83–84, 87–93, 95–98, 101–2, 105–6, 108, 115, 132, 134–35, 143, 145, 149, 165, 174, 177, 184; of the Other, 88, 95, 99, 101–2, 106, 117, 124, 146, 165; pure, 83, 88; signifier of, 102; of the subject, 88, 145. *See also* psychoanalyst, desire-of-the-
Deutsch, Helene, 166–67, 170
discourse, as what creates social bond, 27
"Discourse at Rome." *See* Rome Discourse

215

displacement *(Verschiebung)*, 134–35
dit-mension, 60, 162, 200 n. 17, 209 n. 36, 210 n. 2
Dora, 79
drive *(Trieb),* 82, 89, 143–44, 148–49, 154, 165, 173, 206 n. 13; death, 55, 88; objects of, 154, 175; scopic, 143, 154–55, 158, 162; as "*Trieb* to come," 143–44, 162

Ecole freudienne de Paris (EFP), 107
ego, xvi, 4–5, 15, 22, 23, 45, 49, 50–52, 55, 57, 63, 65, 67–69, 72, 132, 159–60, 162–64, 167, 187; bodily, 49, 162; formation of, 29–30, 32, 34; as hole, 164; as narcissistic, 23, 25–26, 29, 36, 56, 153, 155, 183, 185; paranoic structure of, xvi, 36, 190; unity of, 40
ego-ideal, xvii, 49–53, 94, 99–100, 125, 127, 131–34, 136–37, 139, 155, 160, 174, 212 n. 23; analyst's, 72
ego psychology, 4. *See also* Kris, Ernst
einen einzigen Zug, 51–52, 127, 130–31, 160, 169. *See also* unary mark/*trait*
Empedocles, 63, 147
eros, 83, 90–91, 93–95
ex-egesis, 5, 46

father-being, 174; signifier of, 143
Ferenczi, Sandor, 186–87
Fliess, Wilhelm, 10
forgetting, 3–5, 8–10, 133, 135–36, 138, 182
Foucault, Michel, 46, 203 n. 4; on commentary, 46
Four Fundamental Concepts of Psycho-Analysis, xvii, 6, 141–42, 154
fraternal complex, 23–25, 34, 159
Frege, Gottlob, 173
Freud, Sigmund, 1, 4, 5, 60, 67, 77–78, 80–81, 87, 91, 105–11, 115–16, 120, 130, 141–43, 153, 167, 172, 177; castration in, 137; ego in, 15; ego-ideal in, 94, 99; and first topography 5, 15, 80; on *Hilflosigkeit,* 31; on masochism, 21–22; metaphor of the "sack" in, 175; on *Nebenmensch,* 87; on negative therapeutic reaction, 86; on the repressed, 145, 173; on secondary identification, 51, 127, 131, 160; and second topography, 12, 15, 21–22, 26, 29, 32, 41, 48–49, 51, 55, 77, 127, 160; and Signorelli incident, 133–36, 138; on *Versagung,* 147; and Wolf Man, 125. *See also* narcissism; narcissistic object-choice; speaking, Freud's; speech; true-speaking
Freudianism, 3, 10, 46; as reading of second topography, 99
Freudian subject, 111, 113
Freudian text, xvi, 5–6, 9–10, 12, 15, 45–49; lacunae in, xv, xviii, 5, 9
Freudian unconscious, 5, 141. *See also* unconscious

Galilei, Galileo, 118–19
gaze, the, 41, 101, 154–58, 161–62, 189
Gestalt, 28, 31, 51, 55, 91–92, 163
Gestalttheorie, 33, 159
Gracián (Y Morales), Baltasar, 83, 193

Hartmann, Heinz, 4
Hegel, Georg Wilhelm Friedrich, 56, 58, 80
Heidegger, Martin, 54, 61, 88
Heraclitus, 54, 200 n. 32
historicity, 62
historization, 11, 53, 55, 62, 81
hole(s), 123, 138, 144, 146–49, 162–63, 172–74, 183, 188–89; in the body, 173; in body image, 175, 191; and Borromean knot, xvii; ego as, 189; in the imaginary, 162–65; in the Other, 123, 170; in the real, 174; at the root of language, 174; in the symbolic, 141–42, 173; triple, 165, 173, 176. *See also* knothole

ideal ego, xvii, 49–51, 69, 101, 132, 134, 160, 168, 190
identification, xvii, 24, 32, 37, 40, 134, 139; with the analyst, 99; in Freud, 51, 160; and gaze, 162; and *Gestalt* of body, 163; idealizing, 155; imaginary, 20, 33, 36, 39, 49, 53; narcissistic, 29; symbolic, 52–53; very limit of, 145
imaginary, xvi, xvii, 12, 15, 33, 41, 46–51, 53–57, 63–65, 69–70, 73, 77, 79, 100–102, 107–8, 144, 148–49,

153, 159, 160–62, 164–65, 168–73, 175–77, 182–83, 185, 188–90, 193; another, 162–64, 171, 183, 185, 197 n. 11; with consistency, 175; corporeal, 155, 159, 173, 176; hole in, 162–65; irreducibility of, 63–64; linked to narcissism, xvii; not linked to narcissism, 163; topological, 184, 190; topological function of, xvii
imago, 15, 29–30, 32–34, 37, 39, 47–49, 54, 62, 77–79, 82, 91, 97, 139, 185
impossible, 8, 11, 118–19, 122, 142–44, 147, 191; unconscious as function of, 8; visual, 175
International Psychoanalytic Association (IPA), 3–4, 66, 105, 106–7

Janet, Pierre, 25
jouissance, 22, 89–90, 168; of the father, 105, 126; feminine, 2; of the Other, 87, 89, 106, 167, 174–75; phallic, 154, 174
Jung, Carl Gustav, 141

Kant, Immanuel, 84, 89–91, 163, 192
Kierkegaard, Søren, 106
Klein, Melanie, 34–35, 100
knot-hole, 173, 184
knots, 165, 172–73, 175, 183; topology of, 172, 183; trinitarian, 179. *See also* Borromean knot
knowledge *(savoir),* 9–11, 60, 87, 93–94, 107, 109, 112–16, 118–20, 126, 138, 167–68, 174–75, 179–82, 189, 191, 193, 195 n. 13; literal, 115; in the real, 116; unconscious, 116–17
Koyré, Alexandre, 118–19, 142
Kretschmer, Ernst, 25
Kris, Ernst, 4, 65–73

Lacan's return to Freud, xv, xvi, 2–3, 5–11, 46–47, 99, 107
lack: border zone of, 139; eros as, 94; in the imaginary, 173; in the order of speaking, 122; in the Other, 115, 124, 137, 145–48, 165, 167–68, 170; phallic, 138, 157, 161–62; in the real, 146–48, 153, 165, 173; in the specular image, 153, 162; subject as, 132; in the symbolic, 143, 146, 148, 153, 165, 173

Lagache, Daniel, 48, 54
language, 56, 57, 59, 61–63, 90, 100, 110, 114–15, 120, 126–27, 129, 131–32, 140, 145, 183, 192; wall of, 56–57, 59, 108
letter, 118–32, 135–39, 160, 183; materiality of, xvii, 129–30, 136, 139
Lévi-Strauss, Claude, xvi
literal, 5, 122
littoral, 122
litura, 121–22, 125, 138, 206 n. 12
Loewenstein, Rudolph, 4, 16

Magritte, René ("This is not a pipe"), 130
Maritain, Jacques, 175
masochism, 21, 24–25, 39, 89–90
mathematization: and analytic discourse, 183; and Borromean knot, 183
matheme, 149
May 1968, events of, 64
Merleau-Ponty, Maurice, 155–56
metalanguage, 61, 126, 174, 183
metaphor, 95, 97, 98, 123, 125, 127, 133, 139, 174, 191; and Borromean knot, 183
mimesis, 160
minus small phi, 153, 158, 161, 163, 165, 175, 191
mirror stage, 15–16, 28–32, 34–36, 39–41, 48–49, 51, 78, 155–56, 158, 160–62, 176, 185, 188, 197 n. 1, 198 nn. 7, 20; topological treatment of, 41
misrecognition, 36, 38, 71, 78, 108

narcissism, 15, 39, 41, 49, 94, 97, 99, 135, 143, 155–56, 167–69, 172, 188; in Freud, xvi, 24, 29, 33, 49, 67, 155, 167; primary, 29, 33; secondary, 24–25
narcissistic object, 154–55
narcissistic object-choice, in Freud, 23–24, 29, 34, 155
negation *(Verneinung),* 69–70, 73, 88, 121–23, 130; signifier of, 147; and writing, 130
new covenant: established by Rome Discourse, xv, 6–7; as failed, xv, 7, 10; La-

new covenant (*Continued*)
  can's return to Freud as, 6–7; as noncovenant, 7
Newton, Isaac, 57

objet petit a, 41, 77, 99, 101, 124, 139, 154–55, 158, 160–62, 165–66, 168–69, 170–71, 184, 188, 189; and the analyst, 77; and the body, 188; as cause of desire, 184; and Freud's second topography, 208 n. 9; and the gaze, 154, 158; as residue, 188; as scopic object, 161; as what makes the image hold, 162, 168
ocelli, 156
Oedipus at Colonus (Sophocles), 88, 90, 147
Oedipus complex, 9, 25, 46, 105, 154
one-slip *(l'une-bévue)*, 63, 112, 116, 133, 141–42
other, 23, 25–26, 31–32, 34–36, 38–39, 49–50, 55, 63
Other, 50, 54, 63, 65, 70–73, 80–82, 86–90, 101, 115, 120, 123–24, 126–27, 131–32, 134, 137, 143–47, 167, 174–75, 179, 189–90; barred, 99–101, 115, 145–46, 174; desire of, 50, 53, 55, 88, 90, 95, 98–102, 124, 136, 145, 148, 162; field of, xviii, 70, 72–73, 80–82, 101, 127, 143, 145, 154, 157–58, 160–62, 168–70, 187–88, 190–91; and gaze, 189; and hole, 170; and knot-hole, 184; and look, 161–62. See also *jouissance*, lack

Papin sisters, 15, 19, 21, 23, 24
paranoia, xvi, 15–17, 20–23, 27, 35–39, 41; analytic process as controlled, 39; as crisis of personality, 16–17; self-punishment, 17, 21–22, 25
paranoic knowledge, 36–38, 55
Paranoid Psychosis and Its Relation to Personality (Lacan's thesis), xvi, 15–21, 23–27
pas, 121–23
paternal function, 105–6, 144, 174, 204 n. 3
Paul, Saint, 175
Paulhan, Jean, 192–93
penis envy *(Penisneid)*, 153

Pericles, 58
personality, science of, 25
Petit-Jean, story of, 157–58
phallus, 124, 137, 153–54, 172, 174–75
Picasso, Pablo, 118, 188
Plato, 59, 84, 91–92, 95–97
plus-de-jouir (surplus-enjoyment), 124, 154, 168, 206 n. 14
projection, 23; narcissistic, 53
proper name, 127–29, 131–32, 134–36, 139, 173, 180–81, 183, 212 n. 23
Proust, Marcel, 128
psychoanalysis, 60, 91, 95, 99, 101, 107, 112, 114, 116, 118, 120, 139, 149, 178, 182–84; compared to a game of bridge, 100; didactic, 7, 187; ethics of, 83, 89, 91–92, 100; process of, 50–54, 62, 185, 188–89, 198 n. 17; purpose of, 2, 4, 63, 78, 81–82, 101, 108–9, 141, 148, 175; and religion, 179–83, 212 n. 13; as a science, 1, 9, 34; termination of, xvii, 9, 62–64, 101–2, 170, 190
psychoanalyst: as applied to the mirror, 189, 194; birth of, 192; as blank page, 40; compared to ancient master, 58–60; desire-of-the-, xvii, 4, 11, 12, 53, 83, 91, 95, 98, 100, 115; ego of, 54, 70, 72, 186–87; ego-ideal of, 72; and gaze, 154; and gift of full speech, 58–61; as hole, 189; image of, 78–79; and knowledge *(savoir)*, 113, 115; libido of, 187; position of, 95, 98–100, 102, 116, 149, 187, 192; presence of, 6–7; role of, 50, 73, 120, 170, 173, 177, 178, 183–88; as social symptom, 7; and specular image, 212 n. 23; transition from analysand to, 64, 190, 212 n. 23
"Purloined Letter, The" (Lacan's seminar on), 61, 127

Rat Man, 179
real, xvi, xvii, 2, 15, 46–48, 63, 73, 78, 102–3, 107, 112, 116–19, 122, 131–32, 134, 138, 141–44, 146–48, 164–65, 169, 172–78, 182–83, 185; of the body, 126, 167, 169; as failed encounter, 112, 141, 143, 157, 165, 173, 191; as the impossible, 118; lack in,

146–48, 153, 165, 173; as locus of knowledge *(savoir)*, 116–17; pulsional, 173
reality, 69–72, 78
rebus, 127, 136
repetition *(Wiederholung)*, 78, 80–82, 142, 171
repetition compulsion (automatism of repetition), 141–43
repressed: irreducible *(urverdrängt)*, 73, 82, 99, 112, 132, 141–42, 144–45, 173–74; return of the, 5, 73
repression, 56
Rimbaud, Arthur, 60
Rome Discourse (also "Discourse at Rome" and Rome Report), xv, 6–7, 48, 62–63, 107–8, 147, 149
Rousseau, Jean-Jacques, 27, 38
Russell, Bertrand, 128

Sade, Donatien-Alphonse-François, marquis de, 89–91
Safouan, Moustapha, 131
Saussure, Ferdinand de, 127
schema L, 57, 61, 69, 82, 100
schema of the inverted bouquet, 160
Schmideberg, Melitta, 67
Schreber, Daniel Paul, 18, 198 n. 13
science, 9, 108–9, 116, 142
sign, 122, 129, 132, 160
signifier, 110–14, 123–24, 126–27, 131–32, 141, 143, 145, 160; of the barred Other, 99–101, 145–46, 149, 161, 174; of desire, 102; master, 141; of the Other, 145; of the Other's desire, 99, 145; phallic, 99, 124; pure, 160; structure of, xvii
Signorelli incident, 133–36, 138
Société française de psychanalyse (SFP), 105, 107
Société psychanalytique de Paris (SPP), 66
Socrates, 92–93, 95–98, 115, 185
speaking, Freud's, 5, 46
specular image, xvi, xvii, 50, 153, 155, 159, 161–62, 167–69, 176, 188, 190–92, 212 n. 23; cut in, 190–91; lack in, 153, 162; mobility of, 190; reversal of, xvii, 190–92, 212 n. 23

speech, 2, 50, 53–54, 56–57, 59–63, 69–70, 79–82, 97, 100, 108, 110, 114, 118–20, 122, 141, 182–84, 187, 192, 200 n. 17; Freud's, 46–47; full, 46, 57–58, 61–62, 80; of the Other, 69
Spinoza, Benedict (Baruch), 196 n. 7
Spitz, René, 52
subject, 101, 108, 114–16, 145, 147–48, 155, 166–69, 208 n. 24; barred, 99, 112, 124; Freudian, 113; of science, 108–9, 112, 119
suture, 9–10, 124, 133–34, 136
symbolic, xvi, xvii, 15, 41, 46–59, 61–65, 69, 71–73, 79–82, 99, 101–2, 107–9, 116–17, 119, 134, 138, 141–44, 146–49, 159–60, 164–65, 167–74, 176–77, 182–83, 185, 188, 190–91, 212 n. 23; hole in, 141–42, 148, 165, 173–74; incompleteness of, 101; lack in, 101, 143, 146, 148, 153, 165, 173; primacy of, 47–48, 64–65, 73, 101, 108, 116, 171, 176, 185, 187; refusal of, 147

Themistocles, 58
theoria, 177, 181–82
Tiresias, function of, 188
topology, xvii, 8, 65, 163; of Borromean knot, 182; of knots, 172, 183; of the subject, 8
tragic hero, 85, 87
transference *(Übertragung)*, 5, 46, 49, 54, 73, 77–83, 91–92, 95, 97–98, 102, 113–15, 117, 120, 172
transitivism, 32, 36, 101
true-speaking, 2, 5, 181
truth, 61, 70, 79, 98, 101, 108–9, 112, 118–20, 132, 175, 178–83, 191, 200 n. 17; effects of, 9, 108; psychoanalyst established in, 85

unary mark/*trait (einen einzigen Zug)*, 121, 130–31, 133–34, 139, 160, 167, 169, 174, 190–91, 212 n. 23
unconscious, xv, 2, 4–8, 47, 55, 57, 67, 69, 80, 82, 100, 107, 109, 111–12, 116–17, 122, 125–26, 128, 135, 138–39, 143; as discourse of the Other, 145, 159; formations of, 6, 15, 80,

unconscious (*Continued*)
111–12, 120, 132, 136, 141; Freudian, 141; as function of the impossible, 8; gap in, 173; initial structure of, 141; as lost cause, 7; as *l'une-bévue*, 63, 112, 116, 133, 141–42; as Other who has no Other, 190; structured like a language, 62, 126; subject of, 132, 147

Versagung, as refusal, 147
vision, 29, 31, 155

Wallon, Henri, 29–31
Wo es war, 70, 111, 115, 157
writing, 2, 118, 129, 183, 191